ISSEI BASEBALL

ISSEI BASEBALL

*The Story of the First
Japanese American Ballplayers*

ROBERT K. FITTS

University of Nebraska Press
LINCOLN

Portions of chapters 5 and 6 were previously published as "Baseball and the Yellow Peril: Waseda University's 1905 American Tour," in *Base Ball 10: New Research on the Early Game*, ed. Don Jensen (Jefferson NC: McFarland, 2018), 141–59. Used with permission.

Library of Congress Cataloging-in-Publication Data
Names: Fitts, Robert K., 1965– author.
Title: Issei baseball: the story of the first Japanese American ballplayers / Robert K. Fitts.
Description: Lincoln: University of Nebraska Press, 2020. | Includes bibliographical references and index.
Identifiers: LCCN 2019027695
ISBN 9781496213488 (Cloth)
ISBN 9781496220875 (ePub)
ISBN 9781496220899 (PDF)
ISBN 9781496220882 (Mobi)
Subjects: LCSH: Baseball players—Japan—Biography. | Baseball teams—United States—History—20th century. | Baseball—Japan—History. | Japan—Emigration and immigration. | United States—Emigration and immigration. | Japanese Americans—Evacuation and relocation, 1942–1945. | World War, 1939–1945—Japanese Americans. | Green, Guy W.
Classification: LCC GV863.77.A1 F57 2020 | DDC 796.3570952—dc23
LC record available at https://lccn.loc.gov/2019027695

Set in Vesper by Mikala R. Kolander.

In memory of d'Artagnan.
We miss you.

The early history of Japanese immigrants in the United States, far from being a success story, is, above all, a history of a racial minority struggling to survive in a hostile land.

YUJI ICHIOKA, *The Issei*

There has been no greater agency in bringing our different races together than our national game, baseball. Baseball is our real melting pot.

FRED LIEB, "Baseball: The Nation's Melting Pot," *Baseball Magazine*

Contents

Illustrations

Tables

Recurring Japanese Characters

In order of appearance:

Atsuyoshi "Harrry" Saisho (At-sue-yoh-shee Sigh-show)

Shichiji Kikuchi (Shee-chee-gee Kee-koo-chee)

Ken Kitsuse (Ken Keet-sue-say)

Tozan Masko (Toe-zan Mas-koe)

Hanzaburo Harase (Han-zah-boo-roe Hah-rah-say)

Kotan Saito (Ko-tan Sigh-toe)

Takejiro Ito (Ta-key-ji-roe Ee-toe)

Isoo Abe (Ee-Sow Ah-bay)

Sukekatsu Izumitani (Sue-ke-kat-sue Ee-zoo-me-tah-nee)

Shin Hashido (Sheen Hah-shee-doe)

Atsushi Kono (Aht-sue-shee Koh-no)

Tetsusaburo "Tom" Uyeda (Tet-sue-sa-boo-roh Oo-yay-dah)

Junjiro Uyeda (June-jee-roh Oo-yay-dah)

Takatomo "Bob" Uyeda (Tah-kah-toe-moe Oo-yay-dah)

Toyo Fujita (Toe-yo Foo-gee-tah)

Umekichi "Kitty" Kawashima (Oo-may-kee-chee
Kah-wah-shee-mah)

Shoichi Motohashi (Show-ee-chee Moe-toe-hah-shee)

Naito (Nigh-toe)

Kiichi "Onitei" Suzuki (Key-ee-chee Oh-knee-tay Sue-zoo-key)

Isamu Maeda (Ee-sah-moo Mah-ay-dah)

Minori Sohara (Mee-no-ree So-hah-rah)

Riichiro Shiraishi (Ree-ee-chee-roh Shee-rah-ee-shee)

Takizo Takasugi (Tah-kee-zoe Tah-kah-sue-ghi)

Goro Mikami (Go-roe Mee-kah-mee)
Kazuma Sugase (Kah-zoo-mah Sue-gah-say)
Tokutaro Tachiyama (Toe-koo-tah-roh Tah-chee-yah-mah)
Takaji Kubo (Tah-kah-gee Koo-boh)
Kesaichi "Arthur" Shiomichi (Kay-sigh-chee Shee-oh-mee-chee)

ISSEI BASEBALL

Introduction

White-haired and frail, the old men lounged around a large table at Nikko-ro in Los Angeles's Little Tokyo, reminiscing about summer days long past. Chopsticks lay discarded beside empty plates dribbled with soy sauce. The platters were empty, for life had been hard, and they had learned long ago not to waste food. But the beer glasses and tea cups remained full as they sipped and remembered.

Ken Kitsuse took out some photographs—fading images of young men in baseball uniforms taken nearly fifty years earlier. His lifetime friends Atsuyoshi "Harry" Saisho and Kiichi Suzuki leaned over to get a better look at their old teammates—so many of them gone now: the brash promoter Tozan Masko; the friendly Tetsusaburo "Tetsu"/"Tom" Uyeda; Japan's greatest player Shin Hashido. The young Issei (Japanese immigrants) had played together on many teams, becoming the first Japanese professional ballplayers when they barnstormed across the American Midwest in 1906. They had played in front of thousands of people, been featured in hundreds of newspapers, and traveled throughout the country. Kitsuse had been called "the greatest Japanese shortstop in the world bar none."[1] But the exploits of their youth were forgotten by nearly all outside of the room.

Baseball was a vital part of Japanese American culture. During the 1920s and '30s, thousands of Nisei (Japanese born outside of Japan) children and adults played in organized leagues. The games became a meeting place for the community—a place to socialize, discuss local concerns, talk business, swap gossip. The top teams challenged white and African American nines, entered regional tournaments, and occasionally traveled to Japan. Regional stars became local celebrities and heroes to the Japanese American youth. A handful of players even played professionally in the minor leagues, becoming beacons of ethnic pride. This passion for the game became crucial during World War II, when one hundred thousand Japanese Americans were incarcerated in internment camps. *Baseball Saved Us*, Ken Mochizuki titled his award-winning book on the game during internment. The sport provided an outlet for the frustrations of a people unjustly removed from their homes and helped build morale and a sense of normalcy during this difficult time.

This golden era of Japanese American baseball and the game's importance during internment are well documented through the stellar work of many scholars.[2] But how did baseball become such an important part of Japanese American culture? Little is known about the genesis of Japanese American baseball. No historian has examined the topic in depth.[3]

This story will focus on the pioneers of Japanese American baseball: Harry Saisho, Ken Kitsuse, Tozan Masko, Tom Uyeda, and Kiichi Suzuki. They were the sons and grandsons of samurai—their fathers born just before Commodore Matthew Perry's arrival in 1853 led to the collapse of the feudal system and the rise of Modern Japan. To prepare their children for Japan's new place in the world, their fathers sent them to private schools to study Western ideas and knowledge. There they fell in love with the new American game of baseball.

After graduation these young men came to the United States as students, eager to gain an education and start a new life. They soon found that Japanese immigrants were rarely welcome. Faced with intense bigotry and daily discrimination, each worked a series of unfulfilling menial jobs. Seeking camaraderie, they returned to their love of baseball and formed a team in Los Angeles.

Their lives changed when the Waseda University baseball team came to the United States in 1905 to play twenty-six games on the West Coast. Americans became intrigued with the idea that the Japanese, a people from the other side of the globe, had adopted the American national pastime. Capitalizing on this interest in Japanese baseball, Guy Green, the owner of the famous barnstorming Nebraska Indian Base Ball Team, decided to form the first professional Japanese club in the world and barnstorm across the Midwest.

Saisho, Kitsuse, Masko, and Uyeda joined up and spent 1906 playing 150–170 games in seven states until the team disbanded in October. For these men, it was a life-changing experience. They abandoned their aspirations for financial success to focus on baseball.

Tozan Masko and Tom Uyeda settled in Denver, formed the Mikado's, the first Japanese-run professional baseball club in the world, and toured Colorado and Kansas in 1908.[4] Saisho and Kitsuse returned to Los Angeles and created the Nanka Japanese Base Ball Club. For several years the Nanka remained an amateur squad, playing both white and African American teams. In 1909 the team turned professional, changed its name to the Japanese Base Ball Association (JBBA), and planned a cross-country barnstorming tour but disbanded after a disastrous series of games in California. In 1911 Harry Saisho was ready to try again. As both the Waseda and Keio University teams were touring in the United States, Saisho re-formed the Japanese Base Ball Association and spent the summer barnstorming across the Midwest. In subsequent years the members of the JBBA would scatter, joining the ever-growing number of Japanese American teams across the United States, and teach the next generation to love the game.

Along the way the Japanese teams helped break down racial bigotry. With the rise of Japan's military power and the large number of its citizens emigrating to the United States, hostility toward Japanese grew in the first decades of the twentieth century. Anti-Japanese groups, such as the Asiatic Exclusion League, argued that the Japanese were an alien and inferior race that posed a "Yellow Peril" to Western Civilization. These groups and sympathetic newspapers depicted Japanese as dishonest, deviously clever, animal-like, physically small, misshapen, and dirty. The Japanese ball clubs faced bigotry on the diamond and in the media, but their skill and demeanor undercut these stereotypes. The visiting Waseda University squads did this consciously—acting as ambassadors, spreading goodwill on and off the field. Japanese immigrant teams, on the other hand, just wanted to play ball, but as they barnstormed across America's heartland, they earned the respect of their opponents and fans. Baseball became a bridge between the two cultures, bringing Japanese and Americans together through the shared love of the game.

1

Saisho the Dreamer

Atsuyoshi Saisho spent his first week in the United States under lock and key.

On March 18, 1903, the twenty-year-old had boarded the ss *Gaelic* in Yokohama with dreams of finding his fortune in California. He had attended Waseda University in Tokyo and was now off to study at Stanford.

Using both sail and steam, the small ocean liner had run the Pacific route for eighteen years, transporting thousands of Asian immigrants to the New World. On that March 18 it carried about forty passengers in its cabins and ninety-seven Japanese and Chinese crammed together in "Asiatic steerage"—a narrow area just above the cargo hold. As Saisho approached the entrance for the first time, he must have sensed the difficulties of the upcoming trip. Another traveler recalled, "I stood at the head of a dark stairway leading into the very bowels of the ship. . . . Up the stair came a virulent stench, the full-bodied, wettish sweet smell of the steerage. . . . I descended to my doom."[1]

Steerage consisted of a large room filed with bunk beds—often three or four tiers high. The bed slats were spaced so closely together that even Saisho, who stood just 5 feet 1 and weighed a little over a hundred pounds, needed to crawl into bed. Sitting up was impossible. The shipping company did not provide mattresses or linens; most passengers slept on the bare boards or covered themselves with a thin blanket. There was no separate living space, so leisure time and meals were spent in the same room. Reading was difficult as the only light came from grimy, barred portholes and, on some ships, several naked lightbulbs. The reek of cooked food, body stench, and (if seas were rough) vomit filled the enclosed space. Vermin and disease could spread easily.

Disease had already complicated the *Gaelic*'s voyage, making the hard journey even more arduous. A Korean child had developed chickenpox on the passage from Kobe to Yokohama. The ship was emptied and fumigated before Saisho and other passengers were allowed to board, but en route to Honolulu another steerage passenger developed the disease. The *Gaelic* was emptied and fumigated again upon reaching port, and the ship's doctor inoculated all passengers. No symptoms of the disease developed during the leg from Honolulu to San Francisco, but as a precaution the health inspector ordered the *Gaelic*'s ninety-seven Asiatic steerage passengers to the quarantine station on Angel Island.[2] The Caucasian cabin passengers were allowed to proceed directly to San Francisco. It would be the first of many indignities that Saisho would face in the United States because of his race.

At Angel Island passengers were ordered to disembark while dock workers loaded their baggage into large wire cages on specially designed railcars. The railcars carried the baggage to a disinfecting shed where the cages were blasted by high-pressured steam or a solution of formaldehyde followed by ammonia. Contemporaries bragged that the system "so thoroughly permeates all the substances in the boilers that it will cook an egg in a sailor's bag of clothes."[3]

Meanwhile, passengers underwent medical checkups. Inspectors escorted Saisho and his fellow steerage passengers to large bathhouses where they were required to strip, wash with carbolic soap, and redress in overalls provided by the quarantine station. Their discarded clothes joined the baggage in the disinfecting chambers.

Following this ordeal, the Asian passengers were separated by nationality and housed on the island in either the Japanese or Chinese barracks for a quarantine period of about two weeks. Accommodations were rudimentary as the barracks needed to be fumigated with sulfur dioxide and scrubbed with salt water every morning. Twice a day the detainees from the *Gaelic* "were lined up and inspected by one of the medical officers to make sure there were no new outbreaks of disease and to check for escapes."[4]

After seven days, about a week before the end of the usual quarantine period, the medical inspector released Saisho and thirty-three of his fellow Japanese passengers.[5] Before they departed, their baggage and personal effects were disinfected yet again. Many found their items damaged by the process. An observer noted that clothes retained color "but it was never the original color."[6]

Atsuyoshi was arriving at the height of Japanese immigration to California. In the first decades following the opening of Japan in 1853, few Japanese left their homeland for America. The 1890 federal census listed just 2,039 living in the entire United States.[7] But from 1890 to 1907 nearly seventy thousand Japanese immigrated to the West Coast alone.[8] Most were the second or third sons of small farmers or laborers, fleeing the widespread poverty of southern Japan. These men (about 80 percent of Japanese immigrants before 1907 were male) planned to stay in the United States for several years working as agricultural or railroad laborers before returning to their home villages with enough money to buy land and start a family.

Saisho's background differed from most of his fellow immigrants. He was the eldest son of a samurai war hero. Descended from the noble Atsugyo Fujiwara, whom Emperor Go-Ichijo had sent in 1021 to establish and administer the Kirishima Shrine in Kagoshima Prefecture, the Saisho family became samurai retainers of the powerful Shimazu clan, which ruled over most of the southern island of Kyushu in Satsuma Province. Known for superb horsemanship and martial skill, the Saishos rose to prominence during the civil wars of the sixteenth and early seventeenth centuries and became confidants to the Shimazu family and local administrators. Atsushi Saisho, for example, who may have been Atsuyoshi's great uncle or cousin, was an adviser to the last Shimazu daimyo before becoming a Meiji government minister and the grandfather of Yoko Ono, the wife of Beatle John Lennon.

Atsuyoshi's father, Atsumasa, was born three years before Commodore Perry steamed his four warships into Edo Bay in 1853, forcing Japan to end 250 years of self-imposed isolation and wrenching it out of medieval feudalism. Since 1603 Japan had been ruled by the Tokugawa shogunate from its capital of Edo (now called Tokyo). The shogunate maintained control through an elaborate bureaucracy, a rigid social hierarchy, and a closing of the country's borders. No Japanese could leave; no foreigner could enter. As a result, Japan remained an isolated medieval society into the mid-nineteenth century. Unable to defend the country from the modern American steam-driven warships, the shogunate agreed to Perry's demands to open Japan's borders. The signing of the so-called "Unequal Treaties" with Western powers in 1858 caused widespread condemnation of the Tokugawa government, ultimately leading to open rebellion, the defeat of the shogunate, and the elevation of the seventeen-year-old Meiji emperor as the ruler of Japan in 1868.

After the Meiji Restoration the new government enacted measures to modernize and reform Japan. It abolished the feudal system, reforming the clan fiefdoms into prefectures; instituted compulsory education for all subjects; and created centralized state institutions, including a standing national army based on the conscription of all twenty-one-year-old Japanese males. Under these reforms the emperor officially dissolved the samurai as a class, revoking their hereditary privileges and freeing them from their feudal obligations to their clan lords.

With the traditional life as a Satsuma samurai unavailable, Atsumasa Saisho joined the newly formed Tokyo Metropolitan Police Force around 1874 and received the prestigious Order of the Rising Sun for his heroism fighting against Takamori Saigo during the 1877 Satsuma Rebellion. (The war was the basis for the romanticized Tom Cruise movie *The Last Samurai*.) After the uprising Saisho remained in the police force, serving in Kagoshima and Miyazaki Prefectures for fifteen years. By 1882 he had married and settled in Miyakonojo in Miyazaki Prefecture as the town police chief.

Located on a plateau surrounded by steep mountains covered with dense forest, Miyakonojo was a small market town of about eleven thousand people.[9] Walter Del Mar, an American who passed through around 1900, noted that it consisted of "one long and wide street."[10] In truth it was somewhat larger, with several inns, schools, and small businesses. Photographs show unpaved streets lined with one- and two-story wooden houses built in traditional styles. Few, if any, of the Western cultural influences sweeping through Tokyo at the time were felt there. The countryside surrounding Miyakonojo, according to Basil Hall Chamberlain, a British-born professor at Tokyo University who visited in the 1880s, was "sparsely inhabited by a population poor, primitive, and holding little intercourse with the outer world."[11]

While living in Miyakonojo, Atsumasa would have three sons. Atsuyoshi, the eldest, was born on November 11, 1882. Tadashi was born in 1889, and Eiji, in 1892. Later in his life Atsuyoshi would adopt the name Harry. (For the reader's ease, I will use his English name from this point forward.) During this time, Atsumasa completed his tenure as the chief of police and retired to start a silk company. Eventually, in 1904, he would be elected mayor of Miyakonojo and would serve for ten years.

Growing up in the 1880s, Harry most likely attended the local primary school in Miyakonojo, where he probably met his lifelong friends Shichiji Kikuchi and Ken Kitsuse. Little is known about Shichiji Kikuchi's early life. He was born in Miyakonojo on January 18, 1881, and had an elder brother named Takeji. "Kikuchi" was an old samurai name. The Kikuchi clan ruled Higo Province in northwest Kyushu from the eleventh to sixteenth centuries before it was conquered by the Shimazu. By the late nineteenth century "Kikuchi" was such a common name in Miyazaki Prefecture that it is nearly impossible to identify Shichiji's parents. It is likely that Kikuchi's father was one of the region's many poor rural samurai.

Ken Kitsuse was just a few months older than Harry Saisho. His father, Yuitsu, came from a poor samurai family from the village of Shimonagai, just south of Miyakonojo. Even when he was very young, adults remarked on Yuitsu's intelligence, and as a teen he was sent to study languages and science in Nagasaki—most likely with famous Dutch-born scholar Guido Verbeck at the Seibikan. After graduating in the 1870s, Yuitsu Kitsuse worked as a translator for the Mint Bureau and later became an interpreter for the Ministry of Foreign Affairs. Yuitsu had married Nui (last name unknown) by the late 1870s and returned to Miyakonojo to teach and raise a family. The couple had three children: two boys, Takeshi (born in 1879) and Ken (July 1, 1882), and a daughter, Yoshi (born 1886).

Just before his eighth birthday, Ken's life would change. The new Meiji Constitution, created in 1888, established a legislative body, known as the Imperial Diet, to help govern Japan. The Diet consisted of two houses—the House of Peers, filled by nobles, and the elected House of Representatives. The first general election for representatives took place in 1890. As the most educated man in Miyakonojo, locals wanted to nominate Yuitsu Kitsuse as the district's representative, but his lack of both wealth and prestigious birth posed a problem. To overcome the obstacles intermediaries arranged for Yuitsu to be adopted by the wealthy Yasuda family. But there was a catch. Yuitsu's children could neither take the Yasuda name nor be eligible for Yuitsu's possible inheritance from his new family. Thus Yuitsu was required to disinherit his current family. Yuitsu agreed, and on July 1, 1890, Ken's eighth birthday, he won the election to represent Miyazaki Prefecture's Second Constituency in Japan's first Imperial Diet. Yuitsu moved to Tokyo for the first term and for a second term starting in 1893. Ken and his family remained in Miyakonojo.

At the end of primary school, promising students took entrance examinations for the area middle schools, five-year institutions that were roughly equivalent to modern high schools. In the 1890s there were only a handful of middle schools in Miyazaki Prefecture, and competition for entrance could be stiff. Kikuchi, Kitsuse, and Saisho separated at this point. Kikuchi stayed in town, attending Miyakonojo Middle School. Ken (and his brother Takeshi) enrolled at Kagoshima Prefectural Middle School, now known as Kagoshima Prefectural Tsurumaru High School.[12] Harry tested into Miyazaki Middle School (now called Miyazaki Ohmiya Senior High School). One of the top public schools in the prefecture, the school attracted well-off boys from ex-samurai families. It was there that Saisho would learn a new American game that would become his passion.

2

The National Pastime in Japan

Harry Saisho arrived at Miyazaki Middle School just as a baseball craze swept Japan. The game had entered Japan only three years after the 1868 Meiji Restoration. The Unequal Treaties signed between Japan and the Western powers in 1858 opened five ports to European traders. Over the ensuing year the Japanese transformed the small fishing village of Yokohama into a bustling trading town complete with piers, markets, warehouses, a customs house, and dwellings for the new Japanese and foreign residents. Yokohama grew rapidly from an initial 44 foreigners and 400 Japanese in 1859 to 309 foreigners and 12,000 Japanese in 1864 to roughly 1,000 foreigners and 50,000 Japanese in 1870.

With the United States locked in civil war, the foreign inhabitants of Yokohama during the 1860s were predominately young British men. The group recreated the institutions and comforts from their homeland, including an English-language newspaper in 1861, a photography studio in 1864, and a brewery in 1865. Sports played an important role in the community. A racetrack was built in 1862. The first known soccer and cricket games in Japan were played in 1863 and the first rugby game in 1866. The men organized formal clubs—the Yokohama Rifle Association in 1865, the Yokohama Foot Ball Club in 1866, the Race Club 1866, a racquet club, and the Yokohama Cricket Club in 1868.

Americans trickled into Yokohama at the end of the Civil War and were able to field a baseball team when the USS *Colorado*, returning from a punitive attack on Korea, came to port in October 1871.[1] On either October 26 or 30 (contemporary newspapers give different dates), nine sailors from the *Colorado* met nine American civilians from Yokohama on the cricket field known as the Swamp Ground for a game of baseball. Heavy rain on the previous two days made the field slick and muddy, but the teams managed to play four innings before twilight set in. The sailors, "being very smart in the field," emerged victorious, 15–11.[2] Spectators immediately recognized the significance of the event and sent a dispatch to the *New York Herald* stating, "The first base ball match ever played in Yokohama came off on the 26th ultimo, between nine American residents of the place and a picked nine of the United States ship Colorado."[3]

Japanese students began playing baseball soon after this first game was held in Yokohama. Wanting to modernize quickly, the Meiji government invited Western instructors, called *oyatoi*, to Japan to help introduce foreign technology and institutions. In 1872 the Japanese government employed 369 *oyatoi*, including 102 teachers.[4]

Among these teachers was Horace Wilson, a dapper twenty-eight-year-old with slicked-back wavy dark hair, heavy eyebrows, and a full, drooping mustache. Born in Gorham, Maine, a small town about sixty-five miles north of Boston, Wilson had attended Kents Hill, a Methodist seminary outside of Augusta, Maine, before enlisting in the Union Army's Twelfth Maine Regiment and marching south to fight in Louisiana. Wilson became an avid baseball player, picking up the game either at school or in the army. Discharged in March 1866, Wilson returned to Gorham to teach school before relocating to San Francisco in 1870. Perhaps finding his new life as a bookkeeper unfulfilling, a year later Wilson signed a three-year contract to teach English in Japan and sailed to Yokohama with his wife Mary, two-year-old son Harry, and a bat and ball.[5]

In September or October 1871 Wilson began teaching at Daigaku Nanko, a Tokyo-based school for Western studies soon to be renamed Daiichi Daigaku in 1872 and then Kaisei Gakko in 1873.[6] At the time, Japan had no team sports and few individual sports outside of the martial arts. Tradition states that Wilson found his students in such poor physical condition that he decided to incorporate outdoor exercise into their studies and in 1872 brought out his bat and ball and taught them the game of baseball. Wilson and his students were soon joined by Edward Mudgett, a twenty-year-old faculty member at Daigaku Yobimon, a foreign language school located adjacent to Wilson's institution.[7]

About the same time in the United States another group of Japanese was learning America's national pastime. In August 1871 the Yeddo Royal Japanese Troupe of acrobats arrived in San Francisco from Tokyo.[8] The troop of thirteen or fourteen Japanese and two British managers would spend the next six years performing across the United States. In June 1872 during the troupe's stay in Washington DC, a game of baseball was arranged between the troupe and "a picked nine from the Olympic and National Base Ball Clubs."[9] The match was a publicity stunt—advertised as an oddity—as the Japanese had little to no understanding of the game.

For two days the acrobats trained with Asa Brainard, the Washington Olympics starting pitcher and former member of the 1869 Cincinnati Red Stockings (baseball's first professional team). On June 7 the Japanese and Americans met on the diamond. The game lasted five innings and ended in an 18–17 Olympic victory. Impressions of the game differed. The *Baltimore Sun* reported, "The game . . . was a complete fizzle. The Japs did not know the first principle [of] the game, and never would have made a run if the picked nine choosed [sic] to prevent it." Washington's *Daily Morning Chronicle*, in an article republished nationally, added, "The Japs enjoyed the fun, and, through the courtesy of the Olympics, were allowed to make seventeen runs." Washington's *Daily National Republican*, on the other hand, exclaimed, "The game . . . came near [to] being a victory for the Orientals. The style in which they handle the ball and bat somewhat astonished our boys and had not rain stopped the game there was a fair prospect for a ball going to Japan."[10]

The Yeddo Royal Japanese Troupe played a second game on June 14 against an amateur squad calling itself the Dolly Varden Club (this seems to have been a male squad—not to be confused with the African American women's team of the 1880s). Once again the Japanese came up short—either by a 27–23 or 32–21 score (newspaper reports differ). A third game, scheduled for June 18 in Baltimore against the Diamond State Base Ball Club, was cancelled due to "the inability of two of the Japs to play."[11] There is no evidence that the Yeddo Royal Japanese Troupe played ball again during its stay in the United States. Its entry into the annals of baseball was fleeting, and despite the report in the Wilmington, Delaware, *News*

Journal that "the Japs are desirous of learning our National Game, and on their return to their distant home will be the first to introduce it into the ancient Empire of Japan," there is no evidence that the games impacted the development of baseball on either side of the Pacific.[12]

In Japan just a year after Wilson supposedly introduced the game, another American teacher brought out his bat and ball. In early 1873 eighteen-year-old Albert G. Bates arrived in Tokyo to teach English at Kaitakushi Karigakko, a school established to train future settlers of Japan's northern island of Hokkaido. Seiken Oshima, one of the school's early students, claimed in a 1911 *Asahi* newspaper article that Bates had taught his students how to play the game before Wilson, making him the true father of Japanese baseball.[13]

In 1875 Kaitakushi Karigakko relocated to the city of Sapporo in Hokkaido, bringing the American pastime with it. But tragically Bates was unable to make the move north. Earlier in the year, on January 13, the young man suffocated while taking a Japanese bath heated by a faulty charcoal stove. His grave, marked by a large granite obelisk, still stands in the Yokohama Foreign Cemetery.[14]

Despite the game's introduction in 1871–73, few, if any, formal matches were played until 1876. That summer eight members of the foreign community—they were unable to recruit nine men who could play baseball—took on a native nine from the Imperial College at Tokyo in the first documented game played by a Japanese team. The foreign team—which included Edward Mudgett leading off and playing at second base, Horace Wilson batting third and playing in left field, and Henry Willard Dennison, the vice consul of the United States, batting cleanup—won 34–11. A member of the foreign team wrote, "The Japanese take a great deal of interest in the game, and, as they are very quick and generally good throwers, they will make fair players with some instruction."[15]

A few months later, on September 2, 1876, the Yokohamans were able not only to field a full team but also to upset the crack squad from the USS *Tennessee*, 29–26. The unexpected victory made baseball the most popular sport in the foreign community. A team member, who identified himself only as "An Exile in the Far East," wrote in a dispatch to the *New York Clipper*: "For some years we have been trying to get up a baseball club, but without success. . . . However, I am happy to state that, after beating the navy, ball-fever seized on the largest part of the American community, and now we have in Yokohama a club with over forty members, and in Tokio [*sic*], the capital, they have one with over thirty. Of course the largest part of us . . . had not had any practice for a few years."[16]

The Yokohama team began renting a field from the Cricket Club in 1877 and under the leadership of Edward Mudgett created a busy schedule, playing both the Tokyo club and visiting naval squads. In 1884 the club merged with the Yokohama Cricket Club to form the Yokohama Country and Athletic Club. A decade later, under this new name, the club would play a pivotal role in spreading baseball across Japan.

Japanese returning home after living in the United States also helped spread the game in their native land. In its effort to modernize, the new Meiji government not only imported *oyatoi*, but also sent talented students to study in the West during the early 1870s. Many young men sojourning in the United States soon became baseball enthusiasts. For example, Count Nobuaki Makino, who as the keeper of the privy seal would serve as the personal adviser to the emperor from 1925 to 1935, was supposedly the first Japanese to play the game, learning it while attending school in Philadelphia from 1871 to 1874.[17] Few, however, did more to promote baseball than Hiroshi Hiraoka.

The fifteen-year-old Hiraoka had been sent by his father to study in the United States in 1871.[18] He attended the Lewis Grammar School in the Roxbury section of Boston before working at several locomotive manufactories. During his six years in America Hiroshi became a passionate ballplayer and fan. Returning to Japan in 1877, Hiraoka landed a job with the Shinbashi-Yokohama Railroad and immediately introduced his new co-workers to baseball. The following year (1878) he organized the Shinbashi Athletic Club—Japan's first private baseball club. He charged membership dues and used the income to build the country's first true diamond in 1882 (the Yokohama club still played on the cricket grounds). Aisuke Kabayama, an early club member, would play ball for Wesleyan College in 1886, becoming the first Japanese to play for an American college.[19] A second private baseball club, the Hercules Club, was created in 1884, and other teams soon followed.[20] By 1890 at least a dozen Tokyo-area schools had baseball clubs.

At Japan's most prestigious high school, Daiichi Koto Gakko (First Higher School), baseball took on special importance. More commonly known by its nickname, Ichiko, the school was founded in 1886 as a national academy designed to prepare elite students between the ages of seventeen and twenty for the Imperial University. The curriculum emphasized not only academics, but also the moral training of Japan's future leaders. Students were separated from outside society, instilled with a strong sense of school spirit, and subjected to a Spartan lifestyle designed to purify their spirits. Their baseball team adopted a harsh workout regimen designed to strengthen both body and mind. Batters underwent thousand-swing drills while pitchers attempted to throw fastballs through the brick wall of the clubhouse.

The grueling practices allowed Ichiko's team to dominate its Japanese opponents. From 1890 to 1895 the team won six of the seven recorded games, outscoring opposing teams 124–27.[21] Seeking tougher competition, Ichiko repeatedly challenged the Yokohama Country and Athletic Club (YCAC) but was rebuffed each year. Finally, in 1896, the foreign team accepted and invited Ichiko to play in Yokohama on May 23.

For the Ichiko students there was more at stake than just baseball. After being humiliated by Commodore Perry's Black Ships and the Unequal Treaties, by the 1890s Japan was ready to assert its identity. The defeat of China in the first Sino-Japanese War (1894–95) led to a rise in Japanese nationalism and the widespread belief that Japan was ready to join the Western powers as an equal.[22]

For the Ichiko team the YCAC characterized Western arrogance. A student wrote, "The foreigners in Yokohama have established an athletic field in their central park into which no Japanese may enter. There, playing by themselves, they boast of their skill in baseball. When we attempt to challenge them, they refuse, saying, 'Baseball is our national game' or 'Our bodies are twice the size of yours.'"[23] The Japanese were determined to prove that they could beat the Americans at their national game.

Greeted by jeers from some of the foreign spectators when it took the field on May 23, the Ichiko team crushed its hosts, 29–4. After the game the president of the school's student body exclaimed, "This great victory is more than a victory for our school; it is a victory for the Japanese people!"[24]

The YCAC demanded an immediate rematch and although bolstered with players from the visiting USS *Charleston* and USS *Detroit* lost again, 32–9, on June 5. Two weeks later a team from the USS *Detroit* decided to teach the upstart students a lesson. It failed miserably. In front of nearly ten thousand spectators at Ichiko's home grounds in Tokyo, the students embarrassed the sailors by a score of 22–6.

An Ichiko student wrote in the baseball club's annual report, "The Americans are proud of baseball as their national game just as we have been proud of judo and kendo. Now, however, in a place far removed from their native land, they have fought against a 'little people' whom they ridicule as childish, only to find themselves swept away like falling leaves. No words can describe their disgraceful conduct. The aggressive character of our national spirit is a well-established fact, demonstrated first in the Sino-Japanese War and now by our great victories in baseball."[25]

A final rematch was scheduled for July 4. The Americans gathered an all-star team with the best players from the Yokohama settlement, the USS *Detroit*, and the USS *Olympia*, the flagship of the Pacific Fleet which had just arrived in port. In front of a large crowd gathered for the festive Independence Day event, which included a naval band and a twenty-one-gun salute from the warships anchored just offshore, the YCAC edged out a 14–12 victory. But the smugness was gone. The victors gave the Ichiko students cheers "in right good earnest" and the *Japan Weekly Mail* noted, "Competent critics agree that the Japanese team played a neater and better game."[26]

By the end of the series the Ichiko players had become national heroes. Major newspapers, including the *Asahi*, ran front-page articles on the victories, and the team received hundreds of congratulatory telegrams from schools across the nation. Almost overnight Japan became baseball crazy. Teenage boys across the country wanted to emulate their new heroes, and middle schools responded by creating baseball teams.

Although 541 miles from Tokyo, the students of Miyazaki Middle School, Harry Saisho's new school, were among the many to form a baseball club in the wake of Ichiko's victories. Harry arrived in April 1897, soon after the team was created.

Compared to Miyakonojo, Miyazaki must have felt like a metropolis to young Harry Saisho. Built on both banks of the Oyodo River, the city of about thirty thousand was a dense maze of wooden shops, inns, and homes. Amid the rambling traditional Japanese buildings were symmetrical Western-style structures built of stone with paned windows.

But it was still the backwater of Japan. There were no streetcars or trains and few, if any, automobiles. Travelers relied on rickshaws to go long distances. The streets remained unpaved, turning to deep mud during the rainy season, causing rickshaw wheels to sink and stick. Pedestrians used wooden sandals known as *geta* to raise their stocking feet above the squishy filth. Most of Miyazaki's population dressed in traditional Japanese clothing rather than the Western styles popular in Tokyo and Kobe. Everyday life in the city had changed little for the past few centuries.

Miyazaki Middle School was on the northern edge of town, near the famed Miyazaki Jingu, a second-century shrine dedicated to the mythic first emperor, Jimmu, who supposedly descended from the heavens just north of the city in 660 BC. The school was a rambling, ornate stone building, reminiscent of an ancient temple. In front of the gated entrance was a large parade ground, where Harry spent most of his free time playing ball.

Miyazaki Middle had three intramural teams: the Dormitory Club for live-in students; the Moshun Club; and the Shin-en (God Garden) Club, formed by commuting students. We do not know exactly when Harry first picked up a ball or bat, but by 1899 he was the captain and catcher of the Shin-en team. A student recalled, "At first, we didn't have mitts or shoes. The players had nothing but bare hands and feet. They wore white cotton kimono underwear plus a black waistband (an undress belt). They were like uncivilized barbarians, throwing stones. Many were injured by regulation baseballs."[27] Shin-en was known for its hard practices and on June 17, 1899, captured the school championship by defeating the Dormitory Club, 29–11. The core of Shin-en became the official school team the following season, with Saisho once again serving as captain and backstop.

Miyazaki Middle School's crosstown rival, the Miyazaki Teachers' Training School, also created a baseball team in 1896, while three other area schools (Miyakonojo Middle, Nobeoka Middle, and Miyazaki Agricultural School) formed clubs by 1898. In the autumn of 1900 the five teams met in the first Prefectural Schools Joint Great Athletic Meet to fight for the regional championship.

The Miyazaki Teachers' Training School team had beaten Kagoshima Prefectural Middle School (where Ken Kitsuse attended), 11–7, in July, making it the clear favorite. Just before the start of the tournament, Nobeoka Middle and Miyazaki Agriculture withdrew. With only three clubs remaining, organizers held a lottery to see which team would get a first round bye. Saisho and his Miyazaki Middle got lucky and watched as the Teachers polished off Miyakonojo, 20–11. The two Miyazaki rivals would battle it out for the championship.

The two schools were located next to each other but were profoundly different. Whereas Miyazaki Middle catered to the sons of former samurai, Teachers' Training offered generous scholarships and attracted "smart boys of modest means with high aspirations."[28] The boys from Teachers' Training were also older, having had to complete an additional two years of study after elementary school before admission. With this advantage Teachers' Training had never lost to Miyazaki Middle.

The game was hard-fought, both on the diamond and on the sidelines—bleachers came later. A former player named Sasaki (following the Japanese custom of the time, his first name was not recorded) recalled a typical game between the two schools: "They were good rivals, fighting and quarreling continuously. The Middle School supporters routinely booed the Teachers' Training team, and chanted, 'Scholarship! Scholarship!' Teachers' Training and its supporters endured the loud insult with resignation because in those days the students on national scholarships had an inferiority complex, which these days, one would be proud of."[29]

Although Saisho and his teammates no longer played in their

underwear, their equipment was rudimentary. Instead of sporting the flannel uniforms common in the United States and seen with increasing frequency in Tokyo and Osaka, the Miyazaki teams played in their physical education uniforms. Lacking proper spikes, players wore the traditional thick, split-toed workman's socks, called *tabi*, on their feet. Since they also lacked gloves, many players wore *tabi* on their left hands to cushion the sting of hard-stuck balls. Sasaki remembered: "Some pitchers stood on the mound in white cloth socks and threw a ball in a stylish way—although the mound did not rise like now but was only a white line drawn in lime-powder on the flat ground. Just imagine a pitcher's white socks, drawing a line of successive motion in space, before he took a throwing motion. It was a thrill!"[30]

Miyazaki Middle School histories record the game as a glorious victory. No details or box scores survive, but a short contemporary newspaper article suggests that it was a messy affair. "A heavy rainfall prevented the two schools from playing by the regulations. The schools discussed what they should do and decided to limit the game to four innings. The game ended with Teachers' Training [having] 14 runs to Miyazaki Middle's 29 runs. Miyazaki Middle won the baseball championship."[31]

The following year Miyazaki Middle again captured the prefectural crown. This time all five middle schools competed in October 1901 at Miyakonojo. Back in his hometown, Saisho probably visited with his family and old friends. He undoubtedly saw Shichiji Kikuchi, who finished in third place in the 500-meter dash for Miyakonojo Middle School. Harry's Miyazaki Middle School easily defeated Nebeoka Middle, 18–2, in the tournament's first round before facing Teachers' Training in the final. After its loss the previous year, the Teachers' Training team had spent the year practicing hard and, according to one unverifiable source, had even scrimmaged against the famed Ichiko team. Nonetheless, the result was the same. Miyazaki Middle once again upset the older squad, this time by a 7–2 score.

The school celebrated in prose:

Once upon a time, the Emperor Jimmu made the first manifestation in Takachiho, Miyazaki. He was the first and original of all the

Emperors of Japan. Now, no team is equal to our baseball team all over Kyushu. What a glorious history our baseball team is endowed with! Stand up, baseball braves! Do your best, baseball champions!

Look! The players—heroic figures;

Desperately catching a ball, which is driven in the mid sky;

Standing gallantly in a batter's box to defeat an enemy completely.

They are a great example of Japanese imperial military youth, and baseball should not be regarded just as leisurely play. Baseball is a reproduction of combat.[32]

But if truth be told, these early games bore little resemblance to modern baseball. In his 1967 "Miyazaki Prefecture Baseball History" Hirotake Tanimura wrote, "[These games] in reality, were at a sandlot baseball level. If present-day fans had seen the bouts, they would have regarded them as awkward teams, what we call today 'Early Bird Baseball' (a pickup game before going to work). Oh, boy! I ought not to have mentioned them like this; I should apologize. I didn't intend to blaspheme against the holy baseball games."[33]

At some point during high school, an encounter with a famous politician would alter Saisho's life. Count Sukenori Kabayama was born in nearby Kagoshima and was Harry's father's commanding officer in the Tokyo Metropolitan Police Force. During the 1890s he served as minister of the navy, governor-general of Taiwan, minister of education, and home minister of Japan. (Coincidently he was also the father of Aisuke Kabayama, who had played baseball for Wesleyan College.) While visiting Miyazaki, Kabayama spoke with young Harry about Japan's future and the need to prepare for the challenges of the twentieth century. The former minister advised Harry to ready himself by studying in the United States.

In March 1902 Saisho graduated from Miyazaki Middle (the Japanese school year goes from April to March) and headed to Tokyo to study English at Waseda University. One of four universities in Japan at the time, Waseda was founded as Tokyo Senmon Gakko (Tokyo College) by Shigenobu Okuma in 1882. Okuma had played a prominent role in the Meiji Restoration and the creation of the new government. He filled numerous high government positions, including minister of finance, foreign minister, and prime minister. Believing that the education offered at Japan's two national universities was too narrow to develop independent thinking, Okuma based his private school on Western models of education with an emphasis on international studies. When Saisho enrolled in 1902, the school had just transformed from a college to a university. It contained several schools and associated preparatory schools offering special courses such as languages. As Harry is not listed on the roll of regular Waseda students and would only stay a short time, he must have attended one of the preparatory schools to work on his English before leaving for the United States.

After a year at Waseda, Harry Saisho packed his trunk and boarded the ss *Gaelic* in Yokohama, ready to pursue his dreams.

3

The New World

Following the week-long ordeal in quarantine on Angel Island, Harry Saisho rushed ashore to see his new home. Even after the year in Tokyo, Harry was unprepared for the wonders of San Francisco. Tokyo was a city of nearly two million, crowded together in small, traditional wooden houses with the occasional Western-style three- or four-story building. In San Francisco buildings soared. Newly developed steel-frame construction allowed buildings to rise to previously unimagined heights. Five- to ten-story structures lined the city's thoroughfares. Above them all towered the opulent eighteen-story *Call* Building.

Harry gawked at modern streetcars gliding down the center of Market Street as horse-drawn buggies and wagons piled high with dry goods rumbled along. Automobiles, still rare in Japan, weaved around the slower traffic. The stores lining the major streets were filled with plenty and luxury—items available only to the very wealthy in Japan. Men with high, white collars protruding from their dark jackets, their heads covered with derby hats, strode down the sidewalks and dashed across the streets with little regard to traffic rules. Women in long, full dresses with large brimmed hats, often adorned with fresh flowers, strolled in small groups. Some men and women walked together as couples, hand in hand. Occasionally a couple would kiss—shocking Harry or any Japanese immigrant (kissing a "respectable woman" in public was taboo in Japan). "Everything [I] saw and heard was strange . . . and surprising," remembered Harry.[1]

Harry did not stay long in San Francisco as he planned to attend Leland Stanford Junior University, located in the town of Palo Alto, thirty-three miles to the southwest of the city. Saisho was taking a risk. He had not been accepted to the school before leaving Japan.

Japanese students could enroll at Stanford if they passed the school's rigorous entrance exam or if they could pass a test for English competency and had studied at the Imperial Universities of Tokyo and Kyoto or if they were graduates of the Sapporo Agricultural College, the Higher Commercial School, Doshisha College, Keio University, or one of the elite higher schools, such as Ichiko.[2] Saisho had attended none of these schools. As passing the entrance exam was beyond his language ability, Saisho hoped to be admitted as a Special Student.

Stanford admitted a small number of men and women who had "insufficient preparation for regular standing, but for those who are qualified by age, character, practical experience, and habits of study to profit by university courses," provided they could supply "satisfactory credentials and testimonials." These Special Students could enroll in classes but were not eligible for a degree. They were welcome, however, to apply for regular admission at any point.[3]

Although tuition at Stanford was just twenty dollars per semester for Special Students, room and board was significantly more—as much as twenty-five dollars per month.[4] Harry had arrived in San Francisco with only sixty dollars in his pocket, so he needed to find a job.[5] Fortunately the Stanford school newspaper routinely carried help wanted ads, many specifically looking for "Japanese Schoolboys."

The term "Japanese Schoolboys" had originated in the 1880s, when former president of the University of California William T. Reid and his wife Julia admitted several Japanese students to their Belmont School for Boys. In exchange for tuition and room and board, the young Japanese men performed domestic chores. By the first decade of the twentieth century the practice of hiring male Japanese students as part-time domestic servants was widespread across California. In 1906–7 there were about four thousand Schoolboys employed in San Francisco alone.[6]

On a typical weekday Saisho and most Schoolboys would arise at dawn, build the morning fire, boil water, set the table, and (in households that did not employ a cook) start breakfast. After the meal they would clean up and do the dishes before heading off to school. They would return around 4 p.m., help prepare the evening meal, set the table, and do the dishes and odd cleaning after the meal before spending the remainder of the evening studying. On Saturdays Schoolboys were expected to spend the day house cleaning. On Sundays they were free.

Most young Japanese men were completely unqualified for this job, however. In Japan women did nearly all the domestic work. This was particularly true among the former samurai class (such as Saisho's family), who often had servants. As a result, many Schoolboys were asked to do routine chores that they had never done before. Cultural differences and the language barrier compounded the difficulties. Most Japanese were unfamiliar with the daily tasks, customs, and furnishings of an American home. Even basics such as silverware and dishes were unfamiliar—let alone the complexities of late-Victorian table settings and dining etiquette. Novelist and poet Yonejiro Noguchi recalled his first days as a Schoolboy in San Francisco: "We acted . . . barbarously at the dinner table; we took salt for sugar and declared the cheese to be something rotten. We did not know which hand, left or right, had to hold [the] knife; we used a tablespoon for sipping coffee."[7]

The situation led to comical misunderstandings, reminiscent of the trials of the children's book character Amelia Bedelia. Noguchi remembered: "What a farce we enacted in our first encounter with an American family! Even a stove was a mystery to us. One of my friends endeavored to make a fire by burning the kindling in the oven. . . . One fellow terrified the lady [of the house] when he began to take off his shoes, and even his trousers, before scrubbing the floor. . . . It was natural enough for him, since he regarded his American clothes as a huge luxury."[8] Such misunderstandings were so widespread that the Japanese Schoolboy soon became a stereotype in American ethnic humor, epitomized by humorist Wallace Irwin's character Hashimura Togo. Irwin, a staff columnist for the weekly *Collier's*, published fictitious letters from his character, Togo, about his experiences in the United States. A collection of these works, titled *Letters of a Japanese Schoolboy*, became a top seller in 1909.

Not all encounters were lighthearted. Many Schoolboys complained of abuse—long hours, endless tasks, demanding mistresses, docked wages, poor food, and even physical abuse.[9] Missionary Sidney L. Gulick noted, "Most of the young men . . . are the sons of high-spirited samurai. To expect them to make good servants . . .

is quite unreasonable. . . . Such young men, inherently proud and self-respecting, instinctively resent such treatment as servants commonly receive in the West."[10]

Saisho left no record of his experiences as a Schoolboy, but it is possible that he received his nickname of "Harry" during this time. As many Americans had trouble pronouncing Japanese names, Schoolboys usually adopted American nicknames. Sometimes the young man chose his own name; sometimes the American family suggested one; and now and then the Schoolboy position came with a name that each Japanese man took in turn. According to family tradition, Saisho's nickname was given by an American friend who found "Atsuyoshi" too difficult to say.

Saisho began attending classes as a Special Student in the summer or fall of 1903.[11] At the time, there were just nine Japanese regular students enrolled at the school and a dozen or more Special Students. Although the university was generally supportive of its Japanese students, few would graduate. Only five received diplomas from 1891 to 1900.[12] Most found the course work in a foreign language too difficult, and Saisho was no exception. Despite the courses he had taken at Waseda, Harry found his English too weak to complete the classes. In the fall of 1903 he dropped out before the end of his first semester.

As the first son, Saisho should have returned to Japan, followed his father into public service in Miyakonojo, and eventually become the head of the family—an important position in Meiji Japan. But Harry had little interest in the traditional Japanese lifestyle. He was enamored with California and the relaxed American ways. He decided to remain in the United States and follow his own path.

Harry needed a full-time job, but he soon found that his employment opportunities were limited by more than his poor English. Open discrimination against Asians began soon after the Chinese arrived in California during the 1848 gold rush. Over the next two decades nearly sixty thousand Chinese immigrated to the state, alarming white nativists, who viewed these new immigrants as a threat to their jobs and culture. Most urban whites would not rent to or hire Chinese, leading to the creation of Chinatowns, where the immigrants could live together, work for each other, and openly practice

their culture. This process further segregated the Chinese immigrants and further marked them as different, leading many Americans to believe that Chinese were incapable of assimilation and would
always stand apart. The more extreme argued that Asians and whites
could not coexist peacefully as race carried "with it . . . such psycho-
logical, social, and civilizational differences that any attempt to live
together [was] sure to be disastrous."[13] They saw Asians, and Chinese in particular, as a threat to Western civilization, terrified that
the "Yellow Peril" would eventually dominate the world.

Violence erupted throughout the 1870s and '80s. On October 24,
1871, a mob attacked, tortured, and lynched about twenty Chinese in
Los Angeles. Fourteen years later in Rock Springs, Wyoming, white
miners attacked a Chinese community, burning homes and businesses
and killing twenty-eight. During the two decades 153 anti-Chinese
riots occurred on the West Coast alone.[14] Legal attacks on Chinese
began in the late 1860s, culminating with the Chinese Exclusion Act
of 1882, which prohibited the immigration of Chinese laborers for
ten years. The act was extended and amplified in 1892, requiring all
Chinese to carry registration cards or risk deportation. Chinese, as
well as other Asians, were also barred from becoming American citizens, preventing them from voting, serving on juries, and initiating legal challenges to their discrimination. The Naturalization Act
of 1890 had extended the right to apply for citizenship to "aliens of
African nativity and to persons of African descent" but had purposely
excluded other races as legislators feared that it would encourage
Chinese to remain in the United States permanently.

In the 1880s and early 1890s this discrimination against the Chinese did not necessarily extend to Japanese immigrants. Japanese
immigration began with a trickle—the federal census lists only 148
Japanese in the entire country in 1880 and just 2,039 in 1890. Many
of these early immigrants were students, merchants, and diplomats.
Few white Americans objected to these first immigrants, and pains
were made to differentiate Japanese from the hated Chinese. But as
Japanese immigration accelerated, bigotry grew.

Two months before the 1900 federal census recorded over ten
thousand Japanese living in California, the first major anti-Japanese
rally was held in San Francisco. Addressing a crowd at Metropol-

itan Hall, the city's mayor, James Duval Phelan, proclaimed, "The Chinese and Japanese are not bona fide citizens. They are not the stuff of which American citizens can be made. . . . As they will not assimilate with us and their social life is so different from ours, let them keep at a respectful distance."[15]

Organized opposition to Japanese immigration fizzled out soon after the rally, but anti-Japanese sentiment lingered, festering under the relative calm for the next few years. Saisho and other Japanese immigrants lived with daily acts of bigotry. They were turned away from restaurants, barber shops, and other white-owned businesses; refused housing in certain areas; and rejected at many places of employment.

Seemingly mild, but both grating and insidious, was the constant use of the term "Jap." Juhei Kono, who immigrated to Seattle, remembered, "Being called 'Japs' was almost an everyday occurrence for us. Hardly anybody . . . called us Japanese. . . . Some people commented, 'Please don't be offended if we say "Jap." It's only a word. It's almost an abbreviation . . . so just take it as such and don't be offended.' But, of course, it is still distasteful to us anyway. So I used to tell them, 'We don't hear it that way at all.'"[16]

Although many whites may not have realized it, "Jap" was often used in a pejorative manner to ridicule and dehumanize Japanese and to remind them of their inferior place in American society. In a Friday, November 23, 1906, editorial titled "It Makes Them Angry," the *Houston Post* both highlighted the issue and poked fun at the Japanese:

> Whenever an educated Japanese reads the word "Jap" in an American newspaper . . . his gorge rises, for to his sensitive soul the word appears as a term of derision. Furthermore, the Japanese credit the Americans with such intelligence that they never think for a moment that the word "Jap" is used largely as a result of ignorance. It is a fact, nevertheless, that three-fourths of the people of America regard the word "Jap" as perfectly proper. They regard the word "Jap" as they do such words as Pole, Swiss, French, Greek, Turk, etc. But they are all wrong. To call a proud son of Nippon a "Jap" is like calling a German a Germ, an Italian an It, a Belgian a Bel. . . .

It is not strange that the Japanese do not like it, for they are probably the proudest race of people on the globe today, and they are the
most warlike, and we know from history that it is a marked characteristic of warlike races to be sensitive and proud. If the Japanese
were possessed of a sense of humor, which distinguishes the people
of [the] United States from all other nations, it would make a little
difference with them, but lack of humor has always been a characteristic of the Oriental races.[17]

Saisho found that open discrimination within organized labor
precluded finding a job in manufacturing or at many white-owned
businesses. The limited opportunities in San Francisco included
working in one of the small number of Japanese-owned businesses,
toiling as a day laborer, or washing dishes in a restaurant.

Ever the dreamer, Saisho swore to himself to follow the path of
Kinki Ushijima—better known as George Shima, the Potato King—
and become a great businessman. Like Harry, Ushijima had arrived
in San Francisco knowing little English and had first worked as a
Schoolboy. Changing his name to George Shima, he left San Francisco in late 1889 to become a migrant agricultural laborer. He saved
his money, bought and drained undervalued swampland, and began
growing potatoes. Shima reinvested his profits into more swampland, and his operation grew. By 1900 he had more than three thousand acres, soon controlled the potato crop in northern California,
and became the first Japanese millionaire in the United States.

Harry began his life in agriculture as an olive picker near Palo
Alto in the autumn of 1903. Like most pickers, Saisho camped in
the groves in a tent or makeshift lean-to. He worked from dawn to
dusk, starting at the top of the tree, picking the ripe olives by hand
and dropping them on a waiting canvas spread on the ground below
the tree. He probably earned about a dollar per day.[18]

At the end of the olive season in February 1904, Saisho found
himself unemployed. Eager to earn money and not afraid of adventure, he signed a six-month contract to work in an Alaskan salmon
cannery. The pay was good—between $150 and $200 for the season
with free transportation to the cannery, as well as room and board—
but work was difficult and the hours long. Saisho recalled working

seven days a week in sixteen- to twenty-hour shifts. Chinese held the skilled positions, while Japanese, according to a 1911 congressional report, were "employed almost exclusively in the more unskilled and disagreeable parts of the work. They clean and cut fish, operate butchering and soldering machines, truck and pile cans, and act as helpers in the 'bathrooms.'"[19]

The workers were housed in barn-like bunkhouses, holding 50–100 men, segregated by ethnicity. When not working or sleeping, the Japanese tended to stay in their own bunkhouses, socializing, drinking—often to excess—and gambling at games organized by labor contractors, with losses deducted from wages. For workers who wished to spend their wages outside of the cannery, a host of entertainment establishments sprang up within walking distance. Salons, gambling dens, and brothels surrounded nearly every cannery. "Weekends were typical of the wild west," Saisho remembered, "gambling, drinking, cheating, stealing, and fighting." Harry, however, resisted temptations and held on to his wages, sending some back to his parents in Japan—the first and only time he did so.[20]

Saisho returned to California in the fall of 1904 and worked for a season as a day laborer on farms near Sacramento before taking a job in San Francisco as a dishwasher in a restaurant. At some point while living in San Francisco, Harry reunited with his childhood friend Ken Kitsuse.

A small man, standing 5 feet 2½ and weighing just 115 pounds, Ken's delicate, angular features, full eyebrows, and slicked-back, wavy black hair gave him movie-star good looks. Like Saisho, Kitsuse had fallen in love with baseball while attending Kagoshima Prefectural Middle School, which had a strong team, founded before 1890. Unfortunately no information on Kitsuse's scholastic career survives, but based on his later accomplishments, we can postulate that he was the team's starting shortstop from about 1899 until his graduation in 1902.

Poor, with only a high school education and disinherited, Ken's prospects in Japan were limited, so in 1903 he decided to emigrate to California with his brother Takeshi. Takeshi came first, arriving in San Francisco on February 14 on board the ss *Tosa Maru*. In May Ken's father, now known as Yuitsu Yasuda, escorted Ken and his friends Shichiji Kikuchi and Tamaki Masuda from Miyakonojo to the port of Yokohama, where they would board a ship to the United States. Yuitsu had left the Japanese Diet and now worked for the Toyo Emigration Company, placing Japanese laborers around the world. In 1900, for example, he led a group of seventy-seven Japanese to New Caledonia to work in the island's nickel mines. He was, however, still involved in local politics, and before Ken's ship set sail, a telegram arrived. A dysentery epidemic had broken out in a small village near Miyakonojo, and Yuitsu was needed to manage the problem. Father and son said hasty goodbyes, and Yuitsu departed. It would be the last time they would see each other.

On May 23 the three young men boarded the ss *Korea Maru* and arrived in San Francisco without incident nearly two weeks later, on June 8. For the next two years Kitsuse drops out of the historical record. Presumably he lived with his brother and worked in the Bay Area.

Tragedy struck in the summer of 1904. Ken's father had helped negotiate a contract to provide five hundred Japanese to work at the Boleo Copper mine in Mexico. In July Yuitsu accompanied the laborers on board the ss *Akebono Maru*. The ship arrived at Santa Rosalia on the Baja Peninsula on July 19, and the following day the group marched into the desert to the mine. Conditions were unbearable. Outdoor temperatures hovered around 120 degrees Fahrenheit, making the copper ores "so hot that any contact . . . meant an immediate burn," and poor ventilation in the mines led to roasting temperatures and a buildup of poisonous gases. After three days, the new laborers walked off the job and fled to the *Akebono Maru* —some having to swim from the dock to the moored ship. Negotiations between the mine and Yasuda failed, and the ship sailed for Japan with all but fifty of the promised Japanese laborers on board. During the return voyage Yuitsu mysteriously "became mentally deranged" and died at sea on August 23.[21]

On February 8, 1904, a few months before Yasuda's ill-fated voyage, Japan attacked the Russian Navy stationed at Port Arthur in Manchuria, starting the Russo-Japanese War. Tiny Japan won stunning victories against the mighty Russian Empire at Port Arthur (February 1904 and January 1905) and Mukden (March 1905). In general, admiration for Japan was high across the United States. It was a classic David versus Goliath story, and the American public loved an underdog. But for some, Japan's success raised concern. They worried that a victorious Japanese military would continue its march across the Pacific with its eyes on California, where it would be aided by tens of thousands of Japanese immigrants.

Japanese immigration had continued throughout the war, with nearly eight thousand arriving in 1904 alone.[22] This influx of new arrivals, combined with the concern over Japanese military prowess, worried nativists, including *San Francisco Chronicle* editor John P. Young, who argued that "if the 'inundation of Japanese' were not 'checked,' the result would be a 'complete orientalization of the Pacific Coast.'"[23]

On February 23, 1905, the *San Francisco Chronicle* began what historian Roger Daniels called "a crusade against the Japanese."[24] The front-page headline in large type announced, "The Japanese Invasion, the Problem of the Hour for the United States." The article laid out a thesis that the paper would expound upon for the next few months:

> In the accompanying article the *Chronicle* begins a careful and conservative exposition of the problem which is no longer to be ignored—the Japanese question. It has been but lightly touched upon heretofore; now it is pressing upon California and upon the entire United States as heavily and contains as much menace as the matter of Chinese immigration ever did if, indeed, it is not more serious, socially, industrially, and from an international standpoint. . . . The Japanese is no more assimilable than the Chinese and he is no less adaptable in learning quickly how to do the white man's work and how to get the job for himself by offering his labor for less than a white man can live on. Once the war with Russia is over, the brown stream of Japanese immigration is likely to become an inundating torrent and the class of the immigrants is likely to become worse instead of better.[25]

Future headlines would read: "Japanese a Menace to American Women," "Brown Men an Evil in the Public Schools," "Brown Peril Assumes National Proportions," and "The Yellow Peril—How the Japanese Crowd Out the White Race."[26] The *Chronicle*'s stories were just the beginning. In early March the California legislature passed an anti-Japanese resolution calling upon the U.S. Congress to limit Japanese immigration. The resolution concluded, "Japanese laborers, by reason of race habits, mode of living, disposition and general characteristics[,] are undesirable."[27]

Agitation continued, and on May 14, 1905, in a well-attended meeting in San Francisco, representatives from over a hundred civic and labor organizations formed the Japanese and Corean [*sic*] Exclusion League. Later known as the Asiatic Exclusion League, the organization would remain at the forefront of the anti-Japanese movement until after World War II. From the league's birth its organizers objected not only to the use of cheap Japanese labor, but also to the immigrants themselves on racial grounds.

The initial resolutions, passed during the May 14 meeting, held that "the racial incompatibility as between the peoples of the orient and the United States presents a problem of race preservation which it is our imperative duty to solve in our own favor, and which can only be the solved by a policy of exclusion."[28] The league's racial stance would harden, and two years later its proclaimed principles would include the following: "We cannot assimilate them [Asians] without injury to ourselves. . . . No large community of foreigners, so cocky, with such distinct racial, social and religious prejudices, can abide long in this country without serious friction. . . . We cannot compete with a people having a low standard of civilization, living and wages. . . . It should be against public policy to permit our women to intermarry with Asiatics."[29]

As anti-Japanese sentiment grew, a negative stereotype for Japanese emerged. It is not surprising that this stereotype supported the Asiatic Exclusion League's rhetoric and was used not only by the league, but also by sympathetic newspaper writers to stem Japanese immigration. The intertwined and sometimes contradictory traits depicted the Japanese as an alien and inferior race incapable of assimilating into American society. They were seen as inherently dishonest, deviously clever, and animal-like in their lack of sexual morality and ability to withstand appalling work conditions. They were also portrayed as prideful, clannish, and militaristic, with unwavering loyalty to their native country and emperor. Physically, Japanese were depicted as small, often misshapen, and dirty.[30]

As the *Chronicle* attacked the Japanese in print, physical attacks on the Japanese in the streets increased. Nisuke Mitsumori, who worked for the San Francisco-based Japanese newspaper *Nichi Bei*, remembered:

> It was March or April of 1905 when I landed in San Francisco. . . . There was a gang of scoundrels who came to treat the immigrants roughly as soon as they heard that some Japanese had docked. . . . They were a group of 15 to 20 youngsters who shouted, "Let's go! The Japs have come!" We rushed to the inn to avoid being hit. As we went along, we were bombarded with abuses. . . . They even picked up horse dung off the street and threw it at us. I was baptized with horse dung. This was my very first impression of America. . . .
>
> At that time American feeling towards the Japanese was already bad in general, and we were advised not to walk alone during the day and not to go out at night. It was particularly dangerous after school was over. I never went out at night, and even during the day I tried to avoid the streets where American youngsters might be. I felt very insecure, not economically but physically. I remember those incidents in which young Japanese boys who worked for the paper came back to the office beaten up. It happened frequently. Sometimes we celebrated the fact that we were not hit that day. I began to think that San Francisco was not a good place to stay.[31]

Four hundred miles to the south, the smaller city of Los Angeles beckoned. It had grown rapidly since the discovery of oil in 1892 but had a population of just 170,000, half the size of San Francisco. City leaders were anxious to develop business and were decidedly anti–organized labor. As the unions were almost exclusively white, this gave minorities opportunities for employment. The city acquired a reputation for racial tolerance—at least by the standard of the time. Between 1890 and 1900 nearly five thousand African Americans arrived. Soon Japanese began to join them. In 1905 Harry Saisho and Ken Kitsuse decided to try their luck in the City of Angels. There they would meet the enigmatic Tozan Masko and eventually become professional ballplayers.

4

Issei Baseball

Tozan Masko was a precocious young man. He was the third son of Kurobei Mashiko, a large landowner and entrepreneur from the village of Niida in the Iwase district of Fukushima Prefecture. Born on July 4, 1881, his parents named him Takanori. Japanese kanji can be pronounced in several ways, so the characters used to write his name can also be read as "Koji." Throughout his life he would use both variations as his first name but usually went by his nickname, Tozan. He, or his father, also shortened the last name to Masuko. Later in life Tozan would Anglicize the last name to Masko.[1]

Niida was a remote village with a population of just 2,375 in 1889. To pursue his business interests Kurobei maintained a home in Tokyo, where Tozan may have been born and raised. As a young teen in Tokyo, Masko frequented the offices of the *Yamato* newspaper, the third or fourth largest newspaper in the country with a circulation of 20,000–28,000. It was known for its gossip columns and color wood-block prints (*nishiki-e*) of significant events. Young Tozan impressed the reporters with his intelligence and drew the attention of prominent politician and fellow Iwase native Hironaka Kono. A fierce supporter of the Meiji Restoration and democracy, Kono realized that Japan would soon become a world power and advised Masko to study in the United States to master English and receive a Western education.

On April 17, 1896, fourteen-year-old Tozan Masko boarded the ss *Doric* in Yokohama to begin his journey. He traveled without a chaperone or companion in Asiatic steerage. Fortunately the voyage was uneventful and quick. Not making the usual stop in Honolulu, the *Doric* went straight from Yokohama to San Francisco, setting a record for the fastest Pacific crossing at twelve days, twenty-two

hours, and eighteen minutes.[2] After a brief stay at the Angel Island
quarantine station, Masko entered San Francisco on May 1, 1896.

Masko settled at the Japanese Methodist Episcopal Mission at
1329 Pine Street, between Hyde and Larkin Streets, on the southwest slope of Nob Hill.[3] Just a few blocks away, at the crest of the
hill, stood the magnificent mansions of San Francisco's elite. But at
the hill's base the neighborhood was decidedly more modest. Two-
story wooden houses divided into "flats" lined the streets, alongside
larger, three-story boarding houses and light industries—printing,
carpentry, and machine shops. The area was gritty. Coal-burning
furnaces in nearly every dwelling created perpetual smog, exac-
erbated by the city's famous fog. With the smog came a fine black
grime that settled on every surface. A coal yard located just three
doors down made the Japanese mission especially dirty. In these pre-
automobile days horse dung and garbage littered the street. Stables
stood on nearly every block, further assaulting one's sense of smell.
To repair the horses' shoes the local farrier's hammer could be heard
banging throughout the day. On top of this the sickly-sweet smell
of yeast and hops from the large San Francisco Brewery and the
Golden Gate Yeast Company, located just a block away at 1426 Pine,
permeated the neighborhood.[4]

One block north of the mission stood the remarkable Lurline Salt
Water Baths, a large two-story building containing a 150-x-75-foot
unheated salt-water swimming pool with two water slides. Water for
the pool was drawn daily from San Francisco Bay, piped four miles
to the company's five-million-gallon reservoir and then on to the
pool. Private steam-heated baths were available on a balcony above
the pool. Both the pool and baths were open to the public for a cost
of just thirty cents, including a rental bathing suit. Special hours,
9 a.m. to 12 p.m., twice a week, were set aside for women bathers.

Masko, along with about thirty other Japanese men, lived in a two-
story wooden dormitory positioned immediately behind the church.
The residents were fed three meals a day in return for a nominal
fee and chores. No alcohol or gambling was permitted. A national
report of the Methodist Episcopal Church noted that the mission's
"aim is to keep the church abreast of the needs of the people, and
for this purpose there is maintained the Anglo-Japanese Training

School, . . . an English language school . . . [that] seeks to fit pupils for the schools in America." The course of study was challenging, taking three years to complete, and few residents finished the program. In 1900, the only year that still has surviving data, as many as two hundred men enrolled in the school, but only six graduated.[5]

Young Masko excelled at the mission school. Industrious and ambitious, he picked up English quickly and helped organize a student club. When not attending classes, Masko worked at the *Shin Sekai* newspaper, a Japanese language daily founded in 1894 by Hachiro Soejima. Although *Shin Sekai* would become one of the leading Japanese papers in California, at the time it was still a small enterprise with a circulation of just two hundred.[6]

In the summer of 1897 Masko was ready leave the mission and find a job. He took out an advertisement in the help wanted section of the June 26 issue of the *San Francisco Chronicle*: "Japanese boy wishes a situation to do light housework: has good recommendation. Please address G. Masuko 1329 Pine St." Although Masko would use a Japanese surname for most of his life, he would occasionally, especially when interacting with Anglo-Americans, use "George" as his first name. The advertisement ran for only one week as Masko found employment as a chef in the household of Claus Spreckels, the largest beet sugar manufacturer in the United States, whose son owned the neighboring Lurline Salt Water Baths. Masko worked and lived at one of the Spreckels's estates in the Santa Cruz area, where he also attended an American high school and became an avid baseball player.

After four years with the Spreckels, Masko returned to the *Shin Sekai* newspaper in 1902. Newspaper founder Hachiro Soejima placed him at the head of the paper's Fresno office, where he remained for a year and a half until he was forced to resign. The reason for his resignation is lost to time. The record only states that the transgression was another's fault. In 1904 Masko, now nearly twenty-four years old, moved to Los Angeles to take a job with the *Rafu Shimpo* newspaper.

At the beginning of the twentieth century Los Angeles contained a small but rapidly expanding Japanese community. In 1890 fewer than a hundred Japanese lived in the city, but fourteen years later the community had grown to nearly four thousand. By 1907 the population would rise to six thousand. Nearly all these new residents were men. Known as birds of passage—*deseki* in Japanese—they planned to stay in the United States a short time, earn as much as possible, and return to Japan with enough money to purchase a farm or business and start a family.

Japanese-owned boarding houses and supporting businesses sprung up to accommodate the new arrivals. Most were located around North San Pedro Street and First Avenue, an area that would become known as Little Tokyo. By 1907 there were more than sixty Japanese-owned lodging houses and a half dozen pool halls, as well as barbershops, groceries, and other businesses. There were also over sixty Japanese-owned restaurants, which catered to their own countrymen instead of serving the general American-born population. Many were drinking establishments known as *nomiya*. With the large, transient, mostly male population came problems. Public drunkenness and disorderly behavior became nightly occurrences, brawls increasingly commonplace, and gambling and prostitution widespread.[7]

As Los Angeles's Japanese community grew, two young students at the University of Southern California saw an opportunity. There were no local Japanese-language newspapers. To get their news Japanese speakers relied on papers printed in San Francisco. Seijiro Shibuya, a twenty-five-year-old son of a wealthy Tokyo samurai family, and twenty-six-year-old Masaharu Yamaguchi, a graduate of Tokyo Imperial University, created the *Rafu Shimpo* (Los Angeles Currier) in April 1903. The first issues came out sporadically, written by hand and mimeographed.[8]

Within months the newspaper prospered, and Yamaguchi returned to Japan to purchase a set of printer's type in Japanese—an item unavailable in the United States. The founders set up offices in four cramped rooms on the second floor of 128 N. Main St. (where City Hall now stands) and hired a small staff. On February 1, 1904, the paper began as a daily.

The paper soon attracted a number of bright, progressive, ambitious young men as writers and editors. Tozan Masko joined the staff in the spring, and a few months later, in August 1904, Hanzaburo

Harase came on board as a writer and editor. A graduate of either the Japanese Naval School or the aristocratic Peers College (sources differ), Harase arrived in the United States to visit the 1904 World's Fair in St. Louis and then settled in Los Angeles. A brilliant, creative thinker, he would eventually become a successful businessman, engineer, and inventor, holding several mechanical patents. Harase was said to have a "sense of humor so great that he could compete with Charlie Chaplin."[9]

The pay at *Rafu Shimpo* was poor. As chief editor, Shibiya made $25 per month; Harase and the other editors/writers received $15–$18. (At the time uneducated day laborers made one dollar per day.) On these meager salaries the writers could not afford to rent an apartment, so most slept and cooked their skimpy meals in the cramped newspaper offices. When the office was full of sleeping writers and printing supplies, reporters would sleep in the "black only" bathroom (restrooms were segregated at that time) located on the building's second floor.

With the start of the Russo-Japanese War the paper's circulation rose from 250 to 400 as Japanese immigrants wanted to stay abreast of the latest developments. Unable to keep up with the increased demand in the tiny second-floor rooms, the paper moved to the building's larger basement in 1905. Despite its rising sales, the newspaper remained amateur. Articles and editorials were often poorly thought out, recklessly opinionated, and needlessly argumentative. Such flaws led to libel suits and disputes with prominent members of the Japanese community.

The writers were a young, rowdy bunch. Nearly all were sons of ex-samurai families, educated at the top schools in Japan before coming to California to further their education or make their fortune. Los Angeles offered many vices, and *Rafu Shimpo*'s staff sampled them regularly. In 1929 Harase remembered having to rouse hungover writers sleeping in the segregated bathroom. "Tozan Masko and Kotan Saito asked for a few minutes, put their heads into the dirty toilets, and flushed water over their heads. They then claimed that they felt better."[10] Saito's and fellow editor Yoshio Sato's drinking binges would occasionally shut down the newspaper. Without their contributions the paper could not go to press, and after particularly raucous evenings the next day's issue would have to be canceled. The paper kept the type assembled to print a one-page apology "saying that there would be no issue as the printing press was broken" just for these occasions.[11]

The drinking sometimes led to brawling. On Harase's second day at the paper he arrived at the office and "was first surprised by the smell of alcohol, second by groans, and by finding a monster-like person, named Ono, sleeping on the floor wrapped in a newspaper. His face looked just like a bulldog's. Shibuya was sleeping right next to him. He didn't seem to have a nose either. They looked very different from how they had looked the day before. Apparently, Shibuya had gotten into a fight with a police officer the night before. Ono tried to stop them but also got hit. No wonder I couldn't see their noses in their swollen purple faces."[12]

Some staff members frequented Los Angeles's red-light district. A small scandal erupted in late 1904–5, when the rival paper, *Rafu Mainichi*, ran a large article attacking *Rafu Shimpo* founder Masaharu Yamaguchi and another editor under the headline "Elite Gentleman Buying Prostitutes." The motive for the attack soon became apparent. *Mainichi*'s editor was not only a business rival, but also Yamaguchi's rival for the affections of the same prostitute.

On weekend afternoons, when they were not working, drinking, or whoring, the young reporters played baseball. The team began in 1904, probably with informal pick-up games joined by whoever could be convinced to play. Soon, however, a true team coalesced, and players joined from outside the newspaper. An article in the *Los Angeles Herald* noted that the squad was calling itself the Japanese Base Ball Club of Los Angeles by May 17, 1905.[13]

The team included Harase, the drinking partners Saito and Sato, and Tozan Masko. Twenty-five-year-old Takejiro Ito, one of the most respected men in Los Angeles's Japanese community, became the club's first president. From Chiba Prefecture, Ito graduated from Saisei Gakusha Medical School at just seventeen years old in 1895 and passed the national medical board two years later. In 1898 he immigrated to the United States and, after stints in Portland and Fresno, arrived in Los Angeles to open his own medical practice around 1903. Despite his education and stature in the community, Ito meshed well with his *Rafu Shimpo* teammates. A biographical entry noted that he was "very friendly to everyone, having relationships with people in all different social levels. He loves sake and was very energetic and never got a hangover." As he got older, Ito would become known as a community organizer and patron of Japanese sports such as sumo, jiujitsu, and archery, as well as baseball.[14]

Soon after arriving in Los Angeles in late 1905, Harry Saisho and Ken Kitsuse visited the *Rafu Shimpo* office, met with the ballplayers, and joined the team. Finding an open space to play ball near the newspaper offices was difficult. By 1904 office and industrial buildings covered most of downtown Los Angeles. The ballplayers would walk east on First Street, past the domed Santa Fe Railroad depot, across the First Street Bridge, to the open lots on East First Street, just west of Aliso Road and Boyle Ave. In the late 1880s to early 1890s the area held one of the city's first baseball fields. Known as the Old First Street Grounds, the ballpark was owned and operated by Marco Hellman, the son of Isaias Hellman, a wealthy banker, real estate developer, and founder of the University of Southern California. No description of the ballpark survives, although we know that it had a grandstand shaded by canvas because two local boys stole the covering in August 1890.[15] The park was closed in 1895, but maps show that sections remained undeveloped until after 1905.[16] Each Sunday the members of the Japanese Base Ball Club of Los Angeles would meet at the open lot and practice or play against other amateur teams. According to an unidentified longtime resident, these games became "celebrated as a healthy form of entertainment in the Japanese community."[17]

The club was among the earliest Japanese immigrant baseball teams. The first teams emerged in Hawaii, where large numbers of Japanese had immigrated to work on the islands' sugar plantations. In 1896 Reverend Takie Okumura, concerned about the moral and physical welfare of children left on their own while their parents toiled in the fields and mills, established a Japanese kindergarten and the Honolulu Japanese Elementary School. Three years later he organized his students into a baseball team called the Excelsiors. Although just youths, the Excelsiors are the first known all-Japanese team organized outside of Japan. Within a few years other

Japanese youth teams, such as the Asahi, were created. Adult teams followed, and in 1908 the first Japanese baseball league was established in Honolulu with five teams. A decade later the Hawaiian Islands contained dozens of organized Japanese ball clubs at all levels, playing in both Japanese and multiethnic leagues.[18]

On the mainland United States primary sources for early Japanese immigrant baseball are scarce—almost nonexistent. Few copies of Japanese immigrant newspapers prior to 1906 survive, and mainstream American newspapers mostly ignored Asian players and teams. As a result, there is no primary evidence of a Japanese immigrant team on the mainland prior to the *Herald*'s May 1905 reference to the *Rafu Shimpo* club. But oral tradition states that the first Issei team began in San Francisco when famed artist Chiura Obata founded the Fuji Athletic Club in the fall of 1903 and designed the team's interlocking FAC logo. Tradition also states that the following year a group of young men from Kanagawa Prefecture organized the Kanagawa Doshi Club (KDC) in the Bay City.[19]

Two reports of individual Japanese playing in the United States before May 1905 did reach the national press. On June 7, 1897, "Patsy" Tebeau, the player-manager of the Cleveland Spiders, whose outfield already included Native American Louis Sockalexis, sprung some choice news on a reporter from the *Washington Post*:

> By the way, I forgot to tell you that we are going to enlarge the curio department of the Spiders. Sockalexis is the feature of our museum now, barring a necktie that Jack O'Connor brought in Boston and broke the Sabbath with. . . . Besides Sockalexis and Jack's Sabbath breaking neckwear in our museum, I will place a five-foot-three Jap. This Jap is built like little Cub Stricker [the Cleveland infielder who stood 5 feet 3 and weighed 138 pounds] and is a relative of Sorakichi, the Japanese wrestler, who died a few years ago. He was brought to my attention by Pete Gallagher, the old catcher, who is now a politician in Chicago. Jap has played on amateur teams in Chicago. He is swift as a bullet and can hit in the .300 class, so Pete believes. He handles himself like a seasoned veteran. I will spring him on the public next season. These museum attractions on a ball team are box-office successes.[20]

About a month later *Sporting Life* announced, "It is reported that Manager Tebeau of Cleveland has signed a new player in the person of a Japanese athlete and juggler, a half-brother to Matsuda Soraki-chi, the famous wrestler. Tebeau thinks the Jap will be the marvel of the diamond and the greatest player of the century."[21]

Tebeau, however, did not follow through on his plan, and newspapers provide no more information on this mysterious Japanese ballplayer. His reported half-brother, Matsuda Sorakichi, was well known to most sporting fans in the 1880s. Born in 1859 in Japan, Matsuda was a trained sumo wrestler with the name Torakichi before emigrating to the United States in 1883 and becoming a professional wrestler. He wrestled throughout the Northeast and Great Lakes area, facing the world's top wrestlers during his seven-year career. In 1885 he married Ella B. Lodge, a white American widow from Philadelphia, but the two would separate before Sorakichi died penniless on August 16, 1891. No record of Matsuda's having a half-brother or other relatives in the United States has been found. It is, of course, highly possible that Tebeau, or his friend Pete Gallagher, claimed that the Japanese player was a relative of the famous wrestler to help publicize the prospect.[22]

No other Japanese ballplayer would make the news until 1905, when Patsy Tebeau's archrival John McGraw of the New York Giants reportedly tried to sign a Japanese. On February 10 the *New York Times* reported, "When the New York National League players start south on their training trip they will be accompanied by a Japanese ball player, who answers to the name of Shumza Sugimoto. He is twenty-three years old, an outfielder, and played last year with the Cuban Giants. While McGraw does not expect the Japanese to make the team, he has consented to take him South, and see what there is in him. Sugimoto is a jiu jitsu expert . . . [and] weighs only 118 pounds, but it is said can handle a man who tips the scales at 175."[23]

The next day the *Elmira Gazette and Free Press* added that Sugimoto was "a remarkable outfielder, a fine batter and skillful base runner [who] is likely to be put into regular service in center field."[24] Other publications picked up the news and added that Sugimoto "was a masseur at the Hot Springs, where McGraw found him and took him on the field to try him out. The little manager declared he was 'all to the good.'"[25]

Even if Sugimoto had the ability to make the Giants, his eligibility to play in the National League was in doubt. McGraw told the *Sporting Life*, "The question as to whether a Mongolian can play in the National League will be raised in time."[26] On February 25 the *Oakland Tribune* ran an article questioning the validity of barring Japanese. The article noted, "All this talk of drawing the color line on Sugimoto seems rather incongruous when one recalls the fact that Bender, Sockalexis and other Indians have been allowed to play in the big league." Furthermore, "There is nothing in the by-laws and constitution of the National League which would prevent Sugimoto from making his appearance at the historic Polo Grounds."[27] Sugimoto seemed indignant that he could be barred from playing. *Sporting Life* reported that he "does not like the drawing of the color line in his case and says he will remain a semi-professional with the Creole Stars of New Orleans if his engagement by the Giants will be resented by the players of other clubs."[28]

Whether it was on account of race or ability, McGraw did not sign Sugimoto, and he disappears from the records. Attempts to trace his baseball career with the Cuban Giants and Creole Stars or his personal life have been fruitless. A tantalizing document, however, suggests his possible past. On March 10, 1904, the *Louisiana*, out of Havana, docked at New Orleans. Among the passengers was the Sugimoto Acrobat Troupe from Japan. During the voyage one of the troupe "was attacked in the hold of a steamship traveling from Havana to New Orleans by an infuriated panther. His cries for help were quickly answered, but not before he was terribly torn." After disembarking, the Sugimoto Troupe joined the Great Floto Show, a traveling circus, and toured throughout the West and Louisiana. The troupe consisted of forty-four-year-old K. Sugimoto and his five sons, who ranged in age from eight to twenty-three. The eldest son, recorded in the passenger list as S. Sugimoto, born about 1881, would be the same age as Shumza Sugimoto, who would play ball in New Orleans. Although it is possible, it seems unlikely that there were two twenty-three-year-old athletes from Japan named S. Sugimoto living in the New Orleans area during the winter of 1904–5.[29]

Starting in April 1905, Japanese baseball was again in the news as Isoo Abe and his Waseda University Base Ball Club arrived in San Francisco with plans to tour the United States. It would be the first foreign team to play in America. The visit would transform both international and Japanese American baseball and change Saisho's and Kitsuse's lives.

5

Waseda Arrives

Isoo Abe was an idealistic man. He spent his life trying to improve Japanese society, championing women's suffrage, unionized labor, and methods to eliminate poverty. He is known as "the Founding Father of Japanese Socialism" and recognized as one of the greatest intellectuals of the late Meiji era. He was also the founding father of Japanese baseball and the first to use the game to foster goodwill between two nations.

Born Isoo Okamoto in 1865, Isoo was the second son of a samurai and martial arts teacher from the southern city of Fukuoka.[1] At the age of fourteen he enrolled at the Christian Doshisha Seminary in Kyoto, where he became both a Christian and a pacifist. Soon after graduating from Doshisha in 1884, he arranged to be adopted by the heirless Abe family, thereby allowing him to be excused from military service as an only son. Now known as Isoo Abe, he returned to Doshisha as an instructor before leaving in August 1891 for the United States to study at the Hartford Seminary in Connecticut.

Abe lived in Connecticut for three years, graduating in June 1894. During this time he read Edward Bellamy's popular novel *Looking Backward*—a story of a man transported 113 years into the future, when American had become a socialist utopia. Deeply moved, Abe became a socialist. Surprisingly during his three years in the United States, Abe never watched a baseball game. He would not be introduced to the sport until he returned to Japan.[2]

In 1894 Abe traveled to Europe and during a brief stop in England read a newspaper account of a track and field contest between Oxford and Yale Universities. On July 18 nearly fifty thousand people braved the rains and "cold gusty wind" to watch the two universities "struggle for athletic supremacy" at the Queen's Club Grounds in London. The *Los Angeles Herald* reported: "It is probable that no event of recent years in the history of English athletics has attracted half the interest which centered in today's contests on the grounds of the Queen's club. The champion university team of England was to meet the champion university team of America, and this was sufficient to cause the wildest enthusiasm among all admirers of athletic sports, and among sportsmen generally throughout the British Isle."[3]

The excitement surrounding the contest made Abe realize the potential for international athletics to bring countries closer together. "I was inspired by that news," he wrote. "What a nice idea it is! I hope I can organize such international competitions someday."[4]

Soon after Abe returned home in 1895, Ichiko defeated the Yokohama Country and Athletic Club, initiating Japan's first national baseball craze. Walking on the Doshisha campus around 1897, Abe saw a baseball game for the first time. He immediately realized that the game not only developed notions of team unity and fair play, but was also the ideal sport for Japanese to play against the United States. Baseball, he would come to believe, was a tool for eliminating prejudice and thus would contribute to world peace.[5]

In 1899 Abe joined the faculty at Waseda University (then known as Tokyo Senmon Gakko), teaching economics and political science. Focusing on the growing economic inequalities in Japan, he soon became one of the nation's most prominent and prolific social critics. In 1901 he formed Japan's first socialist political party. Advocating disarmament, public ownership of land, and industrial rights for workers, it was promptly banned by the government.[6]

Also in 1901 Abe helped create Waseda's baseball club and became the team's manager. A short, stocky man with a large head and a droopy left eye from birth, the thirty-six-year-old Abe was a poor ballplayer but nevertheless practiced with the students to learn the game. In the evenings he often lectured the team on his philosophy of sport. For Abe baseball and the quest for a socialist utopia were intertwined. "He was convinced," writes historian Masako Gavin, "that team sports, as exemplified by baseball, were the best way to instill the spirit of fair play and cooperation required of citizens in the coming social order."[7]

Soon after forming the team, Abe met with Waseda's founder,

Shigenobu Okuma, to explain his desire to take the baseball team abroad. "He laughed at me," Abe told the Stanford University newspaper, "and told me that we must first have a team that would win the championship of Japan."[8]

Waseda challenged its first opponents in 1903, beating the American members of the Yokohama Country and Athletic Club, 9–7, and losing to its rival school, Keio University, 11–9. After the season Abe promised his players that he would arrange a trip to the United States if they could win the local championship by defeating Tokyo's three major teams: Ichiko, Keio, and Gakushuin (an institute of higher learning reserved for members of the greater imperial family). To help, Abe convinced former University of Chicago player Fred Merrifield, who was teaching at Tokyo Gakuin College, to coach the team.

When Merrifield began, the Waseda players were pretty raw. They understood the basics of the game but none of its finer points. They also lacked up-to-date equipment. They played with makeshift gloves and did not own spikes so wore *tabi* (the traditional heavy split sock used by workmen). Merrifield taught them "scientific baseball," worked on their fielding, and taught pitcher Atsushi Kono how to throw a curveball.[9]

The Waseda players learned their lessons well, going undefeated in 1904, including a 28–3 walloping of the Yokohama Country and Athletic Club. That summer Abe asked the university administration to send the team abroad, but this timing could hardly have been worse.

A few months earlier Japan had attacked the Russians at Port Arthur, starting the Russo-Japanese War. Despite early victories Japan's economy and military were stretched to the limits as the country waited for the Russian counterattack. In October 1904 Admiral Zinovy Rozhestvensky, commanding Russia's powerful Baltic Fleet, set sail for Japan. The armada contained thirty-eight ships— eleven battleships, nine destroyers, six cruisers, and twelve support vessels. They would sail halfway around the world—eighteen thousand nautical miles—from the Baltic to the Sea of Japan with orders to destroy the Japanese Navy. The voyage would take months, and they were expected to arrive in the spring of 1905. To send a group of students across the world to play baseball in the midst of this crisis seemed insane. The Waseda administration promptly rejected Abe's request. Abe, however, was stubborn. He appealed to Okuma, reminding him of their earlier conversation. Harkening back to the Oxford-Yale athletic competition of 1894, Abe argued that the tour would strengthen ties with the United States through the mutual love of sport and fair play. Furthermore, he maintained that Americans would be impressed that Japan was confident enough to sponsor a sporting event in the midst of a major conflict.[10] Okuma, who had served Japan as both prime minister and foreign minister, agreed and approved the tour provided that funding could be procured. Abe later wrote the following:

> I explained to [the administration] that the money would be raised from the admission fees from our games in the United States. I showed them *Spalding's Baseball Guide* and insisted that the professional baseball game held in New York drew 40,000 fans and the other game in Boston attracted 35,000 spectators. I told them that we could earn at least ¥6000 per game, if our game drew 10,000 people and we requested our opponent to yield us two-thirds of the total admission fee.... They believed what I said and finally allowed our tour. If I had known that college baseball in the United States was far less popular than professional baseball at that time, I would not have planned our baseball tour.[11]

On April 4, 1905, Abe and his squad of twelve students boarded the ss *Korea* in Yokohama, bound for the United States. The team traveled in first class, an unheard-of expense for students, to underscore the importance of the trip. "The students are representatives of all Japanese universities," Abe told critics.[12] Three days after they left, the Russian fleet was spotted off Singapore, 3,300 miles southwest of Japan.

Abe would later confess that he worried about the team's reception in San Francisco, and he had reason for concern. The *San Francisco Chronicle* had just begun its attack on Japanese immigration. Abe and his team would soon find themselves the targets of anti-Japanese slurs and bigotry.

When the ss *Korea* docked in San Francisco on the morning of April 20, reporters from most of the city's newspapers gathered to interview and photograph the first foreign team to tour the United States. At the time most Americans were unaware that the game was even played in Japan. Printed references to Japanese baseball were few and far between. The *Sporting News*, for example, contained no stories on Japanese baseball prior to 1905. The visitors made a favorable impression on the reporter from the *San Francisco Call*, although the article's prose makes clear what he thought of most Japanese immigrants: "The Waseda ball team is as compact and sturdy looking an aggregation of athletes as ever graced these shores. The men are far above the average Japanese in height and are possessed of more good looks than falls [sic] to the lot of the ordinary Jap."[13]

The *San Francisco Examiner*, owned by William Randolph Hearst, who would soon be at the forefront of the anti-Japanese immigration movement, ran a story poking fun at the Waseda team. "Our territory has been invaded," wrote E. B. Lenhart. "And what's more—the invaders propose to beat us at our own game. . . . Down the gangway tripped eleven nervously-active subs of the Mick-a-doo." The article continues with several paragraphs making fun of the ballplayers' names. For example, "Kyoshin Hashido represents the short stop of the collection. The name suggests that Kyo stops the ball with his shins and that at bat . . . he manages the leather into the hash."[14]

The *Chronicle* ignored the ball club's arrival in the following morning's paper but instead ran an article titled "More Japs Arrive on the *Korea*," reporting that "Swarming on the lower decks of the liner *Korea*, arriving yesterday from the Orient and Hawaii, were 717 Japanese emigrants . . . as devoid of Americanism as Hottentots."[15]

Black horse-drawn carriages met the Waseda ballplayers at the dock and carried them to the St. Francis Hotel at Union Square. Opened just a year earlier, it was the city's finest hotel. Its two massive twelve-story twin towers rose 198 feet in the air, making it among the tallest buildings in the city. It featured a lavish lobby with marble walls accented by Corinthian columns topped with gilt, carved ceilings, and luxurious leather furniture; an enormous opulent columned dining room; and large suites. In a letter home to his wife first baseman Sukekatsu Izumitani gushed, "It is indescribable how wonderful it is. There are fourteen floors [sic]. There is an elevator, so it goes up to the tenth or fourteenth floor quickly and smoothly. It is like pulling up luggage by a rope."[16]

Leading members of the Japanese community and newspapers met the team at the hotel, took photographs, and treated the players to a Japanese meal. At 3 p.m. the players watched their first professional baseball game as the Oakland Commuters topped the San Francisco Seals, 3–1, in a Pacific Coast League match at Recreation Park. Afterward they stopped by Spalding Sporting Goods to purchase the latest baseball equipment—modern spikes, mitts, bats, and balls.

The following morning the players visited Golden Gate Park before boarding the 4 p.m. train to the Stanford University campus at Palo Alto. There they were welcomed by the school's Japanese students club, which had also rented a local house to lodge them during their visit. "The name 'Stanford' sounds like a big town, but it is not at all," Izumitani wrote to his wife. "It is cold and isolated, and there are only a few houses here and there. . . . The house we live in is one of seven or eight houses located in a vast field. The university buildings are outstanding. The dormitory is bigger than the prefectural office building in Kobe. . . . The other buildings are amazing as well."[17]

Izumitani found Stanford's co-ed policies remarkable as all Japanese universities at the time were single-sex:

> There are about one thousand male and seven hundred female students. It is great that male and female students do things together in the United States. Both male and female students are in a same classroom. . . . Some males and females live in the dormitories, and others share houses . . . living together. It sounds strange to Japanese, but it is normal [in the United States]. . . . [They don't] become involved with each other even if they spend a lot of time together. . . . In the evenings we don't see any male students walking by themselves; we see them as couples with female students. . . . I was told that the female students enter universities with the permission of their parents to look for future husbands, and studying is the secondary purpose. I hope it will be like that in Japan in the future.[18]

Several hundred students crowded around Stanford's varsity field on April 22 to watch Waseda practice for the first time since leaving

Japan eighteen days before. The Bay Area papers covered the practices, and nearly all expressed surprise and admiration at the Japanese players' skill, although several of the writers couched their compliments in racist prose.

E. B. Lenhart of the *Examiner* managed to provide the greatest praise and most offensive comments. Below the headline "If You Think the Japs Can't Play Ball You'd Better Turn on Your Alarm Clock" and a large photograph of second baseman Kiyoshi Oshikawa, he wrote:

> Some . . . [of the Stanford students] are still unwilling to bet that what they saw yesterday morning was a condition and not a theory. You could see intelligent young men gouging their knuckles into their eyes and trying to convince themselves that they were really out of the feathers. . . . That flock of brownskins from Waseda University, Japan was the cause of all this commotion. They were out for a little loosening of their joints and those who watched the proceedings got a shock of about three thousand and three volts. We calculated the Japs knew nearly as much about the great American game as a rooster does of laying bricks. That none of us suddenly died of apoplexy must go into history as one of the wonders of the age. . . .
>
> These Wah! Wah! Wah! Se-Dah! undergrads frolicked with the regulation swatstick and sphere with the ease and agility your distant cousin Orang Outang shows when he leaps from a bare limb to one that promises him a succulent mouthful. . . . They grabbed grounders, snatched throws, seized flies and generally cavorted around that lot like a bunch of individuals sent here by Satan to make us jump out of our heads to drink unto him. . . .
>
> Of truth they were rather tiny, somewhat warp-legged and awkward. But they got there just the same and when they line up against the [Stanford] Cardinal team next Saturday the Occidental young men will have to hustle very hard unless they want to be the subjects of an Oriental trimming. As of this writing, there's no telling how the strangers would loom up in a battle with Uncle Henry's Seals or Johnny McGraw's Giants. But you can stow one fact away for future reference: IF YOU ARE INCLINED TO REGARD THE WASEDA UNIVERSITY BASEBALL TEAM AS A JOKE—Wake up![19]

For the next week the Waseda team prepared for its opening game on April 29 against its Stanford hosts. "We repeat the same routine over and over every day," wrote Izumitani. "We wake up around 8 a.m. and finish eating breakfast around 9 a.m. We then chat and play catch until around 10 or 11 a.m. and have lunch. After lunch a carriage comes to pick us up. All thirteen of us jump on the carriage to go to the university's athletic field. We practice until 3:30 p.m. We are back home at 4 p.m. and have dinner at 5 p.m. Until we go to bed at 10 p.m., we don't even go out for a walk."[20]

Stanford students, faculty and even San Francisco reporters attended the practices. Excitement for the opening game against Stanford built all week, with each of the area papers running daily updates on the upcoming match. "The little brown men have been practicing for the past few days before crowds of spectators, who have gazed in open-mouthed wonderment at their clever fielding and base running," wrote the *Los Angeles Herald*. "It is no joke that at all—the Japs can play baseball. The majority of men are larger than the ordinary Japanese, and are lithe and strong. Team work is developed to a high degree. The only apparent weakness of the 'brownies' is at the bat. They meet the ball squarely but with little force and the longest hits are usually good for only two bags."[21]

Some reporters abandoned the more stereotypical descriptions of the Japanese team and began to focus on individual players. They were enthralled by the dashing shortstop and captain, Shin Hashido, with his distinctive, full chevron-style moustache and thick black eyebrows. At twenty-six years old, the 5-foot-3 Hashido was the oldest and most experienced player on the team. He had learned the game in high school at Aoyama Gakuin, a private Methodist school in Tokyo, where he had been the team's ace pitcher until his graduation in 1901. Among the Japanese he was admired for his intellect. Whereas most ballplayers focused on business, Hashido majored in the humanities and was a top student and talented writer. On the ball field he impressed nearly all observers with his glove work. "Every liner, fly or grounder within reach of the tiny shortstop was nailed and disposed of with unerring precision," the *Call* reported.[22] The *Chronicle* added, "Captain Hashido, the fast fielding little short stop . . . accepts difficult chances with a sureness that shows long training in the game. Besides being one of the best fielders, he is regarded as the heaviest hitter on the field."[23] The mustached short-stop would become known as the best player of his generation and one of the fathers of Japanese baseball for his numerous contributions after his playing days were over.

But the player receiving the most attention was twenty-one-year-old pitcher Atsushi Kono. "He is an athletic looking fellow and has shown great speed in practice," noted the *Chronicle*.[24] In a feature article titled "Jap Pitcher Puzzles 'Em," the *Oakland Tribune* reported, "The diminutive Jap pitcher is a source of continual wonder to the Stanford players. It seems strange that a man with an arm that measures only twenty-four inches in length could attain [such] great speed."[25] In addition to his velocity, the papers praised Kono's "seemingly perfect control" and noted that he also had "good curves and a change of pace that is puzzling."[26] He was also "the personification of good nature and wears a perpetual smile of the variety that won't rub off," added the *Daily Californian*.[27]

April 29, game day, "was a perfect day for a game"—sunny but not too hot.[28] But things began to go wrong for the visitors well before the 2:30 p.m. proposed start time. The team's house was a forty-minute walk from the baseball field, so Abe decided to conserve his players' energy and rent a horse-drawn carriage to transport them to the game. Dressed in their new beige flannel uniforms, with "Waseda" stitched in maroon letters across their chests, maroon stockings and pillbox caps with two horizontal maroon stripes, the players waited by the house as the minutes ticked by. The carriage was late.

When they finally reached the ball field, ten minutes after game time, "a great throng of spectators" packed the bleachers. About 2,500 fans—believed to be the largest crowd the Stanford team had ever attracted—came out for the contest. A special train from San Francisco, run just for the game, brought over five hundred Japanese, "who filled one entire section of the bleachers" (suggesting that there was segregated seating). The group rose from their seats, cheered, and waved maroon "WU" banners as the Waseda squad arrived in the carriage. The tardy visitors hurried through their warm-ups and took the field to start the game. Observers noted that the Waseda players "appeared to be a trifle nervous," and indeed the game began with Kono walking the leadoff batter on four pitches although he would not score.[29]

The Japanese would actually score first. A second inning lead-off walk to Hashido, followed by a wild pitch and a single by Kono put Waseda up, 1–0, but then nerves got the better of the visitors. Eight Waseda errors, nearly all "wild throws due to over-anxiety," led to an easy 9–1 Stanford victory.[30] Despite the lopsided score the Waseda players made a number of fine plays and according to the *Call*, "covered themselves with glory, for they played a much better game than was expected of them."[31]

"While the little brown men cannot handle the leather-covered ball with the same dexterity that they propel the cannon ball, their work yesterday was little short of marvelous," reported the *Pacific Commercial Advertiser*. "They are woefully weak with the willow, however, notwithstanding that they have a good eye at the plate. . . . Most of their drives were of the scratchy variety, as but one or two of the players have acquired the knack of swinging freely at the ball. On the bases the Japs are veritable demons and the manner in which they tore up the earth in sliding to the cushions surprised the onlookers. Taking it all in all the Waseda team put up an excellent article of baseball."[32]

After a day of rain the teams played a rematch on May 2 at Recreation Park, San Francisco's fifteen-thousand-capacity stadium that housed the Seals, the city's Pacific Coast League franchise. "Nearly 3000 spectators witnessed the game," the *Call* reported, "the majority being Japanese. While they did not always applaud at the right time, they showed a deep interest in the game and were quick to see the clever plays." Although Stanford won, 3–1, the *Call* praised the Waseda players: "The representatives of the Mikado . . . play a sharp, snappy fielding game. It is predicted their style of play will be revolutionized during their Eastern trip and that they will get harder and harder to beat as they pick up the finer points of the game. This they are doing rapidly."[33] The *Call* would continue to support the visiting Japanese and avoid blatant racist comments throughout the remainder of the tour. The same, unfortunately, cannot be said for other California newspapers.

The *Examiner*, perhaps the worst offender, reported on the May 2 game under the headline "Japs Hit Like a Team of Spinsters." Supposedly penned by Uknown Imawanda (You Know I'm a Wanda) of Japan but most likely another E. B. Lenhart masterpiece of bigotry, the article is full of pidgin English and false honorifics as it pokes fun at the Japanese even while praising the team's fielding.[34]

The *Chronicle* carried a factual and relatively inoffensive description of the game, accompanied by a cartoon depicting players from both teams and the Japanese fans (fig. 6).[35] The white Stanford ballplayers are represented by straightforward cartoon drawings while the Japanese are depicted in a style now known as yellowface. Like blackface, yellowface emphasized non-white features and used animalistic imagery and symbolism to dehumanize the subject as well as emphasize otherness and inferiority.[36]

Shin Hashido is depicted in a Simian-like pose with overly long arms and huge, ape-like hands and feet. Far worse is the drawing of four Japanese fans. They also have Simian-like poses with long arms held at awkward, ape-like angles and large hands. Their eyes are mere slits; their faces are grotesque and hostile; and their open mouths show pointy, animal-like teeth. The cartoon supports the stereotype used throughout the *Chronicle*'s attacks on Japanese immigrants, depicting them as inferior aliens, incapable of assimilating into American society.

Abe and the Waseda players faced American bigotry head on the following day, May 3. Soon after arriving in California, Abe received a "courteous letter" from Rear Admiral William H. Whiting inviting the team for a game at the Yerba Buena Naval Training School. The Japanese squad traveled to the base on Goat Island in San Francisco Bay to play against a team of naval students from the training ship USS *Pensacola*. The game was a slugfest with ragged fielding, ending in an 11–8 Pensacola victory. Details from the game were not reported in local papers, but it seems that the naval students in the bleachers taunted the Japanese with racial slurs. Abe would later write in his published account of the trip, "The score cannot tell much about what the actual game was like. The rudeness of the naval school's students not only upset us, but also made the umpire make unfair judgments." After the game Abe met with Admiral

Whiting to discuss the situation, but the outcome of this meeting went unreported.[37]

Waseda finished out the week with its first wins of the tour. Staying on the Stanford campus, the team played students from the Encina Club on Thursday, May 4, and the school's faculty the following day. Neither team seriously challenged the Japanese nine, who won easily despite resting their ace, Kono. The Bay Area newspapers barely commented on these meaningless victories, but the *Los Angeles Times* summarized one game under the headline "That Yellow Peril," while the *Los Angeles Herald*, mistakenly reporting that the second win was against "Stanford University's crack team," quipped, "Here is fresh cause for the anti-Japanese crusade in California. Being 'ruined by Chinese cheap labor' is not half so humiliating as being beaten by Jap players [in] the 'favorite American game.'"[38]

While on campus, the Waseda men mingled with the Stanford students to the best of their abilities. Some players, like Kono, spoke a little English, but most could converse only with the Japanese students. Nonetheless, the team attended two Shakespeare plays (including *Hamlet*), a concert, other cultural events, and several parties held in their honor. In keeping with his belief that international exchanges would lead to cross-cultural understanding and empathy, Abe gave a lecture at the Stanford chapel on the development of athletics in Japan and the goals of his baseball tour, telling his audience that "it is not in baseball only that this trip should be a help to our men. It will broaden their views and help them to a better understanding of the world."[39]

Members of the San Francisco's Japanese community showed their support for their countrymen whenever possible. They not only packed the ballparks to watch the games, but also treated the players to meals and took them on sightseeing excursions. On Sunday, April 30, the city's Waseda University Alumni Association threw a party at the Japanese Imperial Hotel to honor the ball club. Over eighty guests attended. Although Harry Saisho spent the spring of 1905 working near Sacramento, it is possible, maybe even likely, that he made the trip to San Francisco to attend the party and watch his college team play.

In their final week in Palo Alto the Waseda nine faced some stiff competition on the diamond. They began with a 16–0 loss to St. Mary's University, the strongest collegiate team in northern California, on May 9; lost a close 7–5 battle with a U.S. Army team from the Presidio, the military base guarding the Golden Gate, on May 13; were thumped, 14–3, the following day by a local semi-pro club; and finished their stay in the Bay area with a 5–0 loss to the University of California at Berkeley.

Waseda played particularly well against the Presidio team, which had joined the professional California State League and featured future Major Leaguer Ping Bodie. "The spry little visitors kept Uncle Sam's lads on the run, as the final result was uncertain until the last brown slugger had been retired," reported the *Call*. Both Hashido, who "nailed and disposed of with unerring precision . . . every liner, fly or grounder within reach," and the catcher, Masaharu Yamawaki, who earned "round after round of applause from the crowds of soldiers and Japanese enthusiasts," impressed the *Call*'s reporter.[40] Former Major League star Bill Lange, who umpired the game, noted, "The Japs surprised me. . . . I had heard they could play the game some, but I had no idea that they were as good as they were. About the only weakness I noticed was the throwing of their outfielders. When they tried to make long throws they usually fell short, but otherwise they played the game as good as the average college team."[41]

Despite lopsided scores in three of the four losses, the tone of the newspaper articles covering the games had shifted. Gone where the racial slurs, the anti-Japanese jokes and innuendos, and the yellow-face cartoons. Instead the articles just focused on baseball. Even the *Examiner* and the *Chronicle* followed the trend. "For five innings, the Waseda Japanese baseball team played like real champions," noted the *Examiner* while covering the loss to Presidio.[42] Abe's team had won respect. His mission had, in some small part, succeeded as the reporters now treated the players as the Waseda baseball club rather than a group of Japanese represented by stereotypes. This respect, however, would need to be earned at each city on the team's American tour.

6

Waseda Tour Continues

Abe had planned to take his team east to play the future Ivy League schools. He had telegrammed Yale, Harvard, Columbia, Princeton, and Cornell, asking if they would host the Waseda team, but received no response other than a decline from Cornell. Wisely concerned about the cost of traveling across the United States without a sponsor or guaranteed games, Abe decided to keep the team on the West Coast.

On Tuesday, May 16, 1905, the team boarded a train for Los Angeles. To Abe's surprise a large group of Japanese men, led by J. S. Ono from the *Rafu Shimpo* and Takejiro Ito "representing the Japanese Baseball Club of Los Angeles," welcomed the team on the station's platform. According to the *Los Angeles Herald*, "The Japanese population of Los Angeles are manifesting great interest in the doing of their ball-playing countrymen. . . . The coming of the Japanese players to this city means a great deal to the Japanese newspapers. Special editions including scare headed extras have been printed and circulated by the management of the two big Japanese dailies. It is a great event in the eyes of the Japs and it will not be a small crowd of local brown men that will attend the different games."[1]

The *Los Angeles Examiner* also welcomed the team to town with a feature article, large photograph, and cartoon executed in the yellowface style, under the headline, "Jap Baseball Team Is Playing Real Ball" (fig. 7).[2] The cartoon depicts five figures in three vignettes. To the left a single Japanese runs awkwardly above the caption "Jiu Jitsu Ball." In the center a Japanese player has thrown a Western man to the ground by grabbing and twisting his left leg. The caption reads, "For the Umpire," and a dialogue box depicts the player speaking in nonsensical kanji. On the right a Japanese pitcher in the midst of an impossibly goofy windup pitches to a Native American batter (probably representing upcoming opponents from the Sherman Institute). The caption reads, "Port Arthur." The Japanese have typical yellowface characteristics—oversized broad faces with gigantic grinning teeth and small, slanted eyes. The players' bodies are shown in ungraceful and even unathletic, comical poses. The message seems clear; the Waseda team is alien—foreign and un-American—and, despite the article's headline, not to be taken seriously.

The accompanying article, under the subhead "Fellow Japanese All over Los Angeles Studying Up on Rules and Are Prepared to Root Countrymen to Victory," focuses on the alleged meeting of a literary society at the Presbyterian Japanese Mission, where the usual erudite reading had been replaced by a copy of the rules of baseball. Although the event could have occurred and the article is devoid of overt racial slurs, the tone is condescending and belittles the Japanese. At the time, when baseball was not only considered the national game, but was also seen as a conduit to American values, not understanding the basic rules was yet another example of how Japanese were unable to assimilate into American society.

The following day, Wednesday, May 17, Waseda won a "sizzling contest" over Los Angeles High School, breaking a 3–3 tie with two runs in the ninth. "The baseball tossers from Tokio [*sic*] proved their ability to play the American game," summed up the *Los Angeles Times*. Each of the local papers praised the visitors. "The Americans were outplayed at every point of the game," noted the *Examiner*. "Not only can they field and bat, but they know the fine points of the game as well."[3] Again the *Examiner* led off its sports page with a cartoon of the Japanese players. But after the victory this second cartoon depicts the Waseda players differently. Whereas the first showed generic stereotypes of Japanese ballplayers, the second depicts individual players from both teams with an attempt to re-create their likenesses. Although the Japanese still have wide, toothy grins, the caricatures are less offensive.

The American reporters found the behavior of the Japanese fans even more surprising than the Waseda victory. Both the *Times* and the *Examiner* focused on the Japanese spectators for large portions of their articles. While the Waseda players may have gained the reporters' respect through their baseball skills, their countrymen in the stands were still held in contempt. The newspaper descriptions abound with stereotypes, pidgin English, and racial humor, portraying the Japanese immigrants as unable to properly assimilate into American life. Both papers noted that hundreds of local Japanese fans, dressed in their finest clothes and carrying copies of the baseball rules and brightly colored pennants, attended the game. Despite vigorous cheering and abusive comments from American spectators, causing the *Examiner* to comment, "The howling of the High School rooters was also very unsportmanlike, considering that the Japanese players are from a foreign nation on a friendly visit," they watched the game in silence for the first eight innings. But in the ninth inning as Waseda surged ahead, they began to stir.

According to the *Los Angeles Times*, "A short, fat, greasy-faced Mongolian in the center of a compact bunch of his countrymen rose and began a strange yell. 'Whatta Matta his high school? He's no good,' he shouted and his fellows, greatly to the amusement of the other spectators, took up the refrain. It was the firm conviction of the Japs that the 'white boys' could not play ball with the men from Tokio."[4] The *Examiner* continued:

> The little crowd of sympathizers could not restrain themselves. They were dancing up and down in their excitement when suddenly a little chap wearing a large Panama raised the hat high in the air and began to yell. That was enough to start the others and the cheer that went up drowned the yell of the high school boys. True it was a mixed yell, some cheering in Japanese and some in English but the little players on the field waved their hats in response. A second later another run was scored . . . and the Japs hugged each other in the exuberance of their joy. So if it happened that your Jap boy dropped eight or ten dishes last night don't be too harsh with him. He was cheering inwardly at every step.[5]

The description of the Japanese fans continued in articles covering Waseda's well-played 6–5 loss to Occidental College on May 18. "The real feature of the game was the genuine American rooting indulged in by several hundred Japanese in the stand," reported the *Examiner*. "The little Jap in the Panama who started the cheering on the first day was in the front row once more, but this time he

came armed with a Waseda flag about four yards broad and a mega-
phone. . . . These men from across the Pacific who call Los Angeles
their home have demonstrated their ability to catch onto the American way of cheering the team as readily as their brothers did in the
playing line. They didn't wake up until the final inning Wednesday
but yesterday they came early and started the rooting at once."[6] But
the *Los Angeles Times* noted that the outnumbered college students
outcheered the visitors: "The Japanese have not yet mastered the art
of rooting. They made quite a deal of noise, but it was less effective
than the concentrated music of the college supporters."[7]

In contrast to their fans' enthusiasm, the Waseda players remained
stony-faced, barely uttering a sound on the ball field. Bench jockeying and shouting encouragements to teammates was not a part
of the Japanese game. When asked about his players' silence, Abe
told a reporter from the *Seattle Daily Times*, "Every player in Japan
is expected to observe strict silence during a baseball game and . . . ,
more than this, the spectators are requested to be absolutely silent,
except for modest applause with the hands . . . [because] the Japanese believe that they can play a better and more scientific game by
not speaking during the playing."[8] Even today Japanese players are
relatively quiet on the field.

The Occidental players, however, were full of pepper, trying to
distract their foreign opponents by bench jockeying. According to
the *Los Angeles Times*, the collegians

> were quite at a loss for a time. They had never before played against
> such silent foes. They also found that the Japs could not be rattled.
> They only grinned when joshed and went on chewing gum. . . . Spauld-
> ing, the Presbyterian catcher, started some rapid-fire talk to rattle
> the man at bat. The Jap never moved an eyelid to the banter, but his
> friends took it up strong. Spaulding came in for a line of funny talk
> that put him to the bad, and he found he needed all his wits concen-
> trated on playing ball. It was all in very good nature, and both sides
> showed a friendly spirit.[9]

After the close loss against Occidental, the Waseda players enjoyed
a well-earned day off at Chutes Park in Los Angeles watching a Pacific
Coast League game between the Los Angeles Angels and Tacoma

Tigers. The team sat in box seats next to the field, allowing Angels owner Jim Morley to talk to the players. Morley struck up an "earnest conversation" with ace pitcher Atsushi Kono.[10] Except for the scrimmages against Stanford's Encina Club and faculty, Kono had pitched every inning of every game on the tour. Reporters had nicknamed him "Iron Man Kono" and featured him in nearly every article, making him the most recognized player on the team and a celebrity.

During the conversation Morley asked Kono to pitch a game for the Angels while the Waseda team was in town. Abe, realizing that this would just be a publicity stunt to attract fans to the ballpark, declined the offer on Kono's behalf. If Kono and Abe had agreed to Morley's proposal, Kono would have been the first Japanese, and the first Asian, to play in Organized Baseball. We are left to wonder if Kono's acceptance would have hastened the debut of Japanese players into the Major Leagues by decades.[11]

Perhaps no game was more anticipated than the matchup with the Sherman Institute on May 20. It "marked an epoch in the history of our national game," wrote the *Sporting Life*, as "the first time a baseball game was played by teams . . . from two races that have adopted a sport heretofore distinctively that of the white man."[12]

Founded and operated by the U.S. government in 1892, the Sherman Institute was the first "off-reservation" boarding school for Native Americans in California. It educated children from five to twenty years old with the explicit goal of assimilating them into white American society. Like many government-sponsored Native American schools, the Sherman Institute encouraged the boys to play football and baseball to help instill "American values." The school soon became known for its outstanding football squad and would produce a number of professionals, but its baseball team was weak. To bolster the team against Waseda the school recruited local Native American John Tortes Meyers. The son of German American former Union Army officer and saloon owner John Mayer and Felicite Tortes of the Cahuilla tribe, Meyers would be raised by his mother, partly on the Santa Rosa reservation and partly in Riverside, before becoming a local semi-pro star and eventually the star catcher known as Chief Meyers for John McGraw's New York Giants.

The game began at three o'clock, and "the largest crowd of the series gathered at Fiesta Park . . . and cheered loud and long."[13] The Sherman players took the field in dark trousers, high white socks, and white jerseys. The visiting Japanese wore their usual buff uniforms with maroon socks. Waseda scored a quick run in the first on an error by the Sherman shortstop Padillo and added three more in both the fourth and sixth innings. Meanwhile, Waseda starter Atsushi Kono shut out the opposition for five innings. "The teams formed a curious contrast," the *Los Angeles Times* noted. "The Red Men, burly and muscular, seemed to tear through their game. The Brown men, lithe and wiry, slipped around them and out-played them."[14]

In the bottom of the sixth, down 7–0, Sherman fought back, scoring six runs as Meyers "tried to remove the cover from the ball by knocking it to the score board."[15] But Waseda's slick fielding held the Native Americans. "The little warriors from Waseda dashed around the field, taking down the long drives of the red man with ease and grace that was surprising."[16] The Japanese padded their lead to win the game, 12–7. All the newspapers agreed that it was a sensational game, "replete with lively hitting, speedy base-running and good and bad fielding."[17]

With the novelty of opponents from different races, the newspapermen could not resist racial stereotypes, allusions, and metaphors in their game descriptions. "Jap Team Scalps Sherman Braves," "Wiry Japs Wallop Reds," and "Japs Stop a Break from Reservation" declared the next morning's headlines. The articles were replete with references to scalping, reservations, and the Russo-Japanese War. Typical was the *Los Angeles Herald*'s lead: "Determined to win against a team which they considered in every way equal in strength to a company of Russian soldiers, nine little Japs from Waseda college across the sea took into camp the scalps of nine of the hardiest braves from the Sherman reservation school of Riverside yesterday afternoon and sent the big bucks crashing back to defeat with a one-sided score of 12 to 7."[18]

Accompanying an article loaded with racial stereotypes and demeaning terminology, the *Los Angeles Examiner* published a contrasting large montage covering the top of the sports section under the headline "Orientals Win Ball Game from the Aborigines."[19] The centerpiece is a drawing of a Native American man and Japanese man in traditional clothing, each holding a baseball bat (fig. 8). Unlike previous illustrations, these are not cartoon caricatures but respectful, even if somewhat fanciful, depictions of men from the two ethnic groups. On either side of this centerpiece are the photographs of three players from the respective teams. This illustration is in marked contrast to the *Examiner*'s earlier graphic as it treats the players as named individuals rather than stereotypes. The visiting Japanese were slowly gaining respect.

Waseda finished off its stint in Los Angeles with consecutive losses against teams from the Los Angeles Pacific Railroad, St. Vincent's College, and Ponoma College before defeating the University of Southern California (USC), 13–6. Overall Waseda played well and had improved greatly during its stay in the city. Members of the Stanford varsity attended the game against St. Vincent's and told the press "they were astonished at the marked improvement" of the Waseda players.[20] Abe, in an interview with the *Daily Californian*, noted, "My players have improved greatly since they came to America. They had great trouble with batting when they first came, but they have improved a great deal and are no more puzzled by curved balls."[21] The *Los Angeles Times* explained, "The little fellows stand up to the bat well, swing quickly and hard, and generally hit on the line. They are splendid specimens physically; each is built from the ground up; and there is not a pound of superfluous beef on the entire team." After the win against USC, the *Times* gushed, "There may be some things the visiting Japs do not know about the sport that Henry Chadwick and A. G. Spalding brought into prominence, but if so the fact did not develop in yesterday afternoon's play. The big little men from across the boundless blue Pacific pounded their runs largely by sharp hitting and swift work upon the bases; they performed like a bunch of leaguers and showed no weakness whatever in the field, handling their chances with the mechanical precision of star professionals."[22]

During these games Waseda also impressed spectators with its sportsmanship. Reporters throughout the tour noted that the Japanese refused to argue with the umpires—even when clearly wronged. In the May 17 game against Los Angeles High School, for example, the umpiring left something to be desired, with calls blown against both teams. "The High School boys kicked at the decisions of the umpire," the *Los Angeles Herald* related, "but no matter how rank a decision was the Japs never made a sound. Once they looked very hard and were evidently thinking a lot when given the short end but never a kick."[23] After the earlier game against Presidio, umpire Bill Lange commented, "They didn't kick over my decisions. They were good fellows. . . . A Presidio player batted the ball along [the] first base line and I called it fair. It was so close that . . . I asked . . . the catcher if my decision was correct. He . . . replied that the ball was fair by about a foot. What American catcher would have made such an admission? Our catchers would have claimed that the ball hit foul five feet."[24]

In each city the team's gentlemanly behavior won over many white American fans. "Most of the Americans in the bleachers yesterday seemed to lend their sympathies to the brown men. Their sportsmanlike game seemed to appeal to them," concluded the *Los Angeles Times* after the game against the Pacific Railroad in Santa Monica.[25]

Waseda's play and behavior also affected the sports reporters. Articles covering the final four games in Los Angeles are devoid of racial stereotypes, derogatory phrases, jokes, and other overtly offensive language with the notable exceptions of the terms "Jap" and "little brown men." Instead the articles concentrate on baseball, treating the Waseda players as individual ballplayers rather than representations of their race.

On the evening of May 25 the team took the overnight train to Bakersfield, California, a small city of just under ten thousand, one hundred miles north of Los Angeles. Arriving at 8:30 the next morning, the players were greeted on the platform by fans and a group of local Japanese. The *Daily Californian* noted, "The local Japanese colony have made great preparations for celebrating the advent of the Jap players. Tonight a banquet is to be given to the team at the Toto restaurant."[26]

Interest in baseball was waning in Bakersfield. Sponsors and fans hoped that Waseda's two games in the city would help revive the sport. Locals decorated Recreation Park with bunting and Japanese flags, making the grandstand "alive in color" for what the *Daily Cal-*

ifornian called "the biggest baseball days of the season."[27] To drum up interest the newspaper ran a detailed article about the squad, complete with original quotes from Abe and Kono, on the morning Waseda arrived in town. The article's tone is complimentary and without a hint of condescension or bigotry.

Abe and his team spent the remainder of the day with members of the Japanese community. They had much to talk about. The headline of the *Daily Californian* announced that seventeen ships from Admiral Zinovy Rozhestvensky's Baltic Fleet had stopped at the Side Saddle Islands off the coast of Shanghai to refuel. The Russian fleet was now poised to enter the Sea of Japan and perhaps turn the war to Russia's favor.

On the afternoon of May 27 Waseda met Bakersfield High School on the diamond. Nearly 1,500 "enthusiastic and curious spectators" packed Recreation Park "to see whether the 'Yellow Baseball Peril' was all that it had been cracked up to be." Two hundred seats in the grandstand had been set aside for Japanese fans, once again suggesting that the seating may have been segregated. This "section was ablaze with the national colors and enthusiasm was intense."[28]

The game itself was a nail-biter. One run separated the teams for four innings before the high schoolers padded their lead to enter the bottom of the ninth up 6–2. But Waseda battled, scoring three runs and threatened to tie the score before the clearly rattled high school pitcher, Charlie Turner, steadied himself and struck out the final two batters.

The next morning Abe and his players awoke to exciting news. Admiral Heihachiro Togo, commanding the Japanese fleet, had destroyed Rozhestvensky's Baltic Fleet as it tried to enter the Sea of Japan. Details of the battle, however, were unknown to Abe as the *Daily Californian* was not published on Sundays.

That afternoon, after spending the morning touring the local oil fields, Waseda took on the Bakersfield Picked Nine—presumably an all-star team of local amateurs—in front of two thousand fans. Waseda played well, impressing the fans, but the local pitcher, twenty-year-old Hal "Sapho" Claflin, who would soon turn pro and play three years in the Northwest League, limited the visitors to just two runs. Nonetheless, the Japanese "played well enough to keep the interest up to fever heat . . . [and] clearly had the sympathy of the people who packed the grand stand. . . . Though they were always behind the game they played with sufficient vim and vinegar and comported themselves with such uniform courtesy as to win for them the admiration as well as the sympathy of the grand stand."[29]

The games were an unqualified success. "If we could see ball like that every Sunday you would see us out there' was a remark frequently heard while [a reporter was] mingling with the crowd as the people walked from the grand stand." The *Daily Californian* concluded, "The game was instrumental in giving baseball in the city a new lease on life, and the fans were jubilant."[30]

On May 29 Waseda traveled north to Fresno, where the players were met at the train station by a large crowd of jubilant local Japanese thrilled by the coincidental arrival of the team and the details of Admiral Togo's resounding victory at the Battle of Tsushima. By a brilliant and risky tactical maneuver Togo had overwhelmed the Russia fleet, sinking seven of its eleven battleships, four of its six cruisers, and six of its nine destroyers. The Japanese had lost only three torpedo boats. The victory effectively ended the war.

Waseda would stay in town for two days, playing twice against the Fresno franchise of the California State League. It was the finest team that the Japanese would face during their trip, and Abe had asked the Fresno club to play its best. The purpose of the trip, he told the Fresno manager, was "to investigate baseball as it is played on its native [soil]," and he wanted his players to experience the difference between professional and amateur ball. The pros obliged and easily defeated Abe's squad, 10–3 and 13–0.[31] Waseda fielded superbly, making no errors in the first game, but was unable to hit the professionals' curveballs.

At the end of the first contest the local *Fresno Morning Republican* praised the visitors: "They are speedy and fearless base runners and with a little more experience no company will be too fast for them."[32] After the one-sided second game, however, the writer's tone had changed and the otherwise factual article ended with an insult: "The crowd left with the same opinion as that held by the spectators of Tuesday—the Jap is a fast little man and a mighty good fighter but he don't know a great deal about baseball."[33]

From Fresno the Waseda team returned to San Francisco. "I felt like I had come home," recalled Abe.[34] Abe still hoped that an eastern college would invite the team to play, but finding no takers, he decided to end the tour with a week in the Northwest. On June 4 the team boarded a train for the thirty-six-hour trek to Eugene, Oregon.

Arriving at 3 a.m. on June 6, the players checked into a local hotel to catch some sleep before their afternoon game against the University of Oregon. The game began as a tight pitching duel with neither Kono nor Oregon's Peter Beck allowing a runner to reach second base until the fifth inning, when a double gave Oregon a 1–0 lead. Beck surrendered just four hits as Oregon won, 3–0, but exhausted from the travel, for the first time the Waseda players lost their gentlemanly composure and argued with the umpire.

The next morning they left early for Portland and were on the diamond at the Multnomah Athletic Club for a 3:30 start. It was another tight game, ending in a 3–2 win for the home team. The *Morning Oregonian* proclaimed, "Talk of your Yellow Peril! Well, you should have been present yesterday afternoon on the Multnomah Club diamond. And for five innings you would have had a sample of the danger that threatens the good old National game from nine swarthy sons of the Mikado. The Japs have proven that they shoot straight, for they have shot up the Russians some, both on land and sea. To a fair-sized crowd during yesterday's matinee, nine students from the University of Waseda at Tokio [sic] demonstrated that they could play baseball."[35]

That evening and the next day Abe took his team to the Lewis and Clark Centennial Exposition. Similar to a world's fair, the exposition attracted 1.6 million visitors during its four-and-a-half month run (June 1–October 14, 1905). There the ballplayers visited exhibits from around the world, including a lavish replica of Louis XIV's drawing room and a recreated Filipino village complete with about two dozen Igorot tribesmen, displayed to visitors as "head-hunters and dog-eaters."[36]

On June 8 the players took the overnight train to Seattle, where a large contingent of local Japanese and Waseda alumni met them when they arrived at 7:30 a.m. The team checked into the Washington Hotel, one of the city's finest establishments. Once again Abe emphasized the importance of the trip and the gentlemanly status of his ballplayers. The hotel's manager told a reporter from the *Seattle Daily Times*, "They are mighty intelligent little fellows and . . . they travel in first-class style, getting the best rooms in the house and insisting upon the very best of everything."[37]

That afternoon a large crowd watched Waseda play the University of Washington at Recreation Park. "The game is exciting much interest among the Japanese of the city," reported the *Seattle Daily Times*, "and . . . a big crowd of them [came] out to cheer their countrymen and see if they could handle Washington as successfully as they have handled the Russians."[38]

Although "the sympathy of the crowd was all with the Japs, and there was an oriental tinge to the grandstand, given by a few hundred Seattle Japs who smoked cigarettes, cracked peanuts and rooted for the Waseda bunch," their fans left disappointed. Not only did the Huskies have a strong team that including two future Major Leaguers (Hunky Shaw and Bill Brinker), but the heavy workload finally caught up to Atsushi Kono causing him to leave the game in the fourth inning with a sore arm. The result was a 9–2 rout of the visiting Japanese.[39]

Following a second loss to the University of Washington (this time by a closer score of 4–0) on June 10, Waseda met the semi-pro Seattle Rainiers on Sunday, June 11, at Recreation Park. With Kono's arm still sore, Shin Hashido took the mound in front of a large crowd mostly rooting for the Japanese. "The Rainiers [who were] disposed to treat the game as a josh in the early innings, believing they could bat it out any time," soon found themselves down 2–0 in the top of the third. Although "they got serious as the game progressed . . . they could not bunch hits on Captain Hashido." At the end of the nine innings the score stood at 2–1, and Waseda "marched off the field as proudly as if they had put to rout a regiment of Russians."[40]

For Hashido the victory was not the most memorable aspect of the afternoon:

While we were staying at the Washington Hotel in Seattle, we got acquainted with two little brothers from Portland. One was 12, the other was 8. They were typical American children who are very friendly and outspoken. When we played against the Rainier Club, they asked me to take them to the grounds as equipment managers. I loved them, so I accepted that offer. . . . When we won the game by 2 to 1, they jumped on me and called me 'Good boy, good boy!' with big smiles. In the meantime, many people came down from the stands and heartily praised our performance, shaking our hands. We were so delighted and would never forget that wonderful moment.[41]

This experience and similar encounters with American fans during the tour would lead Hashido to return to the United States after graduation, befriending Harry Saisho.

That evening the local Japanese threw the team a large party. Over four hundred men crowded into Seattle's Japan Club. They had much to celebrate. The previous day's headline of the *Seattle Star* had read, "Mikado and Czar Are Now Ready to End War and Talk about Peace." The Russo-Japanese War was unofficially over. Togo's victory had destroyed Russia's navy and left it vulnerable to Japanese invasion. The Russians now wanted to end the hostilities quickly. The peace talks would drag on for months before the signing of the Treaty of Portsmouth on September 5, 1905. The party went late into the night as Abe gave a forty-five-minute speech expressing his gratitude to the hosts.

The players woke up early the next morning for their final day in the United States. They boarded a ship at 10 a.m. and sailed down Puget Sound to Tacoma to play against Whitworth College, a tiny co-ed Presbyterian school with just fifty-five undergraduate students. Having difficulty fielding a competitive nine to challenge Waseda, Whitworth recruited Ernest Charles Tanner, the sixteen-year-old African American star of local Stadium High School. Tanner would hit fifth and catch.

Hashido took the mound 3:30 p.m. for Waseda and "went at the affair in a businesslike manner."[42] Despite two hits and a stolen base by Tanner, the Japanese won, 2–0, and Whitworth never really threatened to score. An hour and forty-five minutes later the Waseda players packed up their equipment and hurried back to Seattle to board the ss *Kanagawa* for the trip home. Tanner would go on to attend Whitworth and become the first African American to play football at the college level in the Pacific Northwest. He would be instrumental in the small school's incredible upset of the University of Oregon in 1908. After graduating, he would become captain and manager of Tacoma's African American Little Giants before eventual becoming one of the first black labor leaders for the longshoremen.[43] The game against Waseda made a lasting impression upon Tanner, and many years later he would speak out against both the forced relocation of Japanese Americans during World War II and the discrimination they faced upon their return to Tacoma in 1945.

At 5 a.m. on June 13 the *Kanagawa* slipped its moorings and sailed for Japan.

Once home, Abe and his players revolutionized Japanese baseball. The team brought back new equipment such as cleats, modern gloves, and the latest bat styles. Japanese manufacturers copied the imports, and soon teams across the country had up-to-date equipment. The players also imported the latest techniques of scientific baseball. They taught other teams the hit and run, the art of bunting, the windup, the spitball, and the basics of systematic practice. Team captain Shin Hashido published a book, *Recent Baseball Techniques*, which disseminated scientific baseball throughout Japan.

In the United States Waseda's visit helped establish baseball as an integral part of Japanese American culture. Hundreds of Japanese immigrants had attended the games, bringing many of them together as a community for the first time. For many of the immigrants the games were their first introduction to baseball. They learned the rules together, sharing a common bond. As they cheered for Waseda, they coalesced into a group, united by their pride in their countrymen's ball playing. "Almost every Japanese inhabitant of the town has shown the keenest interest in the success of their favorites," noted the *Los Angeles Times*.[44] "To the Japanese southern California community it was an inspiration to witness a Japanese team," remembered one of the fans.[45] Waseda's success, combined with the victory in the Russo-Japanese War, gave the immigrants a much-needed sense of pride in the face of an increasingly hostile anti-Japanese movement.

This new appreciation for baseball also gave the immigrants the opportunity to participate in a vital aspect of American culture, demonstrating their desire and ability to assimilate. At the turn of the twentieth century many middle-class whites believed that baseball both epitomized and taught the values needed to participate in American democracy and society. "In the United States, success and progress depend chiefly on the presence of certain personal characteristics," wrote H. Addington Bruce in 1913. "Physical fitness, courage, honesty, patience, the spirit of initiative combined with due respect for lawful authority, soundness and quickness of judgment, self-confidence, self-control, cheeriness, fair-mindedness, and appreciation of the importance of social solidarity, of team play—these are traits requisite as never before in the success of the life of an individual and of a nation. They are traits . . . that no other game . . . develops . . . as does baseball."[46]

Many felt that developing a passion for the game would indoctrinate immigrants with these traits and help them assimilate into American society. "There has been no greater agency in bringing our different races together than our national game, baseball. Baseball is our real melting pot," proclaimed sportswriter Fred Lieb.[47] An editorial in the *New York Telegraph* argued, "Our so-called aliens, hyphenates, unnaturalized immigrants, take to baseball before they take out their citizenship papers. . . . The American idea of racial assimilation, of amiable mutuality, of equal opportunity, is epitomized and illustrated in the game. . . . More than any other single influence, baseball remains at once the pleasant and always growing factor in the friendly democratization of our people, molding together all breeds through the elemental love of sport."[48]

At the time, Japanese immigrant community leaders preached that adopting American white middle-class behavior would break down bigotry and lead to acceptance. We "not only must refrain from irresponsible and careless behavior," wrote business leader Kinji Ushijima in 1911, "but we are also obliged to elevate our individual character and moralize our community. We must endeavor to get [whites] to recognize that the civilization of our nation is worthy of the upmost respect."[49] Baseball would serve as a bridge between the two cultures, bringing them together with a shared passion for the game and providing a path toward respect, acceptance and assimilation.

7

Guy Green's 1906 Japanese Base Ball Club

Guy W. Green was always on the prowl for opportunities to make money in baseball.

Green grew up in Stromsburg, Nebraska; studied at Doane College from 1887 to 1891 and the University of Iowa in 1893; and graduated from the University of Nebraska Law School in 1897. He had captained Doane's baseball team but was not destined for a career in pro ball. In 1900 Green wrote:

> I was death to flies, but I had to carry the ball in as I couldn't throw it over fifty feet. I retired in disgust and at the earnest request of the captain after playing a few games. . . . During my stay in Stromsburg I managed and captained the local nine and played first base. My arm was as bad as ever and the only way I ever got the ball from one corner of the diamond to the other was by running half way across and pushing the sphere the rest of the way. I ceased playing baseball altogether in 1897 but have never lost my love for the sport. I consider it the king of athletic amusements.[1]

Instead of playing, Green turned his considerable creative and entrepreneurial talents toward owning and running his own team.

At the turn of the twentieth century baseball was truly the national pastime. In most small towns the game was the primary form of entertainment, offering respite from the drudgery of back-breaking rural life.[2] Games brought scattered farming communities together and provided a lively topic for discussion in town centers. Baseball had spread throughout the country in the 1860s, as soldiers who had learned the game during the Civil War returned home and taught their neighbors. By 1873 the sporting newspaper *The Spirit of the*

Times could write, "In every little town and hamlet throughout the country we find a ball club, generally two."[3]

Most town ball clubs consisted of local players, ranging in age from teenagers to forty-year-old men. At first few teams sported uniforms. Men played in their work clothes—trousers with suspenders, a worn shirt, leather shoes or boots. Bats and balls were usually homemade, gloves nonexistent. Early diamonds were little more than converted pastures or town greens. By the late nineteenth century town ball had become institutionalized, evolving, in the words of historian Harold Seymour, "into an American institution meriting a place alongside such other symbols of America's past as the little red schoolhouse, the fervid revival meeting, and the old fashioned Fourth of July celebration."[4] Towns built formal playing fields, some with grandstands, and clubs mail ordered spiffy uniforms from Spalding's Sporting Goods or Sears, Roebuck and Company. Teams became a source of local pride and for some residents a measure of their town's self-worth. Rival towns settled disputes on the ball fields, with victors claiming moral superiority over their vanquished neighbors. Heavy wagers were often placed on the outcomes. Under pressure to win, some teams recruited outsiders for their ball playing skills and even hired "ringers"—usually pitchers— for important games.

For fans living on the Great Plains in the early twentieth century watching top-notch baseball was challenging. There were no Major League teams west of the Mississippi River—the closest franchises were located in St. Louis and Chicago. Many of the larger towns had Minor League clubs, but despite the extensive railroad system, travel was slow. Most men could not afford to be absent from their farms or places of business for more than a couple of days. Instead fans waited for traveling independent, or "barnstorming," teams to visit their home town and play their local nine.

The early twentieth century was the heyday of barnstorming baseball. Independent teams crisscrossed the country, playing in one-horse towns and large cities. Often organizers created teams around a theme to attract customers. There were all female teams, squads of only fat men, clubs of men sporting beards, and teams consisting of "exotic" ethnicities. African American clubs, excluded from Organized Baseball leagues, supplemented their incomes by also barnstorming against town teams. Some clubs brought along musicians, jugglers, acrobats, and even high-wire walkers.

These independent squads were often called "semi-professional" to differentiate them from teams associated with Organized Baseball (clubs formally associated with Major League Baseball), but they were professional enterprises. Most teams signed players to contracts, paid them salaries during the season, provided transportation and housing on the road, charged admission to games, and were intent on turning a profit. The top teams packed the grandstands in nearly every town they visited and brought in thousands of dollars.

An innovative idea for a barnstorming squad came to Guy Green in 1895, when, as the player-manager of the Stromsburg town baseball club, he organized a game against the Genoa Indian Industrial School. To his surprise, "Even in Nebraska, where an Indian is not at all a novelty, a baseball organization composed of red men drew everyone who was alive. When the Indians came to Stromsburg, business houses were closed and men, women and children turned out en masse to see the copper-colored performers corral the festive fly and chase the elusive grounder. I reasoned that if an Indian baseball team was a good drawing card in Nebraska, it ought to do wonders further east if properly managed."[5]

After graduating from law school in 1897, Green put his plan into action. Recruiting Native American players from the Genoa and Haskell schools, Green's All Nebraska Indian Base Ball Team (soon shortened to the Nebraska Indians) embarked on a forty-seven-game tour of Nebraska and Iowa. Although they lost twenty-six games, the tour was a success, attracting large enthusiastic crowds. Green realized from the start that fans expected more than just a baseball game. Much like the Harlem Globetrotters basketball team, the Nebraska Indians would entertain spectators with ball tricks, gags, and stereotyped "Indian" behavior—such as war whoops. Even in their first game (played against the University of Nebraska on June 25, 1897), "the great feature of their playing . . . was the attention they gave the grandstand. They seldom caught a ball or made a base without making some elaborate gesticulations intended solely for the spectators."[6]

Encouraged by the crowds during the inaugural season, Green led the team in 1898 on a 103-game tour through Nebraska, Missouri, Iowa, and Illinois. Success continued, and in subsequent seasons the Indians added more games and traveled further from their base. From 1897 to 1906 the Nebraska Indians played 1,637 games in seventeen states and Canada. The mainstay of the Nebraska Indians was a blue-eyed blond Caucasian named Dan Tobey. Standing 5 feet 11, "the Adonis of unorganized baseball" usually hit cleanup and often took the mound. In Green's absence Tobey managed the club. After retiring as a player, Tobey would make his fame as a boxing announcer in Los Angeles, eventually being inducted into the World Boxing Hall of Fame.[7]

Green's true brilliance lay in promotion. Capitalizing on the American public's fascination with Native Americans and the rapidly disappearing Wild West, Green gave players "Indian names" and created stories about them. Often these tales were filled with gross exaggerations based on ethnic stereotypes. Naomas, an ancient outfielder, could regenerate limbs after injury, and Juzicanea, "the meanest looking Indian [Green] had ever seen," slept on the ground and ate only raw meat.[8]

Each spring Green mailed a promotional pamphlet to managers of prospective town teams. The pamphlet was four pages long with a picture of Green on the cover under the title "Coming Soon Green's Nebraska Indians" and their slogan, "Only Ones on Earth." The interior pages contained the team's annual records, quotes from newspapers, and pictures of the team playing ball and dancing in war bonnets and loincloths. An accompanying letter stated, "You have heard of Green's Nebraska Indians. Every baseball crank has. . . . They are genuine Indians. Their coming is an event equal to circus day. . . . I will furnish you free of charge an elegant line of advertising matter. If you use this advertising properly you ought to draw out to the game everyone who is alive."[9]

Weeks before a scheduled game Green flooded local papers with advertisements and stories on the team. Ten days before the Indians came to Washington, Iowa, for example, he placed an announcement in the local newspaper: "Genuine, painted, screeching Indians, hailing from Nebraska, played baseball yesterday afternoon. . . . Poor Lo scalped the suburbanites by means of grinning faces, crazy antics and strong right arms. The Nebraska Indians will play the local team at the fair grounds on April 26–27."[10]

When they arrived in town, Dan Tobey would dress as a clown and "[lead the] players in buckskin and headdresses through the town streets in a parade to the ballpark."[11] At night they would pitch tee-pees and "camp right on the grounds where they play and live in true savage style."[12] Spectators loved the act, and the Indians became one of the most popular squads on the barnstorming circuit.

Green helped maintain enthusiasm for his team by publishing two pamphlets. The first, *The Nebraska Indians: A Complete History of the Nebraska Indian Base Ball Team*, was a game-by-game recounting of the team's first seasons. First released in 1900, Green updated the publication several times by adding subsequent seasons. The second pamphlet, *Fun and Folic with an Indian Ball Team*, published in 1907, contains amusing yarns about players and experiences on the road.

Green was a savvy businessman. "Green . . . is in the baseball business strictly for the money he can get out of it," complained a writer for the *Tecumseh Chieftain*.[13] The Indians' popularity allowed Green to demand as much as 75 percent of the gross gate receipts and stipulate, "Under no circumstances will we play for a smaller general admission price than 25 cents. This must be paid by everyone, both men and women. . . . We are not running a charitable institution."[14] He also demanded, "If you desire a date your grounds must be so arranged that all who see the game will have to pay. By this I do not mean that you must necessarily have a high board fence, but you must have some arrangement so that people will have to put up their money to see the game."[15] Green would later claim in a lawsuit against the National Association of Professional Baseball Leagues that he routinely made $5,000 profit a season on the Nebraska Indians' barnstorming tours.[16]

In 1906 much of America was enthralled by Japan and all things Japanese. Since the opening of the country in 1853, Japanese culture and aesthetics had influenced Western art, architecture, fashion, gardening, interior design, literature, theater, and even wrestling, but its spectacular military victories during the Russo-Japanese War created what H. D. Miller called "Japan-o-mania" from 1905 to 1907.[17] As a prominent lawyer in Lincoln, Nebraska, Guy Green was well aware of this fad. He had also followed Waseda's 1905 baseball tour closely, noting the large crowds and extensive local, and even national, press coverage. Even after Waseda returned home, the American press continued to run articles on the Japanese ballplayers, noting that their success on the diamond proved similarities between the two nations. In July 1905 *Tip Top Weekly*, one of the most popular dime novels (selling approximately five hundred thousand copies a week), followed on the tour's success by publishing two issues featuring its sports hero, Dick Merriwell, traveling to Japan to play "baseball in the flowery kingdom."[18]

Green decided to capitalize on the interest in Japan by creating an all-Japanese baseball team to barnstorm across the Midwest. It would be the first professional Japanese team on either side of the Pacific. In early 1906 Green instructed Dan Tobey to recruit a team of Japanese players for the upcoming season.

In May 1904 members of the Uyeda family gathered in their garden. The walled garden was large by Japanese standards, expertly landscaped with granite boulders and highlighted with ferns forming a peaceful, natural setting. Rough-hewn paving stones led from the tiled-roofed two-story house across a narrow ornamental stream to the garden's rear. The spreading limbs of several mature trees provided shade near the home and privacy along the property line.[19]

Eighteen-year-old Tetsusaburo "Tetsu" Uyeda squatted, putting a clump of soil around a camphor sapling. His forty-seven-year-old father, Minoru; his mother, Tamiko; and four brothers and sister watched. The tree was a symbol. Tetsu had just graduated from Yamaguchi High School and was about to leave for California. Two of his four brothers, twenty-one-year-old Junjiro and fifteen-year-old Takatomo, had plans to follow him. Standing up, Tetsusaburo gave a short speech. He had planted the sapling with two desires: "that the family would remember them forever after they left" and that both "they and the tree would have big futures."[20]

Born into the samurai class, the boys' father, Minoru (born 1857), had the second-largest landholding in Yamaguchi Prefecture. At its height the lands produced about six thousand tons of rice per year. Minoru held the traditional administrative positions in the village of Daido, serving as village headman and postmaster; in 1902 he was elected to Japan's House of Representatives and served in the Imperial Diet. Following Japanese law and tradition, Minoru's eldest son, Jo (born 1880), would inherit the entire estate. The younger brothers were expected to build their own lives. Minoru had wanted Tetsusaburo to attend the military academy after graduating from high school. Yamaguchi had a strong military tradition and had produced many high-ranking army officers. Tetsu, however, had other ideas.[21]

The Uyeda brothers had become avid ballplayers in school. Despite Yamaguchi's being located on the southwest tip of Japan's main island of Honshu, nearly five hundred miles from Tokyo, baseball had arrived there at an early date. Local historians believe that the first games were played in the early 1880s, although the earliest surviving reference is a description of a November 3, 1886, Yamaguchi Commercial High School athletic meet where the students competed at baseball, soccer, lawn tennis, and track and field. By 1895 the game was flourishing on the playgrounds and in the schools.

The three middle Uyeda brothers attended Yamaguchi High School (then known as Yamaguchi Middle School)—Junjiro from 1897 to 1902, Tetsusaburo from 1899 to 1904, and Takatomo from 1902 to 1907. The boys were large for Japanese of the time, towering over their classmates. In the first half of the twentieth century the average Japanese male stood 5 feet 3. Tetsu was 5 feet 7, Junjiro a similar height, while Takatomo would grow to 5 feet 11—a giant by the island nation's standards.[22]

All three played on the school's baseball team, recognized as the strongest in the prefecture. The school imported the latest techniques and strategies from clubs in Tokyo, sponsored tournaments, and sent its team to play other top schools in southern Japan. Frustrated by local rule variations, Yamaguchi High School created a rule book in 1899 and distributed it to the other clubs in the prefecture. Known as the "Yamaguchi Rules," they were nearly identical to the modern version except for awarding a base to a batter after five balls instead of four. Despite similar rules, the game in Yamaguchi in the 1890s bore little resemblance to modern baseball. Most teams lacked uniforms, fielders played without gloves, and most went barefoot or wore *tabi*. According to a history of Yamaguchi baseball, "Back then the teams had no managers. The techniques were pretty basic and the rules were often ignored. Brawls after the games were common, and winning the brawl was regarded as more important than winning the game."[23]

During high school Tetsu was drawn to his English teacher—a young American named Raymond Porter Gorbald. A devout Presbyterian, Gorbald had graduated from Cedarville College in 1897 and received a Doctor of Divinity degree from Lane Theological Seminary in 1902. Immediately after graduation he set off for Japan under the YMCA Student Volunteer Movement. After his early death in 1915 the Cedarville yearbook described him as "a man of keen sympathy, rare thotfulness [sic], unselfish, with a zeal to help everyone [and whose] optimistic outlook on life was an inspiration to all."[24] While in college, Gorbald played football and as the school's star shortstop had "the happy faculty of turning base hits into put-outs, and at the bat [made] the pitcher think of home."[25]

At Yamaguchi High School, Gorbald coached the baseball team and entertained his players with tales about Major League stars— probably telling them about the batting prowess of Ed Delahanty and Nap Lajoie, the pitching of Cy Young, and the antics of Rube Waddell. The young teacher would change Tetsusaburo's life. Enamored by Gorbald's stores, Tetsu decided to forgo a career in the military and instead move to the United States to become a professional ballplayer.[26]

Minoru Uyeda was less than thrilled by his son's dream. "When I graduated from high school," Tetsu later told Fay Profilet of the *St. Louis Post-Dispatch*, "I caused a great commotion in my family by announcing that I was not going to the army school—but to America. After six months, I convinced my parents that nothing could change me, for in America I had centered all my hope and ambition."[27]

In late May 1904 Tetsu and his entire family—father, mother, four brothers, a sister, and fifteen uncles, aunts, and cousins—took the train to Yokohama. There Tetsu boarded the steamship SS *Coptic* as his family was "weeping and saying farewell as though I were going to the battlefield." Two weeks later he arrived in California.[28]

Tetsu had intended to enroll at the University of Southern California and play on the school's baseball team. Had his plan worked, he would have played against Isoo Abe's Waseda University team during its 1905 tour, but, like Harry Saisho, Tetsu found that his English was not strong enough to attend an American university. Instead he went to night school to improve his English while working for the Japanese YMCA in Los Angeles.[29]

During his free time Tetsu played baseball, becoming renowned for his speed on the base paths.[30] On February 11, 1905, Uyeda displayed his ability at the celebration of the first anniversary of the victory at Port Arthur in Los Angeles's Boyle Heights neighborhood. Nearly five thousand Japanese immigrants attended the all-day event, which featured speeches, sporting events, and fireworks. According to the *Los Angeles Herald*, in the hotly contested 220-yard dash, young Tetsu "spurted at the finish and took the prize," winning a brass medal with an American flag ribbon (emphasizing the immigrants' affiliation with their new country).[31] A year later another newspaper article would allow him to fulfill his dream.

Although Guy Green's promotional literature would claim that he had sent Tozan Masko to Japan to "scour the empire for the best players obtainable" at a cost of $150–$300 per man, he had done nothing of the sort.[32] Undoubtedly to save money Dan Tobey formed the team from Japanese immigrants living in California. With Tozan Masko's help he recruited Ken Kitsuse, Harry Saisho, Toyo Fujita, and Kotan Saito from the Japanese Base Ball Club of Los Angeles; twenty-one-year-old Umekichi "Kitty" Kawashima from Kanagawa, Japan (he may have been a student at Stanford); Shoichi Motohashi; and four players, Kato, Kimo, Naito, and Nishi, only identified by their last names.

While searching for players, Tobey noticed a newspaper article that described a local high schooler as "the fastest player ever from Japan."[33] He immediately tracked down Tetsu Uyeda and offered him a contract. As an added bonus Tobey also enlisted Tetsu's older brother, Junjiro, who had arrived in the United States just a few months earlier in November 1905. The Uyeda brothers could barely believe their luck. After being in the country only a short time, they would be professional ballplayers.

The two Uyeda brothers, Saisho, Kitsuse, and their new teammates arrived at Lincoln, Nebraska, by train on the afternoon of March 31, 1906, and immediately went to Havelock, a village of about six hundred on the northwest outskirts of Lincoln. A small crowd had gathered on the dirt street outside the two-story clapboard hotel, waiting to catch a glimpse of the exotic visitors.[34] The players settled down on the inn's second floor, two per room, excited by the prospect of three country meals per day. Dan Tobey gave the players the following day to relax. They stayed in Havelock, reconnoitering the two-story wooden shops that lined the village's wide dirt main street, shooting pool at a local pool hall, and playing cards— presumably among themselves at the hotel.

On April 2 the team went to meet Guy Green at his law firm in Lincoln. Just shy of his thirty-third birthday, Green was of medium build and height. He had an angular, almost effeminate pale face with deep-set brown eyes and brown hair parted to each side from just to the left of the middle of his scalp. Saisho noted, "He owns a law firm and was nice and warm yet had the feel of an adventurer."[35] Harry had judged him perfectly.

Green and Tobey took the players to a sporting goods store to buy equipment and pick up their uniforms. The outfits were nearly identical to the Nebraska Indians' uniforms: white pants reaching just below the knees, wide leather belts, maroon stockings, maroon undershirts, and a winged-collared maroon jersey with "Greens Japs" stitched in white block letters across the chest. The caps were white with maroon bills. The team then went to a photography studio. The photographer shot the players in baseball poses against a neutral background. With the images Green would create a four-by-six-inch promotional card with the photographs of ten players under the headline (fig. 12):

Green's Japanese Base Ball Team
Direct From the Schools and Universities of Japan
Guy W. Green
Manager
Lincoln, Nebraska
Owner also of Green's Nebraska Indians

The players ended their afternoon with tours of City Hall and the University of Nebraska campus before being treated to a large dinner. That evening they oiled their gloves, prepared their uniforms, and readied themselves for the start of training.

At 7 a.m. the next day Tobey banged on the door, waking Saisho. He sprung from bed and joined his teammates in the dining room for breakfast. "They didn't serve a gorgeous breakfast," Saisho recalled, "but they brought out two or three Chinese dishes, and we passed them around. Some of the players also had meat, fried eggs, bacon, bread, and coffee. After using the toilet, we went back to our rooms, changed into baseball uniforms, grabbed two bats each, and were taken to a practice field outside of the village."[36]

The field was not a true ballpark, just a diamond surrounded by a fence with a small stand for onlookers. Tobey introduced Sandy Kissell, a Native American who had played on Green's Nebraska Indians and would be the team's assistant coach. Practice began with the players forming two lines and tossing balls back and forth to warm up their arms. Hard throws were forbidden, which, according to Saisho was wise as "[we] Japanese tend to damage our shoulders by throwing balls hard from the beginning to satisfy our vanity."[37] After the warmup the coaches pitched, allowing each of the Japanese a turn at bat while the rest of the team practiced fielding. The team broke for lunch at 11 a.m., returning to the hotel for a meal and rest before reconvening for a two-and-a-half-hour afternoon practice. The team would stay in Havelock for two weeks, following a similar routine each day. For the Japanese, who were accustomed to California weather, it was bitter cold. Players grumbled as the temperature hovered around freezing, rising slightly the second week into the low 40s.

During the lunch break on the second or third day of practice Tobey handed out the club rules, printed in Japanese. With Masko interpreting, Tobey laid out the fines for undesirable behavior: two dollars for being late for a game; two dollars for lazy playing; three dollars for refusing to follow the manager's orders; three dollars for refusing to travel to the ballpark with the team; three dollars for gambling; and five dollars for drinking alcohol. He then produced a stack of contracts for the players to sign.

"Of course, we happily signed immediately," Saisho remembered. "We had been worried that Mr. Green might not be satisfied with our techniques and would send us home, so we were so happy to be offered contracts that we didn't even think about reading [them]." Later in life Saisho realized how careless they had been. "We had to be careful in the white business world. We Japanese often made mistakes because we were too trusting. Fortunately, none of us broke the contract."[38]

Once the contracts were signed, the players relaxed, feeling confident about their abilities. Green and Tobey, however, were concerned. The Japanese players were not as strong as they had expected. Green knew from experience that the uniqueness of a Japanese squad would not be enough to draw big crowds if the players could not perform well on the field.

Tobey intensified the practices, shouting and exhorting his players to excel. Saisho remembered, "His yelling gave us power and he didn't let us rest. We practiced so hard that after ten minutes we were covered in sweat. If there had been coaches like Tobey in Japan, Japanese baseball would have been better developed."[39] Villagers stopped by the training sessions. At first they came from mere curiosity, wondering how Japanese would play the American pastime, but impressed with Tobey's coaching and the grueling workouts, many stayed to watch.

After a few days the Nebraska Indians joined the Japanese at the practice field. Saisho knew the Indians' reputation as top semi-pros, as talented as many Pacific Coast League players. Nevertheless, their skill surprised him. The Japanese were particularly impressed with the shortstop Juzicania, a Yaqui from Arizona whom Guy Green describes as "the meanest looking Indian I have ever seen." According to Green, Juzicania "wore his hair long, surveyed everything suspiciously with piercing black eyes, and when he came down the street people moved to the edge of the sidewalk and apprehensively watched him pass."[40] "Although he was small like us," Saisho wrote, he could throw the ball "like an arrow," so hard that the receiver sometimes dropped the ball from the sting of the impact. "Knowing that a small man could play that well gave us a motive to practice harder. In poor English, we told the Indians' captain that we were newcomers and inexperienced, and our skin color is very similar, so please teach us."[41]

On April 6 Guy Green came to Havelock to watch his new team practice. Although he may have been secretly uneasy about the players' abilities, he bragged to the *Lincoln Daily Evening News*, "I had never seen them practice before and they did a great deal better than I expected they would do. As fielders they can't be beat. They are not so heavy at batting as an American team but are fairly good hitters and I believe they are going to make a fast team."[42]

On a cold Tuesday, April 10, the Japanese squad watched the Indians play the Lincoln Ducklings of the Class A Western League. Tobey started on the mound for the Indians. He gave up two quick runs before settling down and shutting out the professionals for the next four innings. Saisho noted that Tobey was an "honest pitcher" who eschewed curves and "drops." Instead he relied on brains and control, reading an opponent's weakness and exploiting it by changing planes and pitching to the corners, leaving batters "frustrated." Although the Indians lost, 6–2, the level of play awed the Japanese. They returned to the hotel and spent the evening discussing the techniques they had noticed during the game, such as how the Indian left fielder had used his glove to block the sun as he ran down a fly ball. "We wanted to play games like the Indians," recalled Saisho.[43]

The next day the Indians headed east to begin their 185-game barnstorming season. Wanting to avoid the areas where his Japanese team would play, Green sent the Indians to the central states and East Coast, where they would play in Brooklyn, New Jersey, and Pennsylvania. With the practice field to themselves the Japanese felt more relaxed and less inhibited. They refined their skills and tried to copy the techniques of the Indians and Ducklings.

The Japanese barnstorming tour was due to start in just a few days, and Green knew that the team was not prepared, yet some of the players showed real talent. Tobey had placed Ken Kitsuse at shortstop, and he was a phenomenal fielder. Tetsu Uyeda (now known as Tommy), Kitty Kawashima, and Naito also showed promise. But most of the players were not skilled enough to excel at independent professional ball.

Green had already mailed out promotional material to prospective opponents and local newspapers with the team's all-Japanese roster and probable lineup. The release read:

There are in Japan 263 middle schools and 37 universities at which base ball is played and played according to American rules. The prowess of the little Jap on the diamond is attested by every American navy team that has tried conclusions with them. Every traveler who has seen them play declares that they play ball as if it were their national game, and that these games are sometimes attended by as many as 10,000 people.

Guy W. Green, the Nebraska Indians team promoter and owner, has secured a team of full-blooded Japanese players and is touring the country with them. They are all native Japs, speak no English, and do their coaching in the Japanese tongue. He has secured for this club four of the best pitchers in that country. His lineup also includes the champion long-distance thrower of Japan, as well as that country's greatest shortstop, and the whole team is the pick of the Japanese empire's players.

Manager Green sent an agent to Japan for these players who for several months devoted his time to scouring the empire for the best men obtainable. In his search, he had the assistance of the leading base ball authorities of Japan.

The lineup includes Kato, catcher; Toyo, pitcher; Saito, pitcher and outfielder; T. Uyeda, first baseman; J. Uyeda, second baseman; Naito, third baseman; Kitsuse, shortstop; Nish, outfield; Kawashima, outfield; Kimo, infielder; and Masko, pitcher and manager.[44]

Now Green and Tobey would have to make cuts and find replacements.

Despite his love for the game and his high school experience, Saisho was one of the struggling players. He remarked:

During outfield practice, Kissell's hits were very strong. They went high and dropped fast, unlike our short hits. Moreover, the practice field was windy, so it was very difficult to catch the ball. When I went sideways or backward to make a catch, the ball would fall in an unexpected location. I would try to reach out, but it would drop more than 30 cm in front of me. I played foolishly and often disturbed the other outfielders. The manager saw my failures and thought I was a bad player. I confess that except for Tozan Masko, no one was worse than me, so I never blamed Tobey for thinking of me as a bad player. But Tobey didn't tell me that I couldn't play on the team because I was bad. Instead, he said it was because I was near-sighted. I could go on the trip, but he would not play me in a game. I considered returning to Los Angeles by myself but thought it would disrupt the team and would not be a masculine attitude, so I decided to remain.[45]

As Saisho noted, Masko was also a weak player. He "had a smart mouth, but he was not good at play at all."[46] Tozan was soon relegated to be a batting practice pitcher and would help retrieve balls hit outside the playing field. He would also remain on the team as an interpreter, ticket taker, occasional umpire, and emergency player.

Saisho and Masko were not the only players relegated to the bench. Junjiro Uyeda, Kotan Saito, the catcher Kato, and outfielders Kimo and Nishi are listed on the roster and appear on the team's promotional card but do not appear in any box scores or newspaper articles during the tour.

Green decided to replace the cut Japanese players with Native Americans—probably hoping that most spectators would not be able to tell the difference. The coach, Sandy Kissell, would remain with the team and share pitching duties with Dan Tobey. Seguin, occasionally called Sego in box scores, would catch most of the games. Both Kissell and Seguin would play on Green's Nebraska Indians in 1907. Two other men, known only by their nicknames, "Doctor" (first and third base), and "Noisy" (first base, third base, and catcher), joined the squad. Roy Dean Whitcomb, an eighteen-year-old Caucasian from Lincoln, also appears in box scores throughout the tour at first base and catcher. As Whitcomb and Noisy never appear in the same box score, it is likely that they are the same person. At various points during the season local white players would also join the team. Lewis (no first name given) played in games from July through September, and Charlie Farrell, who had played for the Minneapolis Minnies of the Class D Kansas State League the previous year, played a few games in late April.

Rain fell as Guy Green's Japanese Base Ball Team packed bags and prepared to leave Havelock on the evening of April 13. Despite the weather, a small crowd gathered in front of the hotel to say goodbye. During their two-week stay the Japanese players had become friendly with a number of the villagers—a pleasing contrast to the bigotry they often endured in California. "We had a good time talking about our next destination and we wanted to start playing games like the Indians," recalled Saisho, "but at the same time, I didn't like leaving the village—parting with the women, children and the villagers whom we had become friendly with. I would especially miss the five or six young girls, eight- or nine-year-olds, who would wait for us in front of the hotel dining room and give us candy."[47]

8

The 1906 Barnstorming Tour

From Lincoln, Guy Green's Japanese Base Ball Club headed south, beginning a twenty-five-week tour that covered over 2,500 miles through the states of Nebraska, Kansas, Texas, Arkansas, Indiana, Illinois, Iowa, and Missouri, as well as the Oklahoma and Indian Territories. No schedule survives for the tour, but extensive newspaper searches suggest that the team played between 150 and 170 games.[1]

On Sunday, April 15, the Japanese squad warmed up for the tour by playing the high school team in Frankfort, Kansas. Perhaps seeing the game as an opportunity to allow his weaker players to gain experience, Tobey started a mostly Japanese lineup. Yet the schoolboys jumped out to an early 4–1 lead after three innings, forcing Tobey to bring in what the *Marshall County Index* called "five professional American players." The visitors battled back, eventually winning, 11–8.[2] The near loss to schoolboys confirmed Tobey's view that many of his players were not talented enough for independent ball. There is no record of the team using an all-Japanese starting lineup for the rest of the season.

The next day the team moved on to Irving, a cursed settlement of fewer than five hundred situated on the Big Blue River. Despite the town's being located on some of the best agricultural soil in the area, bad luck had plagued it since its inception. In 1860, a year after settlement, severe drought had ruined a promising crop and windstorms had leveled houses. Swarms of grasshoppers destroyed entire crops in 1866 and 1875; tornados flattened the town in 1879, killing nineteen; and a flood washed away much of the settlement in 1903. A newspaper account of the 1879 tornado mentioning the death of one Dorothy Gale supposedly inspired the beginning and name of the main character for L. Frank Baum's *Wizard of Oz*.[3] Today only a stone monument marking the location of the Irving post office remains. The federal government closed the town in 1960 to build the Turtle Creek Lake reservoir.

In 1906, however, Irving was a pleasant community welcoming to the foreign players. "Mr. Tobey is a good social fellow and made a very favorable impression on the people he had dealings with," wrote a reporter for the *Irving Ledger*. "The Japs, and the Americans with them, were all good fellows and the crowd enjoyed seeing them play. [Irving] Manager Keen is to be congratulated upon getting such a nice set of fellows to open the season with." The afternoon game was tight. After Kitsuse led off with a walk, stole second, and scored on a single, the score swung back and forth until it knotted at five from the bottom of the eighth to the bottom of the twelfth, when "the Japs used the same strategy on their American friends as they did with Russia and pushed three men over the home plate." Following the antics of the Nebraska Indians, the Japanese "kept the crowd amused by their actions and talk." After the game both teams attended a "Pie Social" to benefit the high school baseball club. Tobey auctioned off homemade pies as the event raised $12.80 for the boys. The *Irving Ledger* pointed out that the pie baked by high school senior Miss Etta DeShazer was purchased by "Tommy [Uyeda], the favorite of the Japanese boys."[4]

Two days later, on April 18, at 5:12 a.m. PST, the third largest recorded earthquake in the contiguous United States struck San Francisco. The primary tremor shook the earth for forty-two seconds and was felt from southern Oregon to southern California and as far west as central Nevada. Buildings swayed and collapsed throughout the city as deep fissures ran through streets, buckling paving stones and sidewalks. Almost immediately fires caused by broken gas lines and open kitchen flames spread out of control across the city. The fires burned for three days as broken pipes robbed firefighters of water to extinguish the flames. The downtown section from Franklin Street on the west to Townsend on the south—nearly 25,000 buildings on 480 blocks—burned to the ground. The destroyed area included the Episcopal Methodist Japanese Mission, Tozan Masko's first home in the United States, and the Lurline Baths. China-town and the Japanese community were hit especially hard. In all over 3,000 people lost their lives and over half of the city's 410,000 inhabitants became homeless.

News of the disaster reached eastern Kansas by telegraph soon after the initial quake. Traveling in the Topeka area, the Japanese players would have heard about the catastrophe during the day but would have to wait for a copy of the *Topeka State Journal* for details. "San Francisco Is Burning Up/Earthquake Shock Destroys a Large Portion of the City/Thousands of Lives Are Believed to Have Been Crushed Out" headlined the paper's late edition. Articles detailed widespread death and destruction. Although no surviving source documents their reaction, the players must have been worried. Many had lived in the city and were undoubtedly anxious about friends and perhaps family still living in San Francisco.

Despite the disaster and the players' concerns, the following day the team played the professional Topeka White Sox of the Class C Western Association. Topeka citizens were infatuated with Japanese culture. Women held Japanese tea parties and dressed in Japanese-inspired clothing, while newspaper advertisements often used Japanese imagery. An ad for Jap Rose [laundry] Soap depicted an Asian woman in a kimono and *geta* (wooden sandals) pinning dolls in Japanese dress to her clothesline. Two days before the game a local amateur theater group performed the musical *A Japanese Fete* at the Opera House. The well-received performance featured American women dressed as geisha with the "most wonderful imitations of Japanese coiffures and flowing kimonos of kaleidoscopic hues." On game day the Palace Clothier proclaimed a "Jiu-Jitsu Suit" sale.[5] An editorial in the *Topeka State Journal* on April 10 condemned California's anti-Japanese immigration movement, arguing "the Jap . . . is honest and honorable. He is hard-working and thrifty. He is not a drunkard and he is seldom seen in courts. He is far more desirable in every way as a citizen than those who are pouring through Castle Garden. . . . If the Kansas farmers could get some of those Japs to help in the harvest fields and with the general farm work, it would be a great boon to Kansas."[6]

The game itself disappointed the fans. Green's team was "outclassed," 10–0, by the White Sox, who had three men who would make the Major Leagues. Tobey once again used only five Japanese players—Kitsuse, Uyeda, Kawashima, Naito, and Fujita. A reporter for the *Topeka Daily Capital* noted that the Japanese played as well "as that of the average semi-professional team." At the plate they were able to make contact but were unable to place the ball. The *Topeka State Journal* praised Kitsuse as "fast as a whip" and Kawashima as "easily the star of the team," and it noted that Naito and Fujita were "artists in catching fly balls." The writer added, "In fact the catching of flies is where the Jap shines at the ball game. He dances around watching the ball in the air, and just as he is about to nail it, he jumps off both feet. At stopping hot, fast grounders, he is not a success. At the hitting game he is not much better."[7]

Tobey excused his team's deficiencies by telling reporters, "We have only had the Japs together since April 14" and claimed that the use of American players was just temporary. "In the course of a month we will have an entire Jap team." He also retold the false tale of how Green had sent Masko to Japan to recruit the players, this time adding that the Japanese all came from "Waseda College at Tokyo."[8]

After narrowly defeating the town team at Hoyt, Kansas, 8–7, Green's Japanese faced a formidable squad at Fort Riley on April 22. The army base, founded in 1853, had housed Gen. George Armstrong Custer and his famous Seventh Cavalry before becoming the site of the U.S. Cavalry School in 1887. In 1906 the sprawling military complex held nearly 1,300 soldiers.[9] The soldiers took their sports seriously and fielded two baseball teams—one from the cavalry and one from the artillery.[10] Both squads were among the stronger amateur teams in the region, able to challenge regional independent and college nines.

A week before the game a short article in the *Fort Riley Guidon* exclaimed, "The Japs will undoubtedly prove a great attraction. The team is one of the strongest from the island nation and is now engaged in a tour of the country, having landed only recently at San Francisco. None of the players can speak or write English."[11]

A few days before game day, posters advertising the game were plastered throughout the base and nearby Junction City. The *Junction City Union* ran several articles—full of hyperbole—promoting the game. "The baseball game tomorrow between the Japanese and Fort Riley teams should prove one of the greatest baseball attractions that the vicinity has ever had the good fortune to witness. The Japs are graduates of the leading Universities of the Mikado's island empire. . . . Fort Riley has the fastest team in its history . . . and the game should prove a battle royal, fast though the visitors may be."[12]

For the first time the press directly connected the team to the Russo-Japanese War to capitalize on the public's interest in Japan's surprising victory. Based on information undoubtedly provided by Tobey, the *Junction City Union* claimed, "Green's Japs have in their ranks men who fought Russia doggedly for months during the great Russian-Japanese war. They bear upon their bodies scars of hand-to-hand engagements on the Russian frontier. The team has also beardless boys whose skill no other race can hope to equal."[13]

The hyped-up advertising worked as 1,200 people, paying twenty cents per regular seat or ten cents to sit in the grandstand, came to the afternoon game at the fort's ballpark. According to the *Fort Riley Guidon*, "Many came from mere curiosity." Tobey's exaggerations, however, were soon revealed. "The Japanese ball team," complained a reporter, "was not what the Jap's advertising manager cracked it up to be." The soldiers "lambasted the visiting pitcher in a heart-breaking manner," jumping out to a quick 8–0 lead. As the blow-out continued, the disgruntled fans began to leave. By the end of the 22–5 slaughter, the stands were nearly empty.[14]

In both *The Nebraska Indians: A Complete History of the Nebraska Indian Base Ball Team* and *The Nebraska Indians and Fun and Frolic with an Indian Ball Team*, Guy Green mentions his Japanese squad only once. The event in the following anecdote, published in the latter pamphlet under the chapter heading "He Almost Dropped Dead," occurred the night before the game at Fort Riley.

> Mr. D. W. Tobey acted as road manager for my Japanese Ball Team in 1906.
>
> He surprised me one day by sending me the following letter. I have no doubt the incident described is true in every particular. The question is could Tobey have been held as the murderer of this hotel keeper had he actually dropped dead, and would I have been regarded as an accessory because I furnished the money which killed him.

Manhattan, Kans., Apr. 22nd, 1906.

Now Guy, the following is certainly the truth. I have one eye witness to this, Kissell. When I paid my hotel bill last night at Riley, $18.75, the proprietor fell into a swoon; his heart failed him and it was several minutes before he was able to sign receipt. Guy, I tell you I was scared. I counted out the eighteen bones and I was getting the seventy-five cents when I noticed he was acting very strange. He started to bend over like a person having a fit; he kicked the desk a hell of a jolt and closed his eyes, his face all wrinkled up. I tell you I thought his day had come. I yelled to Kissell. He was on the porch. He came in and was badly scared and wanted to know what I had done to the man. He came to after a short while, signed the receipt, then he told us he was subject to heart failure. I shall never forget this affair as long as I live. You know you and I used to say we knew of or about people dropping dead when we paid a hotel bill. Well, this was close enough for me. It was a rotten hotel, no towels, no water and no grub to speak of. I do believe the $18.75 was a lifesaver to him; yes, I am sure it was.[15]

The team headed west from Fort Riley following the route of present-day I-70, disappointing a "very fair crowd" at Minneapolis for playing only four Japanese alongside five whites, as well as the inhabitants of Marquette for its unenthusiastic play during a 10–3 loss to the town's team.[16]

On Thursday, April 26, Guy Green's club arrived in Salina to take on the Kansas Wesleyan College varsity team. Tobey and Green had flooded the town with the usual advertising, claiming that the team represented the best players in Japan and evoking the Japanese victory against Russia, but this time they created stories about specific players. Pregame newspaper articles told readers that Ken Kitsuse "left school in Japan to serve during the last great war with Russia. He was wounded at Mukden so severely that he was compelled to go home and even yet he limps slightly."[17] Kitsuse, of course, had arrived in the United States nearly two years before the Japanese defeated the Russians at the Battle of Mukden in March 1905. Another story claimed that Tozan Masko was the nephew of Admiral Heihachiro Togo, commander of the victorious Japanese fleet. As no reliable source mentions this connection and Masko's parents came from Fukushima Prefecture, about seven hundred miles north of Togo's hometown of Kagoshima in Satsuma, the relationship is undoubtedly fictitious. Nevertheless, the press would repeat these stories for the remainder of the tour.

Once again spectators were disappointed that Tobey did not field an all-Japanese lineup. Using just Kitsuse, Naito, Kawashima, and Masko (in a rare appearance), the visitors won, 9–5. Reporters differed on the quality of play. The *Salina Evening Journal* claimed, "As a whole the game was very interesting and a good crowd cheered from start to finish." The *Salina Daily Union* disagreed: "It was really not such a good exhibition game. The Japs are fair players but it is generally believed that the posters which announce them as the greatest in Japan yarn slightly. In fact there are several thousand in Japan who can beat them all hollow. The nephew of Togo, Masko, is alright and so is Kitsuse but the remainder of the team did not amount to so much."[18]

A similar story played out the following day at Haven, Kansas. The *Haven Weekly Journal* and nearby *Hutchinson News* had been advertising the game for a week. A long article, repeating Green's advertising verbatim, appeared in the *Weekly Journal* on April 21. Two shorter blurbs appeared in the same issue. "The Japanese on their own island have defeated every team that has gone against them!" "Green's Japs have with them four of the best pitchers of Japan, the champion long distance thrower of the Empire, the greatest Japanese short stop in the world bar none, and the pick of all players from the various schools and universities of Japan. This great team will play the Haven team at Haven on Friday, April 27." "The chances are that not one of our citizens has ever seen a Japanese team play baseball. An opportunity which no one can afford to miss," reminded the *Hutchinson News* the day before the game. Once again the game itself was a letdown. Green's Japanese squeaked by the local squad, not remotely resembling the advertised undefeatable Japanese champions. "They played four Japs and the other five were white men. . . . The crowd was disappointed as they expected to see a full team of Japs play."[19]

As the team finished its first two weeks on the road and prepared to head south to Oklahoma, Tobey faced a dilemma. Spectators were repeatedly disappointed that he did not field an all-Japanese team, but they also wanted to watch a close game. Even with the five non-Japanese in the starting lineup, the team was weak. If he used more of his Japanese players, he risked lopsided losses that would also upset paying fans. The exaggerated advertising, however, attracted large crowds, even if they left disappointed. As long as he kept the team moving, not staying in an area long enough for word to spread that the nine were not particularly good, the barnstormers could continue to make money.

The team spent May in the Oklahoma and Indian Territories, areas that would be combined in 1907 to form the state of Oklahoma, as well as northern Texas, Arkansas, and Missouri. Learning from the difficulties in Kansas, Tobey challenged small town teams, avoiding both larger towns and other independent teams. The team had a run of victories, going 17-3 in recorded games, results that Tobey announced through dispatches to the *Omaha World Herald* and the *Dallas Morning News*. Few feature articles have been recovered from this part of the tour, but these suggest that the games were well attended and well received.

In late May the squad crossed the Mississippi River and entered Illinois. Other than occasional games with border towns in Indiana and Iowa, the team would stay in the Prairie State for nearly seven weeks, playing more than fifty games in the southern and western parts of the state. Tobey followed the strategy established in May, playing small-town nines and avoiding city, semi-pro, and independent teams. Of the nearly fifty towns visited, all but six had fewer than three thousand residents. Only two, Quincy and Springfield, had over thirty thousand inhabitants.

The squad also avoided Chicago and its suburbs. At the time Chicago was a center for semi-pro and independent teams. Every weekend thousands would pay twenty-five cents for a seat or fifteen cents for general admission to watch the city's top teams compete at one of the four enclosed "amateur" ballparks. The top three white independent clubs—the Logan Squares, Gunthers, and West Enders—were stocked with the best players from the Midwest (including many former Major Leaguers) who were making as much as $200 per month. Chicago also boasted several of the nation's top African American teams, including the Leland Giants and Columbia Giants, filled with Major League–caliber players.[20] Below these elite teams ranked dozens of strong semi-pro clubs. Although the Nebraska Indians were competitive in this class, Green's Japanese were no match. Tobey wisely kept his team far away.

In the small towns of rural Illinois, however, a visit from the Japanese team was an exciting event. "The greatest event of the baseball season!" proclaimed the *Stark County News*.[21] Tobey and Green had prepped the region with their usual advertising, but perhaps learning from their mistakes in Kansas, they rarely boasted in the published blurbs that the team was the "fastest in Japan." Instead newspaper articles emphasized the foreignness and exotic nature of the Japanese players and the uniqueness of the team. A typical announcement read, "Green's Japs are the most novel baseball organization the world has ever known. Every player is a genuine Japanese. Not one of them can speak a word of English. They do all their coaching in Japanese."[22]

Spectators came from outlying farms and towns to see the games. Rural newspapers usually included a section for local personal news. Scattered through these papers in the summer of 1906 are references of individuals traveling to see Green's Japanese team. We know, for instance, that John Rackaway Jr., known to everyone as Edwin, although just shy of his sixteenth birthday, made the twelve-mile trek from his home in Mt. Vernon to Belle Rive, Illinois, to see the Japanese team for himself. He joined the crowd who watched the visitors defeat the local boys, 13–5, on June 8. We also know that later in the season Gus Wilson made the seventeen-mile trip from the village of Roland, Iowa, to slightly larger Jewell Junction to watch the game. He decided to make a weekend out of it, staying until Monday.[23]

The team's visit to Toledo, Illinois, was typical of many of the stops. The seat of Cumberland County in east-central Illinois, the town had only about 850 citizens in 1906. A week before the June 16 game the weekly paper noted, "On next Saturday afternoon Green's famous team of Japanese ball players will be here for a game with the local team. If you miss this game, you will perhaps regret it. This team is made up entirely of Japanese players and they have defeated some of the strongest teams in this country."[24]

Facing the visiting professionals was a ragtag group of local men. Lauren M. Wood, a thirty-seven-year-old printer, organized the team and played center field. Wood's eighteen-year-old type compositor, Guy Castelo, came off the bench to spell his boss late in the game. They were joined by twenty-two-year-old farmer Frank Hallett at second base; thirty-five-year-old German butcher Frank Ariens in right field; twenty-year-old barber John Carlyle (known as Lyle) Baichley at first; and Baichley's eighteen-year-old brother, Sidney Lewis Baichley, at third. Lyle and Sidney's younger brother, Grover Cleveland Baichley, was just sixteen years old and did not play in the game, but he would later pitch for the All-Army team in the professional Manila, Philippines, League (1912–14); in the Central Association of the Class D Minor Leagues (1914–16); and in four games in 1914 for the Major League St. Louis Browns.[25] With the future Major Leaguer not ready to take the mound against the Japanese, Manager Wood recruited Halsey Clark, a twenty-one-year-old blacksmith and local star pitcher for Shelbyville, to fortify his team.[26]

On Saturday afternoon, June 16, the two teams and villagers gathered in front of the town's stately red brick, two-story Georgian-style courthouse at the center of town. As the clock in the oversized white central tower struck 2 p.m., the Toledo Military Band began to play, and the teams formed up to march to the ball grounds.[27] When his team took the field, Tobey once again elected to start just four Japanese—Kitsuse at short, Uyeda at second, Kawashima in left, and Naito in right. Tobey would pitch.

Acting as the home team, the "Japanese" jumped out to a first inning 3–0 lead and remained ahead until Toledo scored four in the top of the sixth and another in the eighth. The ringer, Halsey Clark, pitched well, striking out eleven and holding Green's team to just eight hits, but "ragged" fielding led to the Japanese scoring four in the bottom of the eighth to win, 7–5. All agreed that it was "a close and exciting game," and the spectators went home happy.[28]

Just as Green connected the team with the Russo-Japanese War in his advertising, newspapers continually alluded to the war in their reports on the games. After a 3–2 win by the local team on July 11, the *Dwight Journal* bragged, "The Dwight Boys Done What Russia Couldn't Do—Cleaned Up the Japs."[29] Similar references and the occasional metaphor followed the team across Illinois and the Midwest. For example, reporting on the local Newport, Indiana, team's 5–1 loss to Green's Japanese on June 22, a local reporter explained, "We thought our team was as strong as Port Arthur, but it seems like the baseball players of Japan are like the soldiers—sweep everything before them."[30]

Capitalizing on the public's fascination with the Japanese military, during the tour of Illinois the team added a new attraction.

> The Japanese baseball team arrived in the city [of Quincy] last night at 10 o'clock . . . and were driven to the St. James hotel. . . . Manager Hoffer of the Reserves met the train at the depot and concluded arrangements with the manager of the Japs to have two of the little brown men give an exhibition of their native art of jiu jitsu which will be given in front of the grandstand before the game is called. The jiu jitsu exhibition of the Japs' mode of self-defense will be a decided feature and as that mode of wrestling was never seen here it will be greatly appreciated by the fans.[31]

The United States was in the midst of a jiujitsu craze. The Japanese martial art, developed to combat armored samurai, consisted of a series of throws and holds rather than striking attacks. The techniques allowed a small individual to use an opponent's momentum to overcome a larger, heavier adversary. Although Americans had known about jiujitsu since the 1860s, it did not become popular until the publication of H. Irving Handcock's *Japanese Physical Training* in December 1903. In early 1904 both boxing champion Jim Jefferies and President Theodore Roosevelt began taking lessons with recognized masters. Newspapers across the country immediately began printing articles on "the mysterious oriental art."[32] The martial art's popularity soared with Japan's success in the Russo-Japanese War. By 1905 jiujitsu exhibitions and matches were being held throughout the country, and numerous Americans were studying the martial art.

Small-town midwesterners were eager to witness the amazing techniques for themselves. Luckily for Tobey, he had an expert on hand. Ken Kitsuse, schooled in the bellicose Satsuma region, had mastered the art.[33] Four years later he would win a jiujitsu exhibition held before a mostly Caucasian audience at a championship wrestling match held at Naud Junction Pavilion—Los Angeles's premier boxing venue.[34]

Starting in July the team routinely demonstrated jiujitsu prior to games. In Colfax, Illinois, the demonstration and the game against the local team were the highlights of a fun-filled Independence Day celebration that included a shooting contest, band music, an oration by a local lawyer, and foot races featuring the much anticipated "fat man's race," with a bunch of bananas as the first-place prize.[35] Most of the spectators enjoyed the show. A reporter for the *Muscatine Journal* noted that the visiting Japanese pleased the largest crowd of the season with "a good demonstration of playing ball" that was "about as good as the Jiu Jitsu exhibition which the visitors gave before the big show."[36]

Not all games, however, went well. In a brief foray across the Ohio River on June 11, Green's Japanese were leading the local squad from Mount Vernon, Indiana, 5–3, in the top of the eighth inning, when, according to the *Evansville Courier and Press*, "the game broke up in a row . . . when an avalanche of Mount Vernon runs seemed to be imminent. Winston Menzies, the umpire, gave the game to Mount Vernon 9–0."[37] Details and the reason for the "row" are not recorded in any of the local newspapers.

Nearly two weeks later the team once again crossed over into Indiana and left with ill feeling. The June 23 game at Covington, a town of about two thousand, had been well advertised. Local newspapers began reprinting Green's promotional releases nine days before the game. Readers were promised that the team would "give a jiu jitsu exhibition on the diamonds that alone is worth the price."[38]

After the great buildup the citizens of Covington were disappointed with reality. Headlining his article "That Japanese (?) Game," a writer for the *Covington Friend* complained that the Japanese were "aided by five first-class American players . . . [who] filled the most important positions." Furthermore, the Japanese players, far from being the best in Japan, "compared favorably with the average American high school player." Threatening weather had discouraged spectators, resulting in such a low attendance that Tobey refused to put on the jiu jitsu exhibition, further annoying fans. On the good side, however, the reporter praised the Japanese umpire, probably

Masko, as "exceptional good," whose "work [was] the best we have seen on the Covington ground since the days of 'Army' Van Cleave [an umpire active in the 1880s]."[39]

Several newspapers were blunter with their condemnation. The editor of the *Bradford Stark County Republican* complained:

> It is a misnomer to call this team a Japanese team. . . . Their manager is perpetrating a fraud upon the public, is obtaining money under false pretenses by his advertising as he does. What this paper said previous to the game in regard to the personnel of the team we said in good faith and now ask to be absolved from the evident disparity between the advertising and the real facts as to [what players] make up this bunch of pretenders. Before the game [local] manager Leadley should have made a public announcement to those who had paid out their money to see a Japanese ball team that only four of that nationality were to appear in the game, that on part of Bradford he was ready to go on with the entertainment but those who desired it could have their money back.[40]

The editor of the *Carthage Republican*, having run pregame advertising blurbs claiming that the team was "composed entirely of genuine Japanese direct from Japan [who] can speak no English," was also outraged at Tobey's lineup. "The Jap baseball team that played here Saturday was a fake. Four alleged Japs that spoke Clabber Alley [a notorious St. Louis slum] English and [the] balance Americans." Despite the complaint, the game was "quite largely attended" as the visitors won easily, 15–4.[41]

Two weeks later in the town of Plymouth, just twenty miles southeast of Carthage, the team won on a bizarre play. The *Carthage Republican* explained:

> The Jap ball team played our local team on the west side grounds last Friday (August 10). The Japs winning by a score of 3 to 5. Our home team would have won out, if their pitcher had not suddenly been seized with a violent thirst and abandoned his position to get a drink of water. The incident was particularly unfortunate, as the bases were about full, and the Japs took advantage of the situation and run in. He is a splendid catcher [*sic*], but a little erratic at times, and likely

to go off at a tangent on a hot day. A recurrence of this incident will be avoided in future, by having a boy with a bucket of ice water easily available. Some of us boys, who had some stuff up on the result, feel a little sore about the unfortunate occurrence.[42]

Overall the junket through Illinois and Indiana was a great success for Green's Japanese. In the fifty-seven games with recovered scores, the team won forty-eight and lost nine outright, while it forfeited one. Most of the spectators were pleased with the quality of play. The newspapers are filled with accolades: "One of the most spirited and hotly contested games"; "an exciting game"; "a fine aggregation of ball players."[43]

Nearly every article reports a large turnout for the games. Eight hundred came out to watch Doc Leedy's Trolley Dodgers defeat the Japanese in Danville on June 24. With sixteen thousand inhabitants, Danville was one of the largest towns visited, and the game attracted 5 percent of the city's residents. At the usual price of twenty-five cents per ticket, the gate receipts would have been about $200, giving Green's team roughly $150. Turnout was even greater in small towns. On June 29 in the village of Mansfield, with a population of about 700, gate receipts totaled $97, suggesting that at least 388 people, more than half the town, attended the game. After paying $14.55 to rent the ballpark and $9.70 (10 percent of the gate receipts) to the local opponents, the Japanese made $72.75—their usual 75 percent cut.[44]

Perhaps no fans were happier than the spectators of the July 20 contest in Toulon, Illinois. Newspaper advertisements for the game began over a month before the event. On June 13 the *Stark County News* ran a paragraph featuring the story about Kitsuse at Mukden and announced that Green's Japanese would appear at Toulon. For the next three weeks the newspaper published blurbs on the upcoming game, repeating Green's standard advertising text.[45]

The advertising worked. A week before the game the *News* reported, "From Wyoming, Kewanee, Galva and LaFayette word has come that many are already planning to see the Japs play ball here. . . . The people are becoming much interested and a big crowd is assured. Arrangements are being made to have the business houses close from 3 to 5 o'clock on the day of the game." The word continued to spread, and on June 18 the *News* revised its prediction: "From present indications an enormous crowd will see the Japs play the Toulon team."[46]

The *News* was correct. Although Toulon had only about 1,100 inhabitants, "an orderly" and "enthusiastic" crowd of "fully a thousand saw the game." The crowd soon filled the grandstands, forcing many to watch from the outfield, where spectators had also parked their coaches and wagons. Nine-year-old Johnny Walker was probably in the stands that day. Fifteen years later the Toulon native would be catching and playing first base for the Philadelphia Athletics in a brief Major League career.

Tobey started four Japanese—Uyeda at second, Kitsuse at short, Naito in right, and Kawashima in left (Fujita would later substitute for Naito), while Kissell took the mound. Masko drew umpire duties and, according to the *News*, "quickly gained favor of the crowd" as he was "certainly a good one. His decisions were fair and impartial."[47]

The game was a tight pitchers' duel. Inning after inning went by with no score. Kissell would strike out nine while Arthur Lundin, who had spent the past two seasons pitching for the Class B Minor League Rock Island Islanders, would fan fifteen for Toulon and surrender just two hits.

In the eighth it looked like the Japanese would finally break up the shutout. Uyeda led off with a grounder that third baseman Johnson failed to handle, and Kitsuse sacrificed Uyeda to second. Lundin then walked Fujita. With one out and runners on first and second, Kawashima grounded to short for what should have been an inning-ending double play, but the shortstop bobbled the ball, loading the bases with the top of the lineup coming to bat. According to the *News*, "Lundin merely smiled and struck out the next man" before forcing Doctor to ground to second for the third out.

The pitching match continued. "As the game advanced beyond nine innings and on to the tenth, eleventh and twelfth, the excitement became intense." The Japanese had a second opportunity to win as Kawashima began the twelfth with a long fly over the left fielder Strahorn's head. Strahorn seemed to have a chance, tracking the ball as he ran back before running out of room as the ball disappeared behind a team of horses attached to one of the coaches that ringed the outfield. By the time he recovered the ball, Kawashima was on third with a triple. Determined to score on even a grounder, Kawashima led off third, moving down the line with the pitch. But he strayed too far. A quick throw from the catcher caught him by surprise, erasing the threat.

Finally, in the bottom of the thirteenth with a runner on first, Osborne, Toulon's second baseman, hit a hard drive into left field. Kawashima ran toward the ball and tripped, allowing the winning run to score. It was, according to the *News*, "the best ball game ever played in Toulon."

Green's Japanese moved on to Iowa in the third week of August. After dropping their first game to the Muscatine Independents, they went on a winning streak, taking at least ten straight games until they reached the tiny town of Prairie City on August 23. With just 764 inhabitants in 1910, the local nine did not have a large pool of players to fill out their team. To tackle the visiting professionals, the locals turned to fourteen-year-old Burton A. Baird. The blue-eyed youth shocked everybody by striking out twelve. The town team rallied around Baird, supporting him with eight hits and an upset 9–8 win over the Japanese.[48] Baird would later attend the University of Iowa, becoming the Hawkeyes' star pitcher. A professional career, however, was not in his future. He would graduate from Iowa with a BS in 1914 and a MD the following year before practicing at the Mayo Clinic and dying at the young age of thirty-one of an undetermined cause.

Green's team returned to its winning ways the following day, taking the next nineteen games.[49] Most fans still came to the games for the unique opportunity to see a Japanese ball club, but as the season progressed, spectators also came to see a strong team. Papers referred to "Green's crack Jap baseball team" and "the team of genuine Japanese which is attracting so much attention this season."[50] Prior to the August 26 game at Perry, the *Perry Daily Chief* noted:

> The ball game scheduled for this afternoon between the Perry team and Green's famous bunch of Japanese has been the principal topic of conversation among lovers of the national game in this city for sev-

eral days. With good weather, today the crowd will be one of the largest ever seen at the local park. Few if any of the Perry fans have ever seen the Japs play ball and as they have proven that they are first class men at the game there will be more to see than just a Jap with a uniform on. So far this season they have lost but four games and Manager Green has not hesitated to take on the best teams to be found.[51]

The *Perry Chief Reporter* also remarked, "They will be an attraction on account of being the only team of Japs playing in America and also because they are good ball players picked from the best men in a country that is noted for its athletes."[52]

Although cool temperatures and strong winds limited the crowd to just six hundred, the spectators were treated to a good game as Green's team won, 5–1. As in other towns, the Perry fans were disappointed that the visitors were "by no means an all Jap team as Green advertised it to be" but were nonetheless more than satisfied with the quality of play:

> Green's team of Japanese ball players . . . won by superior ball playing—scientific playing. The team work of the Japs, especially in the matter of bunting, was the best by far ever seen in Perry and opened the eyes of some of the fans to the possible benefits to be derived from this kind of ball playing. In the matter of batting out safe hits or individual fielding the Japs had nothing on the local men but when it came to making runs they certainly had the Perry boys out-classed. Their base running was of the best and each player worked hard to help his teammates across the plate.[53]

Fans from other towns also seemed willing to forgive the use of non-Japanese players as long as the team played well. Spectators of the game at Alta were "quite well pleased over the result," while the *Atlantic Cass County Democrat* noted, "A big crowd . . . witnessed some of the best ball playing they have seen this year. The heavy playing on the part of the Japs was done by the white men on the team but they all played fair ball."[54]

The racist and bigoted language common in the newspaper coverage during the 1905 Waseda tour was nearly absent in the midwestern papers covering Green's Japanese. None of the papers relied on offensive stereotypes when describing the Japanese players with the exception of the *Journal Enterprise* of Waverly, Illinois, which referred to "the sly little Japs" during an otherwise inoffensive report on the team's 9–8 victory over the local nine.[55] Although anti-Japanese sentiment in the Midwest at the time was negligible, the players helped to perpetuate a positive image. "The Japs were a nice quiet lot of fellows," reported the *Windsor Gazette*.[56] "They are a manly lot of young fellows," added a reporter from the *Pontiac Leader*.[57]

The team, however, did experience open bigotry at the ballpark at least once. On September 4 the team arrived at Garner, a town of about a thousand. Ten years earlier former-baseball-player-turned-evangelist Billy Sunday had held his first revival meeting at the town, but there would be little Christian charity on game day.

It was a beautiful day for a game, and about six hundred fans packed the small ball park. Having won at least nine straight, Tobey seems to have started the game with a mostly Japanese lineup. The Japanese jumped out to an early lead in a hard-fought game. Garner's seventeen-year-old star pitcher, Charles Forsythe, was particularly good, and by the end of the day would strike out twenty-four. As the game progressed, play on the diamond became contentious and the crowd increasing hostile. The *Des Moines Register*, in a report probably filed by Tobey, claimed "the unruly crowd rushed into the diamond several times during the game and called the Orientals harsh names." In the ninth, Garner battled back, tying the game at three. Fans "went wild and cheered and yelled until they were hoarse."[58]

What happened next is disputed. The local *Garner Signal*, the *Hancock Country Democrat*, and two articles in the *Des Moines Register* all provide different accounts. Combining aspects of each suggests the following scenario. During Garner's comeback or immediately afterward, words were exchanged between the opponents. The crowd got ugly, rushed onto the field, and somebody threw a baseball at Tobey, supposedly knocking him unconscious. A member of the Japanese team returned fire by "throwing the ball maliciously into the crowd." At that point the Japanese walked off the field, and the game was "much delayed by wrangling and disputes." After fifteen minutes Green's team agreed to retake the field but made several substitutions, leaving "only about four or five Japs playing." The teams battled for another four innings until the fortified visitors scored twice in the thirteenth to win.[59]

At some point, probably after the game, the Garner sheriff arrested the unidentified Japanese player who had thrown the ball into the crowd and fined him one dollar plus "costs which amounted to $4.50." Despite the ruckus, the *Hancock County Democrat* declared it "the best game of the season," noting, with the exception of the arrested player, that "the Japanese were all gentlemanly fellows and behaved nicely."[60]

Eleven days later Tobey's team got into another altercation. After winning nine straight games, Green's Japanese played the local nine from the village of Gladbrook, population 850. In the bottom of the eighth, Gladbrook was on top 6–4 when the Japanese disputed a decision by the umpire. The argument escalated and the visitors walked off the field, forfeiting the game.[61] Had they faced bigotry again? Were the players' tempers on edge due to the long, tiring season on the road? Or was a forfeit better than an outright loss? The reason for the team's behavior is lost to time. But disagreements with umpires continued. On September 22, about a week after the Gladbrook forfeit, a writer for the *Alta Advertiser* complained about "the continuous work wrangling over decisions" during the otherwise clean and well-played game against Alta.[62]

Not counting the game forfeited to Gladbrook, Green's Japanese won 35 straight identified games in Iowa after their loss to Prairie City on August 23 and posted an overall 43-4 record in the state. As local reporters commented on their skill, the players had undoubtedly improved since their first games in Kansas. Yet Green and Tobey had also picked their opponents well. Despite the *Perry Daily Chief*'s claim that "manager Green has not hesitated to take on the best teams to be found," they once again avoided cities and strong clubs.[63] Of the forty-two places the team visited in Iowa just seven had three thousand or more inhabitants.

Often the squad overmatched the local nines, making for one-sided, even dull, games. The townspeople of Dow, for example, were excited about the Japanese team's visit. All businesses closed for the afternoon so that everybody could attend, and the local manager hired a German band to play before the game. But the game itself was a 15–0 blowout, called by the *Dow Advocate* "too one sided to be interesting."[64]

During the month of September Green's Japanese outscored their opponents 229–64. Most town teams were just happy to keep the game close. After the contentious game in Garner the local paper concluded, "Our boys did splendid work from start to finish. They were playing against professionals who make ball playing a business and we were agreeably surprised that they did as well as they did."[65] Similarly the *Essex Independent* noted after a 13–8 loss, "It started out to be a good game but before it was very old the spectators saw that our boys were somewhat outclassed. When it comes to a team, who play[s] once in ten days, playing with a team that play[s] every day, and sometimes twice a day, they simply are not in it."[66]

Despite dominating local teams, Green's squad was still not strong enough to beat other independent or city teams. Other than the upset in Prairie City behind the superb pitching of fourteen-year-old Burton Baird and the forfeit, the team's only losses came against teams from large towns: a 5–1 loss to an independent club from Muscatine (town population 16,045) and a doubleheader sweep by a Clarinda club (town population 3,832 in 1910), which played Class D Minor League ball in 1903, 1910, and 1911.

Overall Guy Green's Japanese Base Ball Club's 1906 barnstorming tour was a success. The team won 122 of the 142 games for which results are known.[67] Reporters concurred that Kitsuse was the best of the Japanese ballplayers. He was repeatedly singled out for his stellar fielding. The *Brown County Republican* noted, "The Japanese short stop, a mere boy, was a great favorite with the crowd. With hot grounders throwing up the dust in his direction during the entire game, he covered his entire position without an error."[68] The *Perry Daily Chief* added, "Kitsuse, the Jap who played short stop, certainly did some pretty work. When a ball started toward him the other players would go for their respective places and no attempt was made to back him up."[69]

Throughout the tour the team drew well. Almost every newspaper account commented on the large crowds. The size of the audience is known for thirteen games. The 1,200 fans who packed the Fort Riley stands is the largest recorded crowd, while the smallest known turnout came in Pocahontas, Iowa (town population 625 in 1900), with just 230 spectators. The average attendance for the thirteen games was 541, with a mean of 400. If we extrapolate the mean over the estimated 150–170 games played during the tour, about 60,000–70,000 people witnessed the Japanese team play. From newspaper articles we know that the standard admission price was twenty-five cents and that Green's team took 75 percent of the gate receipts. The Japanese ball club, therefore, took in about $12,000 during the tour, equivalent to about $300,000 in 2019 dollars. The team's expenses are unknown, so we do not know if the tour turned a profit or lost money.

No matter what the financials were, Green elected to disband the team in early October. Its final known game was a 22–2 victory in King City, Missouri, on October 10. Green would not continue the experiment in subsequent seasons. Despite the large crowds and many entertaining games, Green could not revisit the same region with a squad from Japan. Unable to field a competitive all-Japanese team as advertised, he had left many midwestern towns disappointed and had sullied his reputation. "The long looked for Jap game has come and gone, and people are wondering why they had such a desire to see the Japs play," lamented a writer for the *Pella Chronicle*. "The management, like Barnum circus, failed to produce everything advertised. Instead of it being a full Jap team, the Japs only held the minor positions while four Americans did the nice playing. Tobey, the pitcher for the Japs, was the same fellow that came through here with Green's Indians a couple of seasons ago."[70]

In 1907 Green's Nebraska Indians would avoid most of the towns the Japanese team had visited. They would play only a handful of games in Iowa and Illinois as they headed east to Indiana, West Virginia, and the mid-Atlantic states. In September 1907 Green decided to enter Organized Baseball and purchased the Lincoln franchise in the Class A Western League. He controlled the club for just two years, selling it in July 1909 in the midst of the team's second consecutive losing season. Green continued to run the Nebraska Indians through the 1911 season before selling the team to James Beltzer on January 18, 1912. The famed team would continue to exist until the early 1930s. Green would take one more shot at baseball, promoting a barnstorming tour of Hawaiians in 1913 before retiring from the game. After stints as a real estate developer, photographer, and journalist, Green spent the last twenty years of his life as a Presbyterian evangelist, delivering sermons across the Midwest until his death on February 11, 1947.[71]

In mid-October 1906 Saisho, Kitsuse, Masko, Uyeda, and their teammates headed back to the West Coast to resume their lives. But they were forever changed. Each would now forgo plans of striking it rich in California. Instead they would pursue the game they loved.

9

The Mikado's Japanese Base Ball Team

Tozan Masko may not have been much of a ballplayer, but he could recognize a great opportunity and had the audacity to pursue it. The gate receipts from Guy Green's Japanese Base Ball Club were too low for the Lincoln lawyer to continue the team, but they were more than enough to satisfy a Japanese newspaper writer like Masko. He decided he would form his own Japanese team and continue barnstorming. It would be the first Japanese-operated professional baseball team on either side of the Pacific.

After Green disbanded his team, the players headed back to the West Coast and found day jobs. Masko rejoined the staff at the *Rafu Shimpo*; Harry Saisho became a janitor at the Myer Siegel Department Store; Ken Kitsuse became a gardener. Saisho decided to form a new ball club from the core of Green's squad. No longer affiliated with the *Rafu Shimpo*, the players called themselves Nanka—short for Nanbu Kariforunia or Southern California. The team continued to practice near the banks of the Los Angeles River.

The falls of 1906 and 1907 were difficult times for Japanese immigrants living on the West Coast. In the wake of the San Francisco earthquake anti-Japanese sentiment flourished. Assaults on Japanese immigrants in the city's streets increased as nativists blamed them for the spread of disease, unfair labor practices, and even the earthquake itself. In October 1906 the Asiatic Exclusion League led a three-week boycott against Japanese-owned restaurants, vandalizing many.

On October 11 the San Francisco Board of Education barred all Japanese and Korean students from attending local schools, instead requiring them to attend the city's lone Chinese school. Many Americans and the Japanese government were outraged, demanding that the board retract the decree. As the rhetoric grew heated, President Theodore Roosevelt intervened. During the winter of 1906–7 the parties reached a compromise. The Board of Education rescinded its policy to exclude Japanese from the schools (Koreans and Chinese remained segregated). In return Roosevelt and the Japanese government reached the 1907–8 Gentlemen's Agreement, whereby Japan agreed to issue passports to the mainland United States "only to non-laborers, laborers returning from a visit to Japan, and the parents, wives, and children of domiciled laborers."[1] The agreement slowed Japanese immigration to a trickle.

Violence toward Japanese immigrants on the West Coast continued throughout 1907. In San Francisco mobs destroyed Japanese-owned businesses in both May and October. Following a large rally of the Asiatic Exclusion League in downtown Vancouver on September 8, a crowd of two thousand moved into Chinatown and Japantown, vandalizing and looting businesses before Japanese immigrants, armed with sticks, knives, and pistols, fought the mob off. Dozens were seriously injured, but amazingly there were no fatalities.

In 1907 the *Rafu Shimpo* relocated Masko to Denver to cover its growing Japanese community. The 1900 federal census listed just forty-eight Japanese in all of Colorado, but as Denver emerged as a railroad hub, Japanese came to work in the railroad yards, the nearby mines, and local farms. By 1909 nearly six thousand Issei lived in the state. Denver's Japantown, centered around Blake, Market, and Larimer Streets, contained sixty-seven Japanese-owned businesses, including boarding houses, restaurants, grocery stores, and a Japanese Methodist church.[2]

Soon after arriving in Colorado, Tozan decided to press forward with his plans to promote a Japanese baseball club. In early 1908 he created and printed customized stationery. The letterhead announced in bold black ink, "Annual Tour of Mikado's Japanese Base Ball Team. Direct from the schools and universities of Japan. The most marvelous team of genuine Japanese ball players on earth and the only one in America. Tozan T. Masko, Proprietor, Denver, Colo. Telephone Purple 306, 1232 Twenty-First Street."[3] To the right of the header is a 1.75-inch -square head shot of Masko. He wears a dark suit and tie with a high starched white collar. He has a youthful, honest-looking face with impeccably groomed black hair parted stylishly down the middle.

The stationery's reverse side is covered in text printed in red ink. Titled "Some information regarding Mikado's team," the page provides the team's background and sets forth conditions for potential games. Following the lead of Guy Green, Masko invented a history for his team and lifted much of the language directly from Green's advertisements and from his Nebraska Indians contract. Full of grammatical miscues and non sequiturs and cheeky to the point of rudeness, the text reads:

THE TEAM'S HISTORY

Mikado's Japanese Base Ball Team was organized in Japan during 1905 by Tozan T. Masko. They kept their reputation as "Tiger Team" for several seasons. In the December of 1906 he came to the United States. Everyone has heard of Green's Nebraska Indians who have been playing throughout the United States for several seasons, and are still on the road stronger than ever. It is needless to say that when he heard of that he went back to his own country, bearing in mind the reputation of the Nebraska Indians, and was instructed to secure the very best talent available. He fulfilled his instructions. This team of Japanese represents the investment of a small fortune for transportation and other expenses.

Every Japanese player is full-blooded Japanese. Not one of them can speak English. They do all their conversing and coaching in Japanese and is certainly the most Japanesy Japanese you have ever listened to.

There are, in Japan, 265 middle schools and 35 universities at which baseball is played. Mikado's team is composed of the pick of the players from these institutions, and they have crossed the 4,000 miles of Pacific Ocean in order to reach America for this tour.

CAN JAPANESE PLAY BASEBALL?

This question will be answered to your own satisfaction when you see the team. Every returned naval officer and traveler, who has seen the contests in Japan, which are often attended by 10,000 people, brings back great tales of the prowess of the Japanese players. Every American naval team which has tried conclusions with the Japanese has been badly defeated. It is safe to say that the playing of the Japanese will be a revelation to you.

A FEW FACTS TO REMEMBER

1. Under no circumstances will we throw a game. Leaving entirely out of consideration the moral aspect of the question, dishonesty with the public is bad business policy.

2. Under no circumstances will we play for a smaller admission price than 25 cents. This must be paid by everyone, both men and women. If the game is worth seeing it is worth paying for.

3. We will positively not admit free of charge the relatives or friends of the ball players, managers, magnates, stockholders or officers. We are not running a charitable institution.

4. We will positively not admit at any stage of the game children who are unaccompanied by their parents. Children must be pretty small to get by our ticket taker.

5. We will positively not recognize season books or stockholders passes. The owners may have paid you, but that doesn't do us any good.

6. Keep your gates closed until we are on the ground ready to sell tickets and see that we get all that is coming to us. We know, of course, that everyone is honest, but business is business you know.

7. We carry our own tickets for both gate and grandstand. We sell and you take. When you are ready to settle, count the tickets you have taken in, figure out your share of the receipt and we pay you instantly.

8. We always reserve the right to use two umpires, one of whom is to be furnished by us.

9. Don't make a contract with us unless you are prepared to abide by it in a straightforward businesslike manner. We expect to act honestly with you. Be honest with us.

10. We are willing to furnish you all the free advertising matter you can use to advantage. But don't expect us to pay for putting it up. You are to have enough energy to look after that yourself.

11. Settlement must be made for each game as soon as it is played. We positively will not wait until the end of a series.[4]

In March 1908 Masko dispatched letters to ball clubs across the Midwest asking for games. Typed on his custom stationery, his letters read:

Dear Sir;

I am calling your attention in this letter to an absolute baseball novelty, viz., Mikado's, a team of genuine Japanese Ball Player direct from Japan. This team has been gathered by myself from various schools of the Japanese Empire and they put up a surprising exhibition of America's great game.

The team will be in your region this season about [date]. I am now arranging my route and would like to know whether or not it will be possible to secure one or more games with you. The Japanese are bound to create a sensation whenever they play.

I have only a few dates. In fact I have two dates offered me for every one I can fill. So if you wish a visit from the Mikado's you should write without delay. I am forced to turn down numerous offers from towns who answer my letter too late. Therefore answer quick. In case you mislay this letter, any letter addressed to Denver, Colorado, will be promptly forwarded to me.

I carry no canvas fence of any kind. If you desire a date your ground must be so arranged that all who see the game will have to pay. By this I do not mean that you must necessarily have a high fence, but you must have some arrangement so that the people will have to put up their money to see the game.

I will play you for 75% of gross receipts, (including grand stand) win or lose, no guarantee of any kind whatever, and I will furnish you free of charge an elegant line of advertising matter. If you use this advertising matter properly you ought to draw big crowd. You must also make arrangements with hotel to furnish our players with a rate of $1.00 a day per player (including room and board).

Kindly reply to this sheet and especially enlighten me on the following points:

1. Name of town.

2. Population.

3. Ability to draw from the surrounding towns and territory.

4. Kind of ground you have, referring especially to the way they are enclosed.

5. Kind of team you have.

6. Arrangements for collecting admissions. Tell just exactly what method you used to make people pay.

7. Do you play Sunday ball? If not, what towns in your region do?

8. Names of other towns in your region with whom I might get games.

9. Best way to get in and out of your city.[5]

Masko's letter was so unusual that newspapers from small towns, such as Logansport, Indiana, and Fort Scott, Kansas, as well as from Chicago, Cincinnati, and Cleveland, mentioned the letter and the possibility of a game with an all-Japanese team. Some reporters seemed excited by the potential of a game. "Something of a treat is promised in a couple of games with the all Japanese team here in July," noted the *Evening News* of Sault Sainte Marie, Michigan.[6] "Arrangements have been made whereby the famous Mikado's Japanese baseball team will play the All-Stars at League Park some midweek day in June, while they are on their tour of the eastern cities this summer," announced Cleveland's *Plain Dealer*.[7]

Not all of the comments were kind. "Manager [Pete] Hollender is being besieged by communications from all kinds of freak baseball teams," reported the *Evening Independent* of Massillon, Ohio. "This morning Manager Hollender received a communication from the Mikado's Japanese baseball team asking for a game."[8] The Tribune Special Sporting Service, in a nationally syndicated article on baseball in Japan, noted the "enclosed piece of stationery used by the Mikado club . . . is rich as well as original."[9] It went on to quote nearly the entire first page of Masko's letter, including all eleven of his "A Few Facts to Remember." The *Leavenworth Post* was blunter. "The letter is somewhat of a curiosity inasmuch as the writer has not sufficiently mastered the language to express himself properly in English."[10]

With the help of Spalding's Sporting Goods, Masko was able to secure games in Colorado in April; Kansas in May; Cleveland, Ohio, in June; and Bloomington, Indiana, on July 30 and 31.

Masko would introduce his new team and upcoming tour in style. On March 21, 1908, he invited Denver's leading Japanese citizens and members of the white press, including *Denver Rocky Mountain News* sports editor E. W. Dickerson, to a Japanese banquet held at S. Kodama's restaurant at 1958 Larimer Street. The guest list for the event does not survive, but in all likelihood it included Dr. Toshio Shimizu, a twenty-six-year-old physician who acted as the Mikado's president, and Denver's leading Japanese citizen, Naoichi "Harry" Hokasono. Hokasono had arrived in Denver in 1898 to open a restaurant but soon moved into labor contracting, becoming the wealthiest Japanese in the city. An ardent assimilationist and founder of Denver's Japanese Association, Hokasono believed that discrimination against Japanese would ease if immigrants could blend into American society. Later in the year he would publish a pamphlet instructing Japanese immigrants on how to behave in the United States, noting "every one of us, as Japanese, should behave discretely to avoid dishonoring the Yamato race, while striving to obtain the sympathy of honest and decent Americans." His guidelines included:

Do not patronize gambling houses, brothels, and other immoral establishments.

When in public, hold yourself up right and do not talk or laugh too loudly.

Do not frequent or loiter en masse in dangerous or crowded places.

Do not appear intoxicated in public or create any disruptive scenes.

Do not disturb our neighbors, or interrupt their sleep, by loud singing or playing musical instruments like the *shamisen* late at night.

Do not make hostile gestures towards whites.

Do not draw unwanted attention to yourself from whites by appearing unkempt, uncapped or carrying soiled items.[11]

Masko shared Hokasono's attitude toward assimilation. The Mikado's, however, were not on a mission to create goodwill through the shared love of baseball but were a business enterprise.

The morning after the banquet the *Denver Rocky Mountain News* ran a large picture of Masko on the sports page with the caption, "Tozan T. Masuko—Manager and captain of the Mikado's baseball team of Japan, which is assembling in Denver." Masko poses in full uniform, with his hands above his head as if in mid-windup. The shot was appropriated from Guy Green's promotional fliers—artists had darkened the beige pants, changed the dark belt to white, erased "Green's Japs," and hand lettered "Mikado" across the jersey in white.[12] "With a team picked as this one is of the greatest players in Japan, a triumphal tour of America is expected," wrote Dickerson.[13]

But not all of the media supported Masko's enterprise. Anti-Japanese feeling was strong in Denver as labor union leaders feared the growing Japanese population. Six weeks earlier union members had formed the Yellow Peril Exclusion League "for the purpose of protecting themselves against the invasion of Japanese labor in Colorado."[14] Kowtowing to the exclusionists, on the day of the banquet the *Denver Times* ran a huge nine-by-seven-inch cartoon mocking the Mikado's at the top of its sports page (fig. 18).[15] Under the headline "What We May Expect When the Mikado's Team Comes," the cartoon montage contains four vignettes. Drawn in yellowface style, the images rely on the stereotypes perpetuated by the anti–Japanese immigrant league to belittle the team and Japanese in general.

The image in the upper left of the cartoon montage depicts a tiny, child-like man with Asian features wearing a catcher's uniform twisting the arm of a Caucasian umpire who is hollering, "Strike!" The caption reads, "A little jiu jitsu may change some unfair decisions." Below this first image, the same miniature catcher converses with his pitcher. The catcher's speech bubble is written in made-up kanji as the pitcher replies in English, "Leave it to me." Both the catcher and pitcher are squinty-eyed with huge, grinning smiles. A fairly inoffensive drawing in the upper right corner depicts "An appropriate flag design." Modeled on the Japanese military rising sun flag (Kyokujitsu-ki), it contains a baseball in the center of the field with four bats, two megaphones, and two sake bottles replacing the sunrays.

The most offensive and largest image covers the center and right-hand side of the montage. It shows a Japanese batter at the plate along with an American catcher in full equipment. The tiny batter, with simian-like features, barely reaches the squatting catcher's midriff. He is bow-legged, long-armed with squinty, shifty eyes, and struggles to hold a bat that is thicker than his waist and longer than he is tall. A speech bubble written in nonsensical, made-up kanji indicates that he is saying something in Japanese. To the right of the two ballplayers is a small African American drawn in blackface and designated as "Pah-Fessor Bone Dice." The caricature has huge lips and feet and is carrying a bucket labeled "Ice Water," suggesting that he works at the ball field. He translates the Japanese for the readers: "He's saying put one over." The cartoon served as a reminder that no matter how hard the Japanese tried to assimilate, they were still viewed by many whites as inferior and un-American.

Masko's players began arriving on April 6, with the last one reporting on the evening of Saturday, April 11. The roster included Kitty Kawashima and Tom Uyeda from Guy Green's squad. Along with Tom came his tall younger brother, Takatomo, now known as Bob. Bob graduated from Yamaguchi High School in 1907 and a few months later boarded the SS *Tango Maru* to join his brothers in the United States. The Mikado's would give him the opportunity to fulfill his dream of playing professionally.

Despite his claim that the Mikado's were a "team of genuine Japanese ball players," Masko added Roy Whitcomb, who had played on Guy Green's club, to the team. The roster listed the other players as George Aoki, pitcher; B. Iwasaki, pitcher; E. Toda, pitcher; M. Ito, catcher; D. Kimura, shortstop; B. Tada, third base; Joe Katow, left field; W. Oya, center field; S. Sato, utility; and T. Horiuchi, utility. Although a George Aoki attended the University of California, Berkeley, from 1905 to 1907, and a Paul Oya was active in Denver athletics in the early 1910s, none of these players can be positively located in the historical record.

For the next two weeks Masko and his Mikado's trained at Denver's Union Park as they readied for their first game on April 19, Easter Sunday, against the Cottrells Clothiers. Sponsored by the city's largest men's store, the Clothiers would be strong opponents. One of Denver's best amateur teams, they were "made up of local players of considerable reputation" with "one of the strongest batteries in local amateur ranks."[16]

Ever the promoter, Masko filled the local press with tall tales of his team's prowess. "It is evident that they know something about the great American game, from the fact that they won 141 out of 186 games on the Pacific coast. . . . On the team [are] to be found representatives of . . . Tokyo University, Kioto [*sic*] University, the Naval College, Yokohama Commercial College and Waseda College [*sic*]. . . .

The members of the team are all lithe, supple young fellows, who ought to play the fastest kind of baseball."[17]

On game day a two-column advertisement appeared in the *Denver Rocky Mountain News*:

JAPANESE BASEBALL
UNION PARK, 3 P.M., TODAY
Cottrells vs. Mikado's Traveling Professionals
Admission, Including Grandstand, 35c Open Seats, 25c

The announcement may have helped as "a crowd of league proportions turned out" at Union Park to watch a "fast and hard-fought" game "full of exciting plays" between the Mikado's and the Cottrells. The game began with a miscue as a catchable line drive sailed over right fielder Bob Uyeda's head for an inside-the-park home run. Pitcher George Aoki then shut down the Clothiers for the next seven innings as the Mikado's scored two in the fourth and three in the top of the ninth to pile up a 5–1 lead. The Japanese offense featured timely hitting and aggressive base running as the players "ran like scared deers [*sic*] when on the sacks and managed to pilfer a total of nine [bases]."[18] It looked like a sure victory, but the Cottrells came back in the ninth with three runs. With men on base and the game in the balance, the Mikado's "showed themselves to be fighters to the end and undaunted," and they escaped the threat with "the finest kind of fielding" to win 5–4.[19]

The "Royal Mikado's from Across the Ocean Prove to Be Baseball Players of Class and Excel at Bat and on Bases" proclaimed the headline in the *Denver Rocky Mountain News*. The article praised the Japanese for proving "to be decidedly clever in fielding, fast on the bases and fairly strong at bat" and singled out the batting of Tom Uyeda and fielding and hitting of Kitty Kawashima.[20] The *Denver Times*, which had run the mocking cartoon in March, summed up the game in a bland paragraph but admitted that "the fielding and batting of the Japs was good."[21] The *Denver Post* in a two-line summary lamented, "The enthusiastic fan can undoubtedly see another form of Yellow Peril looming up."[22]

The *Denver Post* continued the theme the following day, reporting that "Denver University checked the advance of the yellow peril in the baseball world yesterday afternoon at Union Park." To face the strong university team Masko decided to bolster his lineup with two Caucasian Americans. Roy Whitcomb went behind the plate to catch Kitty Kawashima, and Booth (first name unknown) played short-stop. The reinforcements had little effect on the outcome. Although the Mikado's struck for an early 3–0 lead, the collegians scored in the fourth, sixth, and eighth to win comfortably, 7–3. Despite the loss, the *Post* praised the Japanese for playing "a snappy game and [for] fielding their positions in fine shape."[23]

On the next afternoon, April 21, the Mikado's faced Sacred Heart, another collegiate team. Once again Masko padded his lineup with Caucasian Americans, this time adding five. Only four Japanese (Tom Uyeda at first base, D. Kimura at third base, B. Iwasaki in center field, and Kitty Kawashima in left field) played. Once again the ringers could not lead the Mikado's to victory. Sacred Heart pounded the American pitcher, Lindemeyer, in a 12–4 romp. Even though most of the players were American, Denver's *Daily News* could not refrain from Japanese military imagery in its write up. "Japs Are Repulsed on Sacred Heart Battlefield," stated the headline, followed by the lead, "The third fight in the Jap Invasion at local baseball circles took place yesterday. . . . The little brown men were repulsed by the overwhelming score of 12 to 4 and outfought in every way."[24]

The Mikado's played a final game in Denver the next day against an amateur all-star team, but the results went unrecorded in the city newspapers. On April 23 the team headed south to begin its tour in Colorado Springs. The Mikado's were scheduled to play the Colorado College Tigers, but perhaps smarting from the recent defeats, they instead tackled the town's high school team. Aoki took the mound for the Japanese and narrowly defeated the Colorado Springs Terrors, 7–5, in a game marred by numerous errors due in part to strong winds. A day later the squad defeated La Junta High School, 8–4.

Next the Mikado's headed due east through Kansas. On April 26 and 27 they played at Garden City, a thriving regional center of about three thousand. Throughout the month of April the local *Evening Telegram* had been reporting on a potential conflict with Japan. On April 6 the paper ran a front-page article on charismatic Congressman Richmond Pearson Hobson's views on Japan under the subtitle, "White Nations Should be Prepared for Any Trouble with the Nations of the Orient."

A U.S. Naval Academy graduate, Hobson became a celebrity when he was captured in the Spanish-American War after scuttling the uss *Merrimac* in an attempt to contain the Spanish fleet in Santiago Harbor. Treated as a hero for his self-sacrifice by the American press, he returned home after a month of captivity to great fanfare and immediately embarked on a cross-country tour to meet his adoring fans. A handsome man, Hobson was particularly popular with the ladies and soon began offering kisses to his female well-wishers. Newspapers followed his progress as he kissed his way across America. In one evening in Kansas City he reportedly kissed five hundred women.[25] Hobson retired from the navy in 1903 and four years later was elected to Congress as a Democrat from Alabama.

In 1906 Hobson began to view Japan as a military threat. He urged Congress to increase the size of the navy and to plan for conflict. "War between Japan and the United States is inevitable. Japan is only waiting for a pretext on which to make a declaration of war," he told a reporter in July 1907.[26] Allying himself with the Asiatic Exclusion League, he espoused his views at lecture halls and rallies across the country, warning listeners of the "Yellow Peril" and an imminent race war. "The whole trend of events is . . . toward a contest by the yellow race, aided by the other colored races, a struggle to wrest from the white man his present supremacy."[27] Many viewed Hobson as a hero with the courage to speak out against a foreign threat. For others, like the editors of the *Oakland Tribune*, he was "a menace to public peace" with a "well-developed case of megalomania" and "a good deal of an ass."[28] Hobson enjoyed strong support in Garden City, Kansas, where the *Evening Telegram* noted on April 10, "New guns have arrived for the Kansas National Guard. Japan may as well forget any ideas about fighting Uncle Sam."[29]

The *Evening Telegram*'s coverage of the Mikado's visit was decidedly jingoistic and so full of silly military metaphors and allusions that one should wonder if it was written tongue-in-cheek. The paper announced the upcoming game on April 16 with the headline, "Yellow Peril Threatens the Arkansas Valley—Jap Ball Team." The article began, "The view with alarm attitude toward the Japanese, which congressman Hobson has been wearing for the past five or six years[,] is the proper adornment for the baseball fans in this part of the Arkansas Valley for the Yellow Peril has arisen large and ominous and it now hangs threateningly over the Garden City baseball team."[30] The game-day article was even sillier:

> A fleet flying the flag of the Rising Sun was sighted in the offing this morning and Captain Ralph Clark of the good ship "Diamond" has ordered the vessel scuttled, the decks cleared and everything placed in readiness for the engagement tomorrow. The affray will take place on the diamond in the fair grounds and the present prospects point to a sanguinary conflict, with a long list of strikeouts, errors and deaths on second. . . . If the press dispatches from the front count for anything, the locals feel that the opening game will be a stiff contest as the opposition has been leaving goose eggs and vanquished teams in their wake.[31]

Of course the Mikado's had done nothing of the sort—having not shut out an opponent and just squeaking out their victories.

Strong winds blew across the park when the two teams took the diamond on the afternoon of Sunday, April 26. Masko once again fielded a mixed-race team with four whites and five Japanese. Although the wind caused numerous errors, the game was close, with Garden City tying the score, 5–5, in the bottom of the ninth before winning by a run in the eleventh. The *Evening Telegram* praised the Japanese fielding and thankfully included just one silly military allusion in its otherwise factual game write-up: "'The enemy has met us and it is ours.' This message was wigwagged from the flagship of Captain Clark late yesterday afternoon after a close engagement with the sons of Nippon."[32]

After a second loss to Garden City on April 27 the Mikado's moved on for a pair of games at Dodge City, where the military rhetoric in the newspapers continued. "Uncle Sam Will Need More War Ships If This Is a Fair Test of Strength," headlined the *Globe-Republican* after the Mikado's swept the two games from the locals (15–1 and 6–5). "The party of Japs that arrived here Tuesday to war with the little white brothers of Dodge City on the diamond fought two decisive battles, and left to conquer new fields," the article continued.

"It was a case of the Dodge boys not preparing for war in times of peace. The Jap team was drilled for battle, and they won."[33]

Continuing east across central Kansas, the Mikado's stopped in Larned, Great Bend, Ellingwood, Madison, and Burlington, playing at least seven games between April 30 and May 9. The *Emporia Gazette* related, "The Western Union Telegraph Company is receiving and sending a number of telegrams every day for the manager of the Japanese baseball team, which is playing in towns near Emporia. The messages are all in the Japanese language and the operators are kept guessing as to what is coming next."[34]

Masko was also getting telegrams in Kansas City, even though the team was not due to arrive for another week. "Anybody heard about a lost Japanese baseball team?" one reporter supposedly overheard George Mong, the clerk of the Coates House Hotel, ask after being handed a telegram addressed to "The Japanese B. ball game." "That makes about the fourth message I have had for this bunch of Orientals," the clerk said. "If there is a Jap ball team, where is it? I'd like to know myself."[35]

The Mikado's may have lessened some of the anti-Japanese sentiment in the area as the players conducted themselves well. Not a single complaint made the newspapers, while the *Kinsley Mercury* reported that the team from Larned "says the Japs were clean players and [the Larned players] have nothing but good words for the little brown men who are endeavoring to break into the national game."[36] The *Emporia Gazette* editorialized, "The fact that Japs are playing baseball in Kansas should silence at once the foolish war talk that fills the public prints."[37]

On Friday evening, May 8, the Mikado's arrived by train at Fort Scott, Kansas, a town of just over ten thousand. The local newspaper had been plugging the game, publishing five articles in the week prior to the match. Each stressed the uniqueness of a team "composed strictly of Japanese" and their prowess on the diamond, claiming that they had been "winning nearly all the games they have played thus far in this country." Of course that was not the case. In the fourteen identified games since the start of the tour, the Mikado's were even at seven wins and seven losses. "The game will be one of the most interesting affairs in baseball this season," a reporter concluded. "A Japanese team is something hitherto not seen here, and a large crowd is expected."[38]

Indeed 578 fans turned out at Athletic Park for Sunday afternoon's event. The Fort Scott Athletics would be no pushover. They were the town's top amateur squad. Hitting cleanup and playing first base was Lewis "Lon" Ury. Nicknamed "Old Sheep," the thirty-year-old had kicked around the Minor Leagues since 1902. For four days he had even been a Major Leaguer.[39] In 1903 Ury was having a solid season for Dallas in the Texas League when the seventh-place St. Louis Cardinals purchased his contract on August 28. He would play in just two games, starting at first base and going 0 for 3 against Cincinnati on September 9 and singling against Christy Mathewson during one of four at bats against the New York Giants on September 12. Despite getting a hit off one of the greatest pitchers in history, Ury was released soon afterward and would return to Dallas for the next few seasons.

As the Mikado's took the field, observant spectators realized they had been taken. As before, only five of the players were Japanese— Uyeda at first, Kimura at short, Iwasaki in center, Kawashima in left, and Oya in right. "The third-sacker [Green] and the backstop [Whitcomb] were Americans and the pitcher [Yannoga] and second baseman [Pitling] were Indians," complained a reporter for the *Fort Scott Daily Tribune*. Nevertheless, it was an exciting game. Despite fierce winds kicking up the infield dust, it was "filled with snappy playing" as the Athletics came from behind to win, 3–1.[40]

The *Fort Scott Daily Tribune* also noted, "The work of the first baseman [Tom Uyeda] was very fast." Brother Bob also drew attention: "It is the general belief that the Japs are a stunted and runty class of people, but the muscular proportion of one or two Japs here yesterday with the Mikado [sic] baseball outfit offset this conception. One of the Japs was almost as large as Jim Jeffries and was designed on the same scheme as that of the great heavy-weight slugger."[41] At 6 feet 1 Jeffries (1875–1953), the world heavyweight champion from 1899 to 1905, was just a couple of inches taller than Uyeda.

From Fort Scott the Mikado's crossed the Missouri state line, losing 14–12 to the Rich Hill White Sox, before heading north to Kansas City. Heavy rains came on May 13, lasting several days and

canceling games. Stuck indoors, Masko wrote another batch of letters on his custom-made Mikado's stationery to midwestern towns
in search of opponents. One of these handwritten letters survives.
It is dated May 11 and addressed to the manager of the Edwards-
ville, Illinois, baseball team.

Dear Sir,

Can you give us a game on July 1st. If you satisfy with this date please
let me as soon as possible you can. Also your terms too. I remain,

Yours Truly
T. Masko[42]

The Mikado's remained in the Kansas City area for about two
weeks, playing in nearby towns and looking for opponents. Neither
task went well. On May 16 they lost to the Olathe Eagles. The next
day the Kansas City Stock Yards team crushed them, 13–3, in just
five innings. On May 18 they traveled east to Lexington, Missouri.

Located on the Missouri River, forty miles east of Kansas City,
Lexington was the biggest city west of St. Louis in the 1830s and
1840s. Both an agricultural center and a supply depot for westward-
bound pioneers, Lexington developed one of the largest slave popu-
lations in Missouri. In 1860, 25 percent of the area's population was
enslaved. The city saw major fighting during the Civil War and went
into gradual decline as Kansas City rose in prominence during the
second half of the nineteenth century. In 1900 Lexington contained
just 4,190 people—approximately the same number that had inhabited the city in 1860. The town's pleasure industry, however, survived intact. The infamous Block 42, located on Main Street between
Ninth and Tenth Streets, contained a Presbyterian Church, over a
dozen saloons, a pawnshop, a liquor store, flophouses, and several
brothels at the time of the Mikado's visit. With a quarter of its population African American, Lexington was heavily segregated and
sported both white and black baseball teams.

Playing on the grounds of the Wentworth Military Academy, the
Mikado's beat the white Merchants Club, 4–0, on the evening of May
18. The game remained scoreless for five innings before the Japanese pushed runs across in the sixth, eighth, and ninth innings. A

reporter for the *Lexington Intelligencer* noted that "the Japs played good ball" and that "the game was fast, abounding in many thrilling plays."[43]

The following afternoon the Mikado's tackled Lexington's top club, the African American Lexington Tigers. The Tigers were organized in 1898 from the remains of the Lexington Black Sox. They quickly became one of the top teams in the region, due mostly to Peter Lindsay's sons. Peter, a coal miner, and his wife, Maria, would have ten children; nine of them were boys, and all of them played baseball. Supposedly the brothers formed a semi-pro team with a Lindsay at each position, while Maria sold tickets and Peter manned the turnstile. As there was a twenty-one-year age gap between first-born Samuel and William, the youngest, the story is most likely apocryphal, but most of the brothers did play professional ball. On July 12, 1898, for example, a brief article in the *Kansas City Journal* noted that the Kansas City Unions, a black barnstorming team, had signed catcher John Lindsay, third baseman Jim Lindsay, and right fielder Walter Lindsay, formerly of the Lexington Tigers.[44]

By the time the Mikado's arrived in 1908, most of the Lindsay brothers were playing in other towns, but young William may have played against the Japanese. Bill was born on June 12, 1891, making him just shy of his seventeenth birthday. The following year he would join the Kansas City Giants, earning the nickname "the Kansas Cyclone." In 1910 Bill Lindsay would join Rube Foster's Leland Giants, arguably the nation's top black ball club. A master of the spitball, at his death in 1914 after a sudden illness, the *Indianapolis Freeman* called him "one of the five greatest baseball pitchers in America."[45]

As the Mikado's had trouble beating college and town teams, they were no match for the Tigers. The game write-up in the *Lexington Intelligencer*, although racially offensive, suggests that another factor may have come into play: "Those who saw the Indians (for that is what most of the Japs were) put up a good game against the merchants thought that the yellows would at least give the bona fide Negroes a run for their money. Possibly they might have done so, but the allurements of Block 42 were too tempting and consequently with considerable benzai [*sic*] several of the visitors obtained nice, symmetrical jags. At the game, they had little ambish [*sic*] and went through the formalities with apparent apathy. The pitcher lobbed over balls which to the Tigers looked like hen houses. It was soon apparent that the home team had a cinch and the game became a farce. The final score was said to be 18 to 2."[46] This match against the Tigers is the last known game for the Mikado's.

On Thursday, May 21, it began to rain again. Over nine inches had fallen so far in the month—almost twice the average rainfall for May. Farmers' fields, and probably baseball diamonds, across Kansas became waterlogged. Heavy rains continued into June, eventually triggering the Missouri and Kaw Rivers to overflow and flood downtown Kansas City, causing over a million dollars of damage.[47]

With no games to generate income the Mikado's would soon have been unable to pay for their room and board. We must surmise that Masko canceled the remaining tour dates and returned to Denver in late May or early June. We can only imagine his disappointment, but another opportunity awaited him back in Denver.

Naoichi Hokasono, Denver's leading Japanese resident, had decided that it was time for the Mile High City to have its own Japanese-language newspaper, and he wanted Tozan Masko to be the chief editor. They began work as soon as Masko returned from Kansas City, and the first issue of the *Denver Shimpo* came out on Wednesday, June 24. It was six pages long with a supplement, and in addition to news articles it included a cartoon, illustrations of local scenes and Japanese notables, and advertisements. Masko would remain the paper's chief editor until 1916. Unfortunately no issues of the newspaper survive.[48]

Despite his new appointment, Masko would not abandon his true love. As we will see, he continued to organize and promote Issei baseball for another decade.

10

Nanka and the Japanese Base Ball Association

Kiichi Suzuki's father forbade him from joining Waseda's 1905 tour of the United States. Perhaps Minesuke Suzuki considered traveling in the midst of the Russo-Japanese War too dangerous, or perhaps he wanted his son to focus on his studies. In any case, despite Kiichi's longing to accompany his teammates, he had to remain behind. After the team returned to Japan, the players' tales only furthered Kiichi's desire to see California.[1]

Born in Chiba Prefecture, just east of Tokyo, Suzuki was not a particularly talented ballplayer. He enrolled at Waseda a year after Isoo Abe had founded the school's baseball club in 1901. At 5 feet 3 Suzuki was average size for a Japanese man, but as hard as he tried, he could not make the varsity team. He spent his entire four years on the practice squad, and his name is absent from the Waseda baseball club histories.[2]

Suzuki graduated in the spring of 1906 and a few months later, just after his twenty-second birthday, boarded a steamer for the United States. He arrived in August and made his way to Los Angeles. There he encountered Isamu Maeda, an old acquaintance from Chiba and a fellow baseball enthusiast. The two met from time to time to play catch. That fall Suzuki and Maeda noticed an advertisement in the *Rafu Shimpo*: the Nanka baseball team was looking for new players.[3] Nearly fifty years later Suzuki recalled, "We were nervous when we went to apply for the team at the office of the *Rafu Shimpo* on Main Street. [Umekichi] 'Kitty' Kawashima, [Toyo] Fujita, [Ken] Kitsuse, [Harry] Saisho, and other great players were present, so we were shocked. We newcomers had to improve our skills but the older players, especially Umekichi Kawashima and the best player at the time, Kitsuse, trained us."[4]

Although he never became a good hitter, with practice Kiichi excelled as a fielder and student of the game and would become a pillar of the club. Nicknamed "Onitei," Suzuki became lifelong friends with Saisho and Kitsuse.

In 1907 two of Saisho's old friends from his hometown of Miyakonojo also joined the team. Shichiji Kikuchi, who had graduated from Miyakonojo High School and had emigrated with Ken Kitsuse, signed up, as did Minori "John" Sohara. The son of Toshi Sohara and Suku Otomori, Minori was three years younger than Saisho, Kitsuse, and Kikuchi. At 5 feet 5 he was tall for a Japanese but was rail thin, weighing just 112 pounds. Nonetheless, Sohara was a talented fencer—skillful with both the bamboo kendo sword and the razor-sharp steel katana. He left Japan just a few months after graduating from high school in March 1904, sharing the Asiatic steerage compartment of the SS *Kanagawa Maru* with future *Rafu Shimpo* writer Hanzaburo Harase.[5]

Bolstered by Suzuki and the other new recruits, the Nanka team officially parted ways with the *Rafu Shimpo* (although several players continued to work at the newspaper). The team continued to practice every Sunday at the open lot on the east side of the Los Angeles River at First Street until moving to Highland Park in 1907. "We were crazy about baseball," Suzuki wrote in 1956. "Nothing was more interesting than playing baseball on Sundays and holidays when we were young. We never took jobs that would prevent us from taking Sunday off, no matter how good the opportunity was."[6] But there were not many opportunities open to them. Despite their strong Japanese educations, both the legal restrictions and the language barrier relegated the players to menial jobs. Suzuki and Kitsuse toiled as gardeners for white American families while Saisho continued to work at the Myer Siegel Department Store.

By the fall of 1907 results of Nanka's games routinely began to appear in the amateur baseball column of the *Los Angeles Herald*. The club lost three of the four recorded games that fall but seemed to play respectable ball. "There were no other Japanese teams," Suzuki recalled. "Our opponents were Caucasians, Blacks and foreigners such as Mexicans." The games were arranged in an ad hoc manner. Amateur teams contacted each other through newspaper advertisements.[7]

In December 1907 Montmorency "Red" Perkins, a supposed millionaire and baseball columnist for the *Los Angeles Herald*, organized the amateur Los Angeles–based Valley League. Perkins recruited eight teams and created a ten-week schedule with games played on Sundays. On the evening of Wednesday, December 11, Perkins met with league officials to discuss admitting the Nanka team and seven other clubs. When Perkins announced the accepted teams two days later, the Nanka team was not included. No explanation was given for the rejection. We are left to wonder if some league members objected to admitting Japanese or if there was a less insidious reason for the exclusion.[8]

Following their unsuccessful bid to join the Valley League, the players decided to dedicate more time to the team. In the early days of Japanese baseball members of the Ichiko high school team in Japan had segregated themselves from their classmates in a special dormitory to focus on the game, strengthen team bonds, and instill the "samurai" values of frugality and discipline. An Ichiko player wrote, "The dormitory . . . is a place for practicing self-discipline, the spirit of our baseball club. Both the club and the dormitory should collaborate to train the player's mind to achieve self-discipline as an objective."[9]

In early 1908 the Nanka players decided to follow Ichiko's lead, living together so that they could focus on baseball and, in Saisho's words, "unite the players."[10] The club's headquarters became a bungalow at 635 South Maple Avenue, between Sixth and Seventh Streets in downtown Los Angeles. Although located just a few hundred feet from bustling Main Street, the block on South Maple remained lightly developed—a throwback to an earlier Los Angeles, when streets contained a mix of dwellings, small businesses, light industry, and open spaces. The team's bungalow stood in a row of six small wooden houses sandwiched between the brick Los Angeles Art Glass Company and a livery stable.[11]

The bungalow must have been cramped with a dozen young men packed into a one-story twenty-by-sixty-foot house. It did, however, have several redeeming features. The rent was just twenty-five dollars a month; it was conveniently located to most of the players' jobs; and behind the house was an open lot, providing the young men with a place to practice. The practice area was a 330-x-300-foot sand lot at the corner of Los Angeles Avenue and Sixth Street. A few odd trees, knee-high weeds, and a rail fence separated the field from the streets. Just across Los Angeles Avenue loomed the ten-story Huntington Building. Built in 1905, just a few years before Saisho rented the house, it was the largest building by square footage west of Chicago. It also housed the terminal for the Pacific Electric trolley line. The company had plans to extend its tracks through Nanka's playing field, but the lot remained undeveloped until the end of the decade.

Every evening after work the Nanka players changed into their flannels and gathered on the lot for practice. In the large sandlot they could take batting practice and even scrimmage. When the wind blew or a player slid, dust billowed, temporarily blinding the players, but they continued, thrilled to have their own "stadium." Suzuki remembers Kitsuse's intensity. Ken "was short, but he was indeed a great player, hitting well and defending well. His base running was exceptional. We considered him a god of baseball. But when someone made a mistake, he would give him hell ('drop thunder' in Japanese). So, we nicknamed him Thunder." With Kitsuse's instruction and the constant practice, the team jelled and began beating local amateur teams.[12]

After spending the first half of 1908 training, the Nanka players would have a chance to prove themselves at Venice Beach's "Monster July 4th Program." The all-day event (10 a.m. to 12 p.m.) featured a "Grand Naval Sham Battle," a half-mile swimming race, boat races, pleasure trips on the steamer *Golden West*, a carnival, fireworks, and a free baseball game between the Americans and Japanese.[13]

The Fourth was gorgeous—sunny, temperatures in the seventies, with a light breeze. Thousands swarmed to Venice for the festivities and a day at the beach. At 10 a.m. the Nanka team took the field against the Venice Athletic Club at the town's athletic grounds. To fortify his team for the big game Saisho had recruited Tozan Masko and players from the Mikado's who had just returned to Denver following their abortive tour. They formed a strong squad. Most had been members of Guy Green's traveling team: Toyo Fujita at first, Kitty Kawashima at second, Saisho at third, Ken Kitsuse at short, Sato in left, Takeshi Kitsuse (Ken's older brother) at center, newcomer Senichi Morii in right, Saito at catcher, and Oya on the mound. Tozan Masko would umpire.[14]

Probably to the surprise of most of the spectators, Nanka dominated the American squad. "The Venice Athletic Club baseball team yesterday proved easy meat for the little Los Angeles Japanese nine," reported the *Los Angeles Times*. "The brown men were handy with the bat and succeeded in hitting the beach team's pitcher, Shepherd, all over the field." By the end of nine innings, every Japanese player had scored at least once as Nanka won, 19–3.[15]

The Japanese players spent the rest of the day in Venice, enjoying the amusements. The evening ended as "thousands gathered around the pier to see the sham battle between twelve improvised battleships. Floating out in the water, outlined by fire, the ships shot skyrockets at each other, until the toy boats burned up." The Nanka players then delighted the crowd by setting off seven large fireworks as the finale to the show.[16]

The next morning the *Times* ran a three-column-wide picture of the team, listing the players' names, along with an article headlined, "Japs Beat Venice, Show Fine Batting Work." The astonished reporter admitted, "The little Japs show a surprising knowledge of the game."[17]

Although Masko returned to Denver shortly after the Fourth, Saisho and his Nanka colleagues continued to play in the Los Angeles area nearly every weekend against semi-pro and town clubs. In November the *Los Angeles Herald* noted that "the Jap team and the Pioneer Stars [a white amateur team] are in great demand these days." Indeed the *Herald* contains numerous announcements from opposing managers asking the Nanka for a game.[18]

By late 1908 Japanese baseball was no longer exotic. That fall three American teams played in Japan, and the press covered each extensively. On September 3 the University of Washington varsity became the first American college squad to visit the country. The team stayed for five weeks, playing ten games against Waseda and Keio Universities, the Yokohama Commercial School, and the Yokohama Athletic Club. Seattle newspapers kept readers updated with dispatches wired from Coach Howard Gillette. Upon the team's return a nationally run article summarized the tour, noting the Americans' four losses in ten games. "The Japanese boys played better ball than we thought they would," Gillette told reporters. "Our reception by the Japanese . . . could not have been more cordial. Every detail and arrangement was carried out harmoniously and the cordiality provided makes us all feel that Japan's ball players and their loyal fans constitute sportsmen to emulate."[19]

A week after the Washington team left Japan the American Great White Fleet arrived. In December 1907, as tensions between the United States and Japan rose over the San Francisco Board of Education's segregation of Japanese students and the continuing violence against Japanese immigrants, President Theodore Roosevelt decided to remind Japan of the U.S. Navy's might. He ordered an armada of sixteen modern battleships, painted white to symbolize peace, to circumnavigate the globe, with stops in strategic ports to both honor allies and display the country's formidable power. Nicknamed the Great White Fleet, the ships would take almost fourteen months to complete their tour.

The fleet arrived in Yokohama on October 18, 1908. As the warships were meant to intimidate the Japanese, their arrival could have been met with hostility and perhaps even conflict. Instead the Japanese welcomed the U.S. Navy with open arms and celebration. "The American battleship fleet enjoyed a wild welcome by the Japanese," reported the *New York Sun*. "Decorations were everywhere, ashore and afloat, and in every direction the Japanese were eager to show their goodwill to the visitors. There was a great display of day fireworks of all sorts of designs. The streets were fairly jammed with thousands upon thousands of natives . . . and on every side could be heard expressions of goodwill."[20]

To emphasize shared values the U.S. sailors played a series of nine baseball games against Keio and Waseda Universities. In an unprecedented display of goodwill the Japanese organized an American rooting section. "More than 1000 Jap[anese] were arranged in a section of the bleachers in the most approved American college style, with rooters' caps and colors. . . . Throughout the battle this rooting section . . . cheered for the Americans, their cheering equaling the spontaneous cheering of the rest of the great throng."[21]

The sailors were no match for the Japanese college squads. Keio won all five of its games, although one went into extra innings before the Japanese umpire ended it with a questionable call that "was good humoredly accepted by the boys of the fleet." Waseda won three of its four games. Newspapers in the United States noted the Japanese victories: "Japs Play Ball with Americans," "Japs Won at Baseball," "Sailors of Fleet Go Down to Defeat at Hands of Hosts," read the headlines. The accompanying articles stressed that goodwill dominated the encounters.[22]

Three weeks after the Great White Fleet weighed anchor, Mike Fisher brought the first professional squad to Japan. Fisher, a former Sacramento detective and owner in the Pacific Coast League (PCL), had organized a professional tour to Hawaii in November 1907. His team of PCL stars played a series of games against Hawaiian all-stars and top teams. The visit was a resounding success, with thousands of fans greeting the visitors at the pier and attending the games. Fisher immediately decided on a more ambitious tour for the following postseason. In early 1908 he announced that he would take a team of Major League "stars of the first magnitude" to Asia, with stops in Hawaii, China, the Philippines, and Japan. Initial reports indicated that the team would include future Hall of Famers Frank Chance, Ed Walsh, and Ty Cobb, as well as stars Hal Chase and Doc White.

In July Tozan Masko wrote Fisher, asking to accompany the tour as an interpreter and guide. In typical Masko fashion he was loose with the truth, bragging to Fisher that he was "one of the first ball players that Japan has ever turned out and has been a fan ever since, acting as manager, umpire and promoter of baseball contests here as well as in the Orient."[23]

Tozan included a copy of the Mikado's stationery, which amused Fisher so much that he circulated it to the press. An article poking fun at Masko and his stationery was published in San Francisco and soon was picked up nationally, as well as in Japan. Some newspapers, including the *Japan Times*, reprinted most of first page of Masko's letter, including his section on the Mikado's history and all eleven of his "A Few Facts to Remember."[24]

By the time Fisher's team, now dubbed the Reach All Americans, arrived in Japan in late November, none of the great stars remained on the roster. All had backed out. Instead of an all-star squad, the team consisted of five minor Major Leaguers and seven players from the PCL. Nonetheless, the Japanese welcomed them enthusiastically, packing the ballparks. The All Americans played fourteen games against Waseda and the other top university teams, winning all. Players returned with a strong appreciation for the country, the people, and the way the game was played. "Baseball has caught on to such an extent that it is now played all over the empire, and on the way to the games we see boys 7 and 8 years old playing our sport in parks and small lots," noted one of the tourists.[25]

The press had been covering preparations for Fisher's tour all season. Hundreds of articles mentioning Japanese baseball appeared in newspapers across the country. Nearly all were favorable, lauding the Japanese for their enthusiasm and how well they played the game. Many gave details on the top college teams, mentioning their style of play and top stars. For example, the *Duluth News Tribune* noted, "Japan's college boys have adopted the American national game as their own and the baseball fever is as epidemic in Dai Nippon as it is here. . . . These college teams put up a game that would be a credit to the team of any American college. . . . They field beautifully. Their teamwork has been perfection. They run bases like little fiends, taking every possible chance. . . . In short, they know all the tricks of the game, and work them."[26]

The articles painted a favorable image of the Japanese, with the underlining message that any nation sharing America's national game was a natural ally. Some writers went further, arguing that baseball could be the key to peace. "It is said that we are going to have to fight Japan sooner or later," wrote Edward P. Irvin, a reporter in Honolulu. "What's the use? If we begin soon enough and each year send over one or two of our crack ball teams, the Japanese will get so interested in the game that they will forget all about their anxiety to fight and will—well, if not beat the sword into ball bat, which might be difficult—at least discard the bayonet and the musket ball for the bat and the horsehide sphere. And then they'll wind up by all becoming Americans through their enthusiasm over our national game."[27]

With the publicity surrounding the games in Japan and the generated goodwill, Harry Saisho decided this was the time to turn the

Nanka into an independent professional team and lead it "in a triumphal tour of the [United] States."[28]

Saisho began laying the groundwork for his tour in late 1908. In search of a sponsor in November, he wrote Henry Berry, owner and manager of the PCL's Los Angeles Angels. The *Los Angeles Times* published the letter to poke fun at Saisho's English, under the headline "Big Leaguers Beware New Jap Team Hatching."

> Dear Sir:
>
> I am going originate a Jap Base Ball Team to play eastern state of this country next season. There are quite good players, some of them even played with the Waseda University team in this state about 4 years ago. But I am very anxious to be short of cash of money when it will be done. I couldn't find any way to find to get our money easily because most of our country men has no interest on that business. If you, or some of your friend pay any attention on it please call me up to your office. I will make all explanation.
>
> Your truely [*sic*],
> Harry A. Saisho[29]

Saisho needed to overcome the flaw of both Guy Green's team and Masko's Mikado's: the failure to field a talented all-Japanese squad. Rather than tour with the Nanka club, he decided to create an all-star team of the best available Japanese players, to be called the Japanese Base Ball Association. By late 1908 there were a half dozen Issei baseball clubs in California from which Saisho could recruit. Los Angeles had three. In the winter of 1907 Kiichi Suzuki had moved to Hollywood. Although he would still join the Nanka for occasional games, he wanted to play ball every day. Accordingly in 1908 he created the Hollywood Sakura. "There were only three people who had played in Japan," Suzuki recalled, "so it was tough. I had to teach [the new players] how to use a glove. Fortunately, most of the players lived close by and there was a practice field nearby. Maybe because of that we improved quickly and had wonderful games with the Nihon Hayato Team, which was founded around the same time."[30]

Sakura team member Kiyotomi Ito remembered, "Our captain Onitei [Suzuki] was quite patient and stable, so the team was united and nobody complained. . . . We were boisterous—everyone was vital and we had fun together. . . . Whenever we won a game, we were treated to Chinese food, but when we lost, we were as miserable as a wet mouse."[31] Saisho asked both Suzuki and outfielder Riichiro Shiraishi from the Sakura to join the JBBA. Little is known about Shiraishi, who does not appear in the immigration or census records.

Sakura's rivals, the Nihon Hayato, consisted of young men born in Kagoshima Prefecture. They lived together in a boarding house at 600 South Olive Avenue, about six blocks from the bungalow rented by the Nanka team. The players were generally younger and less experienced than the Nanka veterans, and there is no record in the city newspapers of the team playing non-Japanese squads. In the early 1910s the team would change its name to Sanshu and start playing semi-pro teams. Over the next few years several of Hayato's players would join Saisho's teams, but for the 1909 tour Harry was primarily interested in their eighteen-year-old infielder, Takao Makimoto.

In 1908–9 the San Francisco Bay Area also may have contained three organized Japanese teams. The two original teams, the Fuji Athletic Club and the Kanagawa Doshi Club, probably still existed, although the devastation from the 1906 earthquake disrupted the city's Japanese community to the extent that the teams may have disbanded. No documentary evidence confirms their continued existence, but as the English-language newspapers often ignored Japanese immigrant sports, the lack of evidence does not preclude the clubs' survival. A third team may have been founded just as Saisho began recruiting players for the JBBA. The *Oakland Tribune* reported in December 1908 that a twenty-five-year-old shoemaker named Kota (or Kato) Suyematsu from the Fruitvale section of the city was organizing "a crack nine composed of all-star Nipponese ball twirlers." According to the *Tribune*, Suyematsu had been playing on white amateur teams in the Bay Area for the past few years.[32]

In November 1908 Saisho and Nanka's president, Dr. Takejiro Ito, went to Oakland to recruit a pitcher. A long article in the *Reno Evening Gazette*, probably republished from a Bay Area newspaper, describes their elusive search:

For three years he [Harry Saisho] has been developing a little squad of Nippon athletes until he has one of the fastest fielding teams in the southern part of the state. He has infielders that are above the ordinary, outfielders that are certain and a good catcher—but the pitcher is lacking. That is the weakness in the Japanese ball team that Saisho must overcome. He has brought pitchers from every town along the coast south of Vancouver and they have failed to develop a pitching arm. . . .

Dr. Ito and Captain Saisho are in Oakland looking for a pitcher. . . . When you ask Ito what is the matter with having a Japanese pitcher, he throws up his hands, bites his underlip suggestively and . . . gives an explanation of his native countrymen. "Japanese are not built for pitching. . . . They haven't a throwing arm. One reason is that the arm is too short, another is that the shoulder is too close set against the body. Our people are the greatest contortionists in the world but they can't stand the strain of pitching for their shoulders always give out. The players can't curve the balls either like you Americans. I thought at first it was the height, but I have seen the boys play against white pitchers smaller than our own and he would beat us. We are simply not people adapted to play ball and I can't remedy the defect."

Furthermore he never expects to develop a pitcher among his people. It is a hopeless task that he has been disappointed so many times that he will not attempt again. The team, which is known as the Nanka Japanese for Southern California will tour the state next spring and will appear in Oakland probably with an Indian pitcher in the box out of respect for a harmony of the complexion of the player.[33]

The gem for Saisho's JBBA lineup came through Kiichi Suzuki. Even though Suzuki had never made Waseda's varsity team as a member of the baseball club, he knew Shin Hashido well.

The former captain of Waseda had left the United States in 1905, enthralled with America. Immediately after graduating in 1906, Hashido returned to California as a reporter for the *Yorozu Choho*. Often writing under the nom de plume Togo Yamashita, he sent dispatches on Japanese immigrant life back to Japan to be published in the Osaka-based newspaper. His articles focused on the injustices faced by his countrymen in the United States. To better understand the trials of Japanese itinerant day laborers, Hashido spent a season working the fields and orchards for a dollar a day—reporting on the experience in a series of moving articles.[34] In early 1909 the famous shortstop was still living in Palo Alto, writing for *Yorozu Choho*. Suzuki persuaded him to take a leave from the paper and join the team as it traveled across the United States. Saisho immediately proclaimed his new star the team's captain.

On April 18, 1909, the *Los Angeles Times* printed a team photo of the JBBA in its Sunday sports section.[35] The men are dressed in dark, probably maroon, flannel uniforms with "J.B.B. Association" in white block letters across their chests. Their caps are of the same dark color with white pinstripes but no insignia. The players posed in three rows. Standing in the back row are Toyo Fujita (first base); Shin Hashido (second base and captain), sporting his trademark bushy dark mustache; Harry Saisho (catcher), wearing a mustache nearly identical to Hashido's; and an unnamed Japanese man in a suit and tie with a jauntily tilted fedora. Standing between and behind Hashido and Saisho is a Caucasian man identified in the caption as Allen. Seated in the middle row are Riichiro Shiraishi (right field), Takejiro Ito (manager [sic]), Ken Kitsuse (shortstop), and Isamu Maeda (pitcher). In the front, seated on the ground, are Minori Sohara (third base), Kiichi Suzuki (left field), and Shichiji Kikuchi (center field). Not pictured but on the roster were B. Iwasaki (pitcher) and Takao Makimoto (infield).

In late March or early April 1909 Saisho recruited Tozan Masko to help promote the upcoming tour. The team would start in the Los Angeles area, move into Denver and the Rocky Mountain region in late April, travel to Kansas in late May and June, and hopefully continue east. The JBBA promised opponents a Japanese fencing and jiujitsu exhibition before each game and would require only half of the gate receipts instead of the usual 75 percent charged by most barnstorming teams.[36]

Masko went right to work recycling the copy and exaggerations used first by Guy Green and then during his own Mikado's tour. Styling himself the manager and the team professional, he flooded their first stop, Riverside, California, with promotional material. The *Riverside Daily Press* announced on April 4:

Arrangements have been completed for a novel baseball game between the Riverside team and a team composed of the best nine players from the Japanese Empire, to be held at Evans park grounds on the afternoon of Saturday, April 17. . . . The Japanese team has been selected from the Japanese Baseball Association of Japan, for a tour of the cities of America. The manager of the association is Tozan Masuko, who has written that the team has had two offers for every single engagement it could fill. The players of the Jap team have been picked from the colleges of Japan and are said to be a corking good lot of players who will make things interesting for some of the best teams on the coast. . . . The Jap baseball team comes straight from the Orient. They played in Los Angeles some years ago and earned quite a reputation as experience players.[37]

Two days later, under the headline "Twirlers are Japanesy, but Not Easy to Defeat," the *Daily Press* printed Masko's usual tall tale that the team was founded in 1905 in Japan as the Tigers and included the top players from the "Flowery Kingdom." In the week prior to the game the *Daily Press* published three short follow-up articles praising the Japanese team's authenticity and skill: "Japan's best baseball talent is represented in Tozan's team, and if Riverside succeeds in holding the team down to anything like even score, the local players will gain prestige that should serve them well for next season's campaign."[38] But the game did not go as expected.

On the morning of Saturday, April 17, Saisho and the JBBA took the Santa Fe Railroad from Los Angeles to Riverside and headed to the ballpark. Prior to the game the Japanese entertained the large crowd with an exhibition of jiujitsu and kendo. Despite Saisho's recruiting efforts, he did not field an all-Japanese nine. Unable to find a suitable Japanese pitcher, a Caucasian named Tally took the mound while a second Caucasian, named Bell, played infield. But the ringers did not help. Riverside pummeled the JBBA, 17–0. Saisho's squad did pull off a nifty triple play in the eighth inning but otherwise was completely overmatched. The *Daily Press* concluded, "The Japanese team was made to realize that the American national game is not their game." Despite the lopsided score and disappointing play, the Riverside fans were "good natured and accorded the visitors the greatest courtesy, giving them the lion's share of applause." In appreciation, the Japanese staged a second martial arts exhibition after the game.[39]

During an interview with the *Daily Press* an unidentified "manager" of the JBBA (either Masko or Saisho) would claim that the beaten team was actually the club's second squad as the top players were in Denver preparing for a tour of the Midwest and East. The garbled names in the lineups published in the newspaper make it difficult to verify the Japanese players, but interviews with Saisho and Suzuki during the 1950s, as well as no mention of a Japanese team in that week's Denver papers, make it clear that Riverside had defeated JBBA's top (and only) team. The unidentified "manager" told the reporter through an interpreter:

> It was quite a disappointing game, our contest with your brilliant team. We shall not forget it as long as we live, as we look at the game as a first lesson . . . in our ever-onward progress in the acquisition of the art of the national game of America. We are most grateful to the Riverside players for the game, and also to the audience for their generous patronage. I admire your pitcher for his wonderful twirls and his cool judgment. We are far too young in the game, although we have beaten many good players in the towns about Los Angeles. . . . Through our journey we will ever remember the occasion of the game at Riverside, and I hope that we will have a chance to meet your players again. . . . I hope that your team is always successful and wish you many good lucks [sic].[40]

That evening the Japanese community of Riverside threw a party for the JBBA players. It had been planned as a victory celebration, but instead the locals tried their best to console the forlorn defeated team. At one point the hosts asked team captain Shin Hashido for a speech. "A defeated General has no words," he snapped. The next day he quit the club and, according to Saisho, "hid in Long Beach."[41] Things quickly went from bad to worse. Before they left Riverside, the team was robbed.

Returning from Riverside on April 18, Saisho's squad went straight to Joy Park in Los Angeles, where it would face another tough opponent—the Los Angeles Colored Giants.

As in most of the United States at the turn of the century, baseball in California was racially segregated. Unlike other areas, however, California had no African American leagues or professional teams. Instead amateur and semi-pro black teams played each other and arranged games with local white teams in an ad hoc manner. The Los Angeles Giants were the best black team in the area, if not in all of California. Although an amateur/semi-pro team, the Giants received national attention in 1908 when they beat the great Walter Johnson. The twenty-year-old future Hall of Famer had just completed his second big league season—finishing with the fifth-lowest ERA in the American League. To sharpen his skills he spent his off-season pitching in the California Winter League, and on October 18, 1908, the Los Angeles Giants pounded out nine hits as they beat him, 6–5, despite the ace raking up twenty strikeouts.[42]

The Giants' lineup against the JBBA contained only two players from the squad that had topped Johnson and just one recognizable player. Wes Pryor, who would play for the Chicago Leland Giants in 1910 and several different eastern black independent teams in 1914, led off the batting order and played left field. The others were local amateurs identified in the newspapers only by their last names. Nevertheless, the *Los Angeles Times* announced, "Fans will be treated to an exhibition of the national game as played by the best talent of the black and brown races."[43]

The game began well for the Japanese. After holding the Giants hitless in the top of the first, Kitsuse led off the bottom of the inning with a walk. Saisho followed with a single. Two batters later the Caucasian pitcher Tally doubled to score both runners. But the lead did not last long. The Giants notched one in the second, one in the third, and pounded out five in the fourth. After that, as the *Los Angeles Herald* noted, "There was not a ghost of a chance of [the JBBA's] winning."[44] The final score was 9–3.

The loss to the mighty Los Angeles Giants probably caused Saisho little concern. Few of the JBBA's opponents during the upcoming tour would be as strong as the Giants. The next game would be easier. The Japanese were slated to play Los Angeles High School on Thursday, April 22.

Opened in the mid-1870s, Los Angeles High School was the oldest public high school in southern California and until 1905 the only public high school in the city. With a large student body, the school routinely fielded a strong ball team that had nearly beaten Waseda University during its 1905 tour (Waseda had scored two runs in the ninth to win). Nevertheless, the now professional JBBA players expected to win.

The Japanese began with a relentless first-inning attack. Kitsuse, Bell, Tally, and Fujita started with consecutive hits as the JBBA erupted for five runs. The high schoolers came back with a run in the bottom of the first off Iwasaki. After a scoreless second inning the Japanese team fell apart. The high schoolers crushed Iwasaki's pitches, collecting seventeen hits, including three triples. At the same time the Japanese defense crumbled. It would make twelve errors while the students ran "around bases until tired out." The final score: Los Angeles High School 15, JBBA 9.

Kiichi Suzuki later recalled, "[Our] team was enthusiastic but incompetent."[45] Utterly disheartened and without his star, Shin Hashido, Saisho canceled the planned tour to the East and returned to his job at the Myer Siegel Department Store.

11

"Japanese Invasion"

Richmond Pearson Hobson was at it again. In the summer of 1910 the congressman from Alabama toured the Midwest, delivering his anti-Japan rantings to packed auditoriums. "Japan covets the Philippines, the Hawaiian Islands, Alaska, and the Pacific slope," Hobson told an audience in Columbus, Indiana. "Her swarming population requires more territory and her military and naval ambition craves the control of all the strategic points on the Pacific. . . . Moreover, the United States is rich, and being unprepared . . . is considered so easy to conquer as to be the most tempting possible prey."[1]

On February 20, 1911, Hobson addressed his fellow representatives on the floor of Congress. "Ever since this Nation went into the Hawaiian Islands and the Japanese nation served notice that they never would acquiesce; ever since we went to the Philippines and Japan asked us to let her go there with us and we refused; ever since her citizens have come to this country in great numbers, and our people, following the natural law of segregation of races, have not given them the treatment they thought they ought to have, they have been prepared for war. The war is already prepared for in every department and has been for months."

"Do I understand the gentleman to say that war is a visible certainty?" asked Michael Driscoll of New York.

"Yes, I say so," declared Hobson, "and it cannot be very far off."

Ten days later, following a meeting with President William Howard Taft, Hobson elaborated. "Japan will never permit the United States to finish the Panama Canal," he told reporters. "Japan . . . recognizes that war is inevitable and that she can choose the time." "Long before the canal is finished Japan will find an excuse for making trouble. Then will come the flash, the sudden attack, and disaster to the United States on every side."[2]

Hobson's warnings received a mixed reception. Supporters of the Asiatic Exclusion League and many readers of William Randolph Hearst's newspapers clung to the former naval officer's statements as justification for eliminating Japanese immigration and curtailing the rights of Japanese already in the country. An editorial in the *Enterprise News-Record* from Enterprise, a town of about 1,200 located in far northeast Oregon, proclaimed:

> Mr. Hobson was correct in his statements. . . . Japan is the menace. Climbing into the United States and swarming like squirrels from Japanese ports, the little yellow man would hold the Hawaiian Islands today . . . if it were possible for the Mikado's regime to precipitate war with the United States. . . . Up and down the Pacific Coast . . . there are in the neighborhood of 100,000 Japanese males, all soldiers, all ready to fight, all anxious to fight for conquest—purely for the lust of conquest, the deep call of gain. . . . There is no question about Japan's intentions. Profuse oriental profession of friendship is so much hogwash.[3]

Despite Hobson's popularity in some quarters, most of the country still viewed him as an alarmist and egotist seeking attention. "Under the constitution it would doubtless prove impossible to provide muzzles for the preposterous Hobsons, but it is open to all level-headed citizens to disregard their ridiculous vaporings," editorialized the *Los Angeles Express*.[4] When *Sporting Life* announced that a Japanese team would tour the United States in 1911, the paper mocked Hobson. "JAPANESE INVASION!" screamed the front-page headline in massive, bold type. The sub-headline explained the joke: "Not in the Panoply of Horrid War, but in Base Ball Uniforms and Armed with Bats and Balls, Will the 'Yellow Peril' Present Itself in Peaceful Aspect to the New World?"[5]

By 1911 most American fans should have been aware that the game thrived in Japan, but the few that did not, certainly would by the end of the year. The year began with rumors that two Japanese would attend spring training. On January 17 New York Giants manager John McGraw announced that Togo S. Hamamoto of Tokyo would be joining the team at Marlin Springs, Texas, to observe American "scientific baseball." A press release noted that Hamamoto, "who has the backing of a number of influential citizens of Tokyo . . . will devote his time to mastering the game. His backers plan to develop players in their own country and make it a national pastime."[6] Newspapers across the country, from large-market dailies to bi-weekly rags in rural villages, reprinted the announcement.

Twenty-six-year-old Shizunobu "Togo" Hamamoto had been living in St. Louis, working as a valet while reporting on Major League baseball for the Nagasaki-based newspaper *Sasebo*. Fluent in English, he had immigrated to Seattle in April 1903 from Nagasaki and made his way to St. Louis in 1906. He attended four or five games per week and became friendly with a number of the players.[7]

About a month later Hamamoto was in the news again. This time reporters had transformed him from an observer into a player receiving a tryout. "Togo is a star player among the Japs, and will work out daily," reported the *Chronicle-Telegram* in Elyria, Ohio. He may play on the second team."[8] Reporters also transformed him from working as a valet to bringing a valet and personal cook to training camp.

"But the Jap . . . may do more than merely learn baseball. He threatens to change the entire social conditions of ball players," joked an anonymous writer. "When the valet is seen trailing Togo's baseball shoes after a workout with the Giants or perhaps pressing his suit and folding it neatly away in the locker to await the next practice it is likely to strike the ball players['] fancy and before the Giants come north it is more than probable that Togo S. will lose the distinction of being the only ball player who has his own private valet."[9]

On March 25 the sports editor of the *Altoona Times* in Pennsylvania asked, "Where is Togo Hamamoto, the Japanese athlete, who was going to train with the New York Giants?"[10] Hamamoto never materialized. Reports from the Giants' spring training camp fail to mention him, and newspaper articles do not provide a reason for his absence. Hamamoto would eventually become a champion amateur golfer, winning several St. Louis tournaments before returning to Japan in 1933.[11]

On January 18, the day after McGraw announced Hamamoto's invitation to spring training, Chicago Cubs owner Charles Murphy

received a letter "in the best of English" from Ito Sugimoto requesting a tryout. According to the message, the twenty-one-year-old
Sugimoto was an infielder from Honolulu who was currently playing semi-pro ball in San Francisco. Murphy supposedly forwarded
the request to manager Frank Chance, who was wintering in Glen-
dora, California, asking him to investigate the lead. Murphy told
reporters that he "favors taking Ito to New Orleans for a tryout."
Papers pointed out that "if the deal goes through the Cubs can claim
the distinction of breaking in the first Japanese in the history of the
major leagues." Sugimoto probably did not meet Chance's standards,
as he never signed with the team or made the trip to spring training. The newspaper reports are the only time Sugimoto enters the
documentary record. He does not appear in census returns; birth,
marriage, or death notices; box scores; or any other primary sources.
Yet two years later he made the papers again. This time Sugimoto
wrote Murphy seeking the position of "official bat boy." Murphy
told reports that he would consider the application.[12]

"Japan Invades America," announced *Collier's Outdoor American* on
April 15, 1911, the day following Waseda University's arrival in San
Francisco. Returning for its second tour of the United States, the
Waseda ball club would stay for four months, playing fifty-three
games against the top colleges and amateur teams across the country. Isoo Abe, now head of the school's athletic department and president of Japan's baseball association, was unable to accompany the
team. Instead Takizo "Frank" Takasugi, who had graduated from
Northwestern and DePauw Universities and now served as an English
professor at Waseda, led the group of fourteen students.

In 1905 the press had met Waseda's arrival with derision, but this
time newspapers depicted the Japanese positively, praising them for
having successfully adopted the American national pastime. Even the
usually anti-Japanese *San Francisco Chronicle* ran a complimentary
article covering the team's arrival. *Outdoor American* went further,
praising the team and Japanese in general for "a fighting spirit certain to win the admiration of the American fan."[13]

Harlan "Pat" Page, a former three-sport athlete at the University
of Chicago and captain of the baseball team, met the team at the

dock in San Francisco. Chicago had invited Waseda to the United States to continue a baseball exchange started the previous season.

In the fall of 1910 the University of Chicago varsity had traveled to Japan to play Waseda and Keio. The players stayed in Japan for about a month, playing ten games. Thousands came to watch each game; some walking more than thirty miles to the ball field, others traveling over two hundred miles by steam locomotive. Although the games were "exceedingly hard fought," Chicago had little trouble with Waseda, winning all six meetings comfortably by a combined 69–10 score. Keio proved more challenging, but the visitors still won all three games (3–1, 2–1, and 5–2). The majority of players on both teams felt that the games built mutual respect and friendship.[14] "We were considered not only as guests of Waseda University, but also as guests of the Japanese nation," wrote team captain J. J. Pegues. "Everywhere individuals put themselves out to make us enjoy our stay in the Flowery Kingdom to the utmost, and to show us that a true feeling of friendliness existed for us as representatives of the Unites States. . . . We had come to know the Japanese students, and . . . they had come to know us, and . . . we had also done at least a little to secure a better understanding and a stronger bond of friendship between their nation and ours."[15]

Eager to continue the friendship, the University of Chicago invited the Waseda team to the United States. The Japanese would play first on the West Coast before traveling to the Midwest to play a three-game series with Chicago, as well as with nearby schools. They would then play on the East Coast before ending the visit in the Northwest.

Waseda's 1911 U.S. tour began with a scrimmage against Waseda alumni living in the San Francisco area in front of a crowd of seven hundred—nearly all local Japanese. The varsity team won easily, 18–0, as the local squad, known as the Pacifics, contained no players with known baseball experience and played a "very crude and awkward" game.[16] Waseda then tackled the top collegiate squads in California. Unlike in 1905, when Americans were just surprised that Japanese could play baseball, sports journalists had high hopes for the current team, noting "their game is a high-class article." But it soon became apparent that the Waseda team still had much to learn. It was blown out by Stanford, 11–2; "completely outclassed" by Santa Clara, 10–1; and after a 4–1 win over the University of California at Berkeley, dropped close games to Sacred Heart College, 10–9, the naval training ship *Pensacola*, 4–3, and the semi-pro Brooke Realties of Sacramento, 3–1. A game against Mission High School of San Francisco ended in a 5–5 draw after Waseda walked off the field to protest a decision by the umpire.[17]

Spectators noticed two characteristics about Waseda's play. The first was obvious: the Waseda players and manager were silent. There were no shouts of encouragement, no instructions from the dugout, no yells of "I've got it" in the field. The team did all of its communicating through silent hand signals. In Japan this both created a sense of decorum and helped disguise upcoming strategies, but in the United States the silence seemed odd and even dour. "The average American crowd attending baseball games would hardly stand for this sort of thing," noted the *Missouri Sharp Shooter*. "What the average crowd wants is loud coaching accompanied by all possible antics . . . [which] has a tendency to liven up the crowd itself and, after all, the real fun of going to a baseball contest is to get in the game a little one's self."[18]

The second point was more nuanced. The Waseda team had developed a different style of baseball than their American opponents—a style that survives in Japanese baseball even today. J. J. Pegues wrote for *Collier's Outdoor American*:

> The . . . Japanese have done much to overcome their handicap in size by a careful study of the game and a development of those features to which they are physically best suited. At bat, they have sought to curb their natural desire to hit hard, and, instead of attempting to slug, stand well up to the plate and try to chop short hits over the infield, or else gain bases by laying down well placed bunts toward either first or third. Once on base they are dangerous, as their teammates sacrifice them along skillfully, and they are quick to take advantage of every opportunity. . . .
>
> Their pitchers seldom have the speed of the average American college pitcher, and so must depend for effectiveness upon control and curves. As a consequence, the Japanese pitcher but rarely risks a straight ball over the plate but seeks to induce the batter to strike

on slow curves over the corners. In fielding, they are often brilliant. They move like a flash when the ball is hit, and often succeed in cutting off apparently safe ones. But it is in the tricks and fine points of the game that the Japanese excel. They may be expected to steal home, attempt a squeeze play, or work a delayed steal of either second or third anytime.[19]

Newspapers across the United States, from the *New York Times* to the *Laredo (TX) Weekly Times*, followed Waseda's progress, noting game results and running occasional articles of various lengths. Starting in mid-May many papers began carrying a series of articles featuring the Waseda players titled "Japs Tell How to Play Ball." Each piece contained a short essay written by a Waseda player on how to play his particular position and a large photograph of the player. Manasoba Fukubori explained that a third baseman must be courageous and agile; ace pitcher Sutekichi Matsuda wrote, "Of three great virtues in pitching in baseball, curve, velocity and accuracy, I find the one greatest to be admired is accuracy"; and Goro Mikami noted that "fearlessness and much confidence help the batter."[20] After fifteen days in California the Waseda squad headed east by train toward Chicago, with stops for games in Ogden, Utah, and Boulder, Colorado.

A week after the Waseda ball club left California, the Keio University team arrived in San Francisco. Established in 1858, twenty-four years before archrival Waseda, Keio was considered by most experts to be Japan's top team in 1911. The two clubs, however, had not met on the diamond for five years as the schools had canceled all games for fear the rivalry would lead to student riots.

Keio had worked hard to surpass Waseda as the nation's top team. The players traveled to Hawaii in the summer of 1908, where they played local teams and California's University of Santa Clara. They returned to Japan in time to take five games from the visiting Great White Fleet and three from the University of Washington. In 1909 Keio invited the University of Wisconsin's varsity team to Japan. Keio shocked the Americans by winning the first three games (by one run in each) before dropping the final game, 8–0. The second game went eighteen innings, the longest game in Japan at the time, before Keio pushed across the winning run. Nineteen-year-old Kazuma Sugase pitched all four games for Keio, including all eighteen innings of the second meeting, when he struck out sixteen and allowed just five hits. The son of a German father and Japanese woman, Sugase would become Japan's top pitcher and be singled out by John McGraw as "one of the greatest all-around athletes in Japan."[21]

The Keio team, however, was not satisfied with its victories over Wisconsin. The players knew that they still had much to learn before they could tackle the top American university teams. In December 1910 Keio invited Arthur "Tilley" Shafer (often spelled Schaeffer) to Japan to coach the team. The twenty-one-year-old Shafer had attended St. Vincent's in Los Angeles, when Waseda played against the school in 1905, and during a trip with Santa Clara College to Hawaii in 1908 he played against Keio. In 1909 he signed with the New York Giants and spent the majority of two seasons on McGraw's bench, hitting just .179 in 1909 and .190 in 1910. Contemplating his future in the fall of 1910, Shafer wrote to offer his services to Keio. Much to his surprise, Keio accepted and made the appropriate arrangements. After returning to the States, Shafer told the *New York Globe*:

> It was the greatest experience of my life. You can't imagine the fun that I had teaching the boys from Keio how to pull off inside base-ball. . . . We'd play a game and when a certain play arose, I would stop and explain it to them. . . . Another thing I did, was to write out 25 pages of different plays—those that ordinarily pop up in the course of a game. They had these translated into Japanese and at night would sit around their little charcoal fires figuring it all out. They would set down questions, and the next day would crowd around me and demand explanations. If a play was pulled off during a game and it proved successful, they would stop the game and write it down in lit-tle books which they carried.[22]

The *Globe* writer further noted, "What amused Schaeffer most of all was the eagerness the Japanese displayed in learning baseball slang. One of the first things they wanted to know was how to shout like big leaguers. Schaefer taught them all the pet expressions, like 'Up on your toes, old boy! That's the stuff! A little more pepper! Look up! That's where you're going to hit it? Come on! A little more of that smoke!' He says they picked it up very quickly and that sometimes when he would be walking down the street with the members of the team, some boisterous fellow would leap into the air and shout, 'That's the stuff, old boy! Step away from it!'"[23]

By the time the team arrived in the United States, it was well prepared. After beginning with a tie against the University of California, Keio won three straight over Springville, Utah; Salida, Colorado; and Denver University. In addition to the ace Kazuma Sugase, the team also boasted two star defensive players—shortstop Katsumaro Sasaki, "a fielder of exceptional ability [who] on the bases is the Ty Cobb of Japan," and center fielder Shigeru Takahama, capable of "covering a vast amount of territory."[24] Like Waseda, Keio would travel across the country facing the top American collegiate teams. The squad would stay for two months, playing forty-four games, before continuing on to Hawaii, where it would play for another month. But the two Japanese teams would not meet on the diamond, even though it would have been an ideal opportunity for the two rivals to face off with little fear of an ensuing riot.

Neither the Waseda nor Keio ball clubs would travel as far south as Los Angeles. The City of Angels would have to make do with its local Japanese squads.

After the disastrous showing during its brief barnstorming tour in the spring of 1909, the JBBA had disbanded. The players returned to their day jobs. Tozan Masko went back to Denver and resumed his post as editor of the *Denver Shimpo*. Shin Hashido, having quit the team, stayed in Long Beach and continued to write for the Japanese newspaper *Yorozu Choho*. Kiichi Suzuki and Ken Kitsuse returned to garden care. In May 1909 Kitsuse announced that he would enter the Los Angeles marathon. Ken claimed that he hailed from New York, perhaps to overcome prejudice against local Japanese. His plan nearly backfired as other runners objected to his entry under the pretext that he was not a local. Kitsuse told reporters that "he would run anyway, even if he was prevented from receiving any compensation . . . if for no other reason than to show the Los Angeles public he is at least the peer of all Japanese runners." In an emergency session the race organizers voted to allow Ken to participate. He would be joined by two other Japanese runners, although none would finish near the front of the pack.[25]

Harry Saisho resumed his position at the Myer Siegel Department Store. Since joining the store, Saisho had moved up from janitor to shipping clerk to window dresser and was now a floor supervisor. Several years earlier Harry had attended a lecture by Kisaburo Uyeno, the Japanese consul to San Francisco from 1901 to 1907 who had urged his Issei listeners to settle in the United States and invest in undeveloped land. Saisho saved his wages and bought real estate in both the San Fernando Valley and Lancaster, California. At the time, Issei were still allowed to purchase land in California, but that would not always be the case. In 1913 California passed the Alien Land Law, forbidding Asians from owning real estate.

In the fall of 1909 a visit to Los Angeles by the African American Occidental team from Salt Lake City brought the JBBA back together. Formed in 1906 as an amateur club, the Occidentals took on local amateur and semi-pro squads. Their snappy play brought both black and white fans to the ballparks, and Salt Lake's mainstream papers followed the team's exploits. By 1908 the Occidentals had transformed into a semi-professional independent club, recruiting professional African American ballplayers and barnstorming throughout the region.[26]

In July 1908 a unique opportunity presented itself. Fort Douglas in the all-white semi-pro Utah State League could no longer field a team. A replacement was needed. The league's board of directors proposed that the spot be filled by "the Occidentals, [the] invincible amateur team of colored boys."[27] It was a radical suggestion. At the time, African Americans were barred from organized professional baseball, and even at the amateur/semi-pro level there were no integrated baseball leagues in the United States. The last black team to play in a white league was the Acme Giants from Celoron, New York, which was part of the Iron and Oil League in 1898.

The team from the city of Murray objected immediately. The *Deseret Evening News* reported, "They are baseball enthusiasts of the most earnest kind but when it comes to playing with the brunette wonders Murray's team say 'No' and the fans say they don't blame the team. . . . The town suggests the substitution of another team, composed of white men."[28] A few days later the newspaper editorialized, "If Murray really wants to make the league a big success . . . it will sacrifice a bit of personal feeling and get in and play ball. . . . The colored boys constitute the best amateur [team] outside of the state league."[29] The teams argued back and forth for several weeks until Murray final relented. "The announcement . . . that the Occidentals were full-fledged members of the league seemed to meet with universal approval of the fans everywhere," noted the *Salt Lake Herald*.[30]

The Occidentals took over Fort Douglas's slot on the schedule and two days after joining the league met the Murray team on the diamond. Revenge was sweet as the Occidentals pounded their foes, 8–3, as they "clouted the ball as though they had an awful grudge."[31] The Occidentals ended up finishing third in the league.

Undermined by a newly created rival league, the Utah State League disbanded in 1909, and the Occidentals reverted to playing games with local teams for side bets and barnstorming through Idaho and Utah. Having strengthened the team with shortstop Joe Robinson—according to the *Salt Lake Telegram* "one of the best colored ball players ever seen in this neck of the woods"—the Occidentals racked up a 94-14 record during the 1909 season.[32] In early October, after winning two straight games in a best-of-three series over the all-white Yampa Smelters, the Occidentals declared themselves Utah state champions. Eager to continue playing and earning money, they made arrangements to travel to Los Angeles to challenge the Los Angeles Colored Giants in a five-game series to "decide the colored championship of the coast."[33]

The championship series was over quickly. The Occidentals overwhelmed the Giants in three straight games. Although they had picked up several hundred dollars in gate receipts and side bets, the Occidentals decided to stay in Los Angeles for the winter season to play other local independent squads. Their first game would be against members of the PCL Los Angeles Angels. Newspapers soon promoted the game as a showdown between the races.

Under the headline "White and Black Play Attracting Interest," the *Salt Lake Herald-Republican* announced:

The "White and Black" match game to be played Sunday at the Chutes between the Angels and the Salt Lake negro club known as the Occidentals is causing more talk in baseball circles than has been indulged in since the [Angels] dropped out of the pennant race. The winning of the game means more to the Angels than the winning of the side bet and the big cut of the gate receipts. It is a matter of personal pride with every man on the Los Angeles lineup. They wouldn't be beaten by the black men for all the money that rolls in at the box office.

The Occidentals are a real ball team. . . . A peep at the . . . lineup shows that the colored captain has strengthened his forces by the addition of Lane at short. Lane is one of the stars of the Los Angeles Giants, a local Negro nine. "Let them strengthen up all they can," said [Angels player-manager] Frank Dillon last night. "That's what we want them to do. We want to wallop these fellas good and hard, we don't want to give them any chance to come back with a holler of any kind. Bill Tozer will pitch as he never pitched before. I think it would break Bill's heart to be beaten by these blacks. Bill is a southerner, you know—comes from the southern part of Utah."[34]

About 3,400 "enthusiastic fans," including a large African American contingent, packed Chutes Park on November 21. To the delight of their fans, who "cheered themselves hoarse," the Occidentals took a 1–0 lead in the top of the first, but the joy was short-lived as the Angels retook the lead in the bottom of the inning and cruised to a 6–1 victory.[35]

After the game Los Angeles Angels catcher Jess Orndorff determined the time was right to begin an off-season business as a sports promoter. "I believe that I can hold successfully baseball games and wrestling contests in the angel city during the next few months," he told the *Los Angeles Herald*.[36] Perhaps inspired by the racial rivalry brought out in the Occidentals versus Angels game, Orndorff decided to pit the African Americans against a Japanese squad.

With the help of Harry Saisho and Nanka player Senichi Morii, Orndorff brought together a team of Japanese from the city's various squads. According to a somewhat exaggerated report in the *Herald*,

Kitsuse, who will do the twirling for the Occidental challengers, is probably the best Japanese pitcher on the coast. Saisho, who will operate on the receiving end of the battery, formerly played with the Nebraska Indians and will be tried out next season by a class "B" league of the middle west. Saisho has a sure peg to the second station, but three men having stolen bases on him during the last six games played. . . . The Japs have witnessed nearly every game which the fast-colored team has played and Captain Morii feels certain that his team will have a little difficulty in bringing [the] dusky champions into camp. . . . [It] promises to be one of the most interesting and fastest games ever played on the coast.[37]

Orndorff expected a large turnout at Chutes Park for the game on Sunday, December 19. The *Los Angeles Herald* ran articles on the event nearly every other day for two straight weeks. Most emphasized the game's racial element. A December 18 article noted, "[It] is an exhibition of the national game in which race supremacy in the art will be settled. . . . This game between the All-Star Japanese team and the colored Occidental champions of the west places the following question before the sporting public: Are the Japanese superior to the negroes in baseball?" As many scientists of the time believed in the linear ranking of ethnic and racial groups and some heralded organized sports, especially baseball, as a marker of higher civilization, fans may have been curious about which team would win at America's national game. The *Salt Lake Telegram*, however, took a less intellectual approach to reporting the game. Relying on sheer bigotry to attract readers, it republished an article from the *Herald* under the headline, "When Jap Meets Coon Then Comes a Baseball Game."[38]

To drum up attendance Orndorff printed two sets of handbills—one in English and one in Japanese—and "flooded" the Japanese neighborhood, centered on San Pedro and First Streets, with the advertisements. "Practically all of Japtown will be seen on the bleachers when the game is called," predicted the *Herald*. Gambling had always been a strong component of Issei culture, and the game provided an opportunity to express the Japanese community's national pride by wagering on its countrymen. "Many of the Jap fans have raked up considerable coin and will go prepared to make a killing," continued the *Herald*. "Should the brown men win, and many believe they will succeed in trimming the negroes, the coming week will be one large holiday in Japtown."[39]

Although lineups had been announced several days before the game, there was a last-minute change. Ken Kitsuse and Harry Saisho, according to the *Herald*, "were unable to complete negotiations [with Orndorff] and the deal fell through." Instead Orndorff himself would catch, while Bill Tozer, the ace of the Los Angeles Angels, would pitch. The twenty-seven-year-old Tozer had been a professional since 1903, pitching briefly for the Cincinnati Reds the previous season. He had just completed his finest season, going 31-12 with a 1.79 ERA in 381.2 innings for the Angels.[40] The battery upgrade suggests that Orndorff may have placed a significant side bet on the Japanese team to win.

December 19 was cold for a baseball game, at least by southern California standards, with highs in the 50s. Nonetheless, nearly two thousand spectators arrived at Chutes Park to witness the heralded event. Facing Tozer, the Occidentals supplemented their usual lineup with the top two players from the Los Angeles Colored Giants. Bill Lane, who had played briefly with Salt Lake that spring, played shortstop, and Bill Pettus, one of the top black players in the West, started at first base. Bert Harrison took the mound. Alongside their two white ringers, the Japanese started Morii at second, Sami in left field, Mokuda at short, Fujita (from Saisho's team) at first, Motohashi (who had been on Guy Green's 1906 roster but saw no or limited playing time) at third, Maeda in center, and Yama in right.

For three innings Tozer and Harrison held their opponents scoreless. In the top of the fourth a triple by Orndorff followed by a Tozer single gave the "Japanese" a brief one-run lead, but the Occidentals tied the score in the bottom half of the inning as Morii dropped a popup and Pettus tripled home a base runner. After the Occidentals pushed home another run, both Tozer and his Japanese defense fell apart in the bottom of the fifth. The Occidentals put the game away with four runs on three singles, a pair of stolen bases, and three Japanese errors. The game ended on a bizarre play as Orndorff and Tozer, who had ended the eighth inning with outs, attempted to bat again at the beginning of the ninth. Each was allowed to swing away before being declared out for batting out of turn. The final score was 7–3.

Opinions on the quality of the game differed. The *Los Angeles Herald*, which had been promoting the match, called it "a well-played game" and added, "Orndorff's first venture in the promoting field . . . was a marked success in every way."[41] Other newspapers, however, were less enthusiastic. The *Salt Lake Tribune* and *Los Angeles Examiner* both praised the Japanese players for putting "up a good game" and "making a surprisingly good showing at the American game," but noted that they were "woefully weak" at bat and thoroughly outplayed by the Occidentals.[42] The *Los Angeles Times*, calling the game just "ordinary," had little respect for the Japanese players. Under the subheading, "Little Brown Men Are Not Wonders at the American Sport," the *Times* complained, "The Jap boys cannot hit the ball and are shy on fielding. . . . The Jap boys were afraid they would be hit by the pitched balls and did their best to keep out of danger. As a result, many of them were struck out." The overtly racist *Salt Lake Telegram* headlined its article "Coons Defeat Japs in Baseball Game."[43]

Although neither Saisho nor Kitsuse played against the Occidentals, the hubbub surrounding the game prompted Harry to reform the JBBA. Saisho traveled to San Diego to arrange games for the squad in late December. The *San Diego Union* reported, "Saisho says he realizes that the San Diego Midwinter league team would be too fast a proposition for his countrymen but that he would like to play any amateur or semi-professional aggregation of hit and run artists."[44] The games, however, did not materialize, and Saisho tried again to schedule a game for February of the following year. This time he intended to combine the baseball game with a wrestling match. The *San Diego Union* wrote:

Harry A. Saisho, the polite little Japanese who was in San Diego about two months ago, is now developing into a manager of wrestlers. . . . Saisho's English is a trifle faulty, but his intentions are good. His letter . . . is reproduced below in full:

Sporting Editor, *San Diego Union*:

Dear Sir:

I am much obliged to you helped us as much as possible past time. I trying to get game (baseball) now in Feb. or first March if possible for we may not stay any longer than March. Here is another sporting matter. My friend Mr. R. Fukada, that jiujitsu wrestler—he matched to Young Johnson, middleweight champion of coast and won about 9 minutes, Jan. 4th at Los Angeles. He willing to get one fight to a wrestler in San Diego in recent. He will be here in a few days. Please let me know a man attend on. He weight about 140 pounds or more. I believe he is more stronger than Yokohama called a world champion. Please notify soon possible.

Harry A. Saisho[45]

The letter worked, and Saisho arranged a jiujitsu and kendo demonstration followed by a wrestling match between Fukuda and Tom Travers on February 26, 1910, as well as a ball game between the JBBA and San Diego's California Winter League team on the following day.[46]

The JBBA would have its hands full. The San Diego squad had won the California Winter League championship for the past two seasons and would win the next two as well. The team featured at least two big leaguers—third baseman Tom Downey, who played for the Reds from 1909 to 1912, and his Reds teammate, first baseman Chick Autry. To be competitive Saisho recruited two ringers: Jess Orndorff, the part-time promoter and back-stop for the Los Angeles Angels, would catch, while Jim Scott of the Chicago White Sox would take the mound. Scott would pitch nine years in Chicago, finishing with 107 wins and a 2.30 ERA, and would accompany the White Sox on their 1913 visit to Japan.

The event became a near disaster. Fans had crowded Athletic Park on Sunday, February 20, waiting in vain for the Japanese to arrive due to a miscommunication between Saisho and Will Palmer, the home team owner-manager. The fans had to wait again the next week as the Santa Fe train from Los Angeles, carrying Orndorff, Scott, and two Japanese players, arrived three hours late. Rather than disappoint the waiting fans a second time, Palmer quickly recruited local amateur players to fill out the Japanese team and play an exhibition game until the stars arrived. The contest, however, was completely one-sided. The Japanese "were unable to get but a few scratch hits," although the San Diego pitcher "merely lobbed the ball across." The

hosts "made the game one long joke." By the time the missing players arrived, "most of the spectators had left the grounds." At 4 p.m.
Scott took the mound for the JBBA, and the feature game began in
front of near-empty stands. Scott dominated, striking out eight in
just four innings before the game was called on account of darkness
after only an hour of play.[47]

Returning to Los Angeles, Saisho, now called "the leading light
in the Japanese athletic colony" by the *Los Angeles Times*, focused
on creating both a Japanese athletic club and baseball league. At the
time, Japanese were routinely barred from Caucasian athletic clubs,
leaving them few places to play Western sports such as tennis or to
swim. The immigrants also practiced the traditional Japanese sports
of jiujitsu, kendo, and sumo. Several times a week scores of wrestlers
and fencers crammed into a small brick tenement at 120 North San
Pedro Street to practice.[48] A larger space was needed. Likewise the
city's Japanese ballplayers decided that after being excluded from
organized leagues, they would create their own league. In the summer of 1910 six teams—Saisho's Nanka, the Sanshu, the Nippon,
the Hollywood Sakura, the Asahi, and the Hayato—formed a league.
Games were played each weekend at the field at Seventh and Alex-
andria Streets. The *Times* noted, "The Japanese colony has much
interest in baseball and the merchants have hung up many prizes
for the team that makes the best showing during the season."[49]

In the winter of 1910–11, as announcements for the upcoming
Waseda and Keio tours hit the newspapers, Saisho decided that his
players were ready to fulfill their dreams of becoming professionals
and barnstorm across the country. Needing money to buy new uniforms, advertise, and pay players, Harry reached out to prominent
Japanese businessmen and professionals as sponsors; organized a
sumo *basho* (tournament) and theatrical play to raise money; and
withdrew his own savings—probably mortgaging his real estate in
Lancaster and the San Fernando Valley.

Saisho's 1911 team contained many from the old guard. Guy Green
Japanese veterans Ken Kitsuse, Toyo Fujita, and Kitty Kawashima
would be back, as would 1909 JBBA stalwarts Kiichi Suzuki, Minori
Sohara, Riichiro Shiraishi, and Shoichi Motohashi. They would be
joined by two young recruits.

At twenty-three years old Tokutaro Tachiyama was one of the youngest players on the team. He had learned to play ball at Kagoshima Commercial High School. After graduating, he immigrated to the United States, arriving in Seattle on November 14, 1907. Immigration records describe him as 5 feet 3, with a small mole above the right corner of his mouth and a dark birthmark under his chin. The other new player was also twenty-three years old but would turn twenty-four in April. Takaji Kubo may have been young, but he had the most formal training. Born in Kosei Mura in Yamaguchi Prefecture, Kubo had played outfield for Keio University in 1907 and 1908. Although he was a bench player, starting only a few games each season, he had played well in his two starts against American teams. In 1907 he had two hits in four at bats against the semi-pro St. Louis team from Hawaii, and a year later he went two for two against the squad from the USS *Ohio* during the Great White Fleet's visit to Japan. In April 1910 Kubo arrived in the United States. He would stay only a few years before returning to Japan.[50]

Saisho himself would act as manager and promoter, taking the field only when necessary. To help run the team Harry recruited thirty-one-year-old Kesaichi "Arthur" Shiomichi to act as traveling secretary. Like Saisho, Shiomichi was from Miyazaki Prefecture and had come to California in 1903. Although he had not attended college in Japan, Shiomichi could speak and write English well.

In early April Harry purchased a 5-x-8½-inch pocket ledger book. On the first page he wrote, "April 8–1911 First Game at Pomona H.S., JBBA vs. Pomona H.S." and began an exacting account of the team's 1911 barnstorming tour.[51] For each day he recorded the income from the gate receipts and the expenses for travel, board, players' salaries, equipment, and medical bills—indeed everything, including stops for ice cream. Saisho began the ledger with a zero balance as he expected ticket sales to cover the team's expenses. He then ordered a thousand printed advertisements, bought stamps and library paste, and mailed them to perspective opponents in the Midwest.

The team spent April and early May honing its skills with weekly games in the Los Angeles area. It warmed up against Pomona and Whittier high schools and then tackled the more challenging San Bernardino Stars, the African American Los Angeles Giants, and the University of Southern California. To differentiate itself from the Waseda and Keio teams, the JBBA advertised itself as "the only professional Japanese team which has ever appeared in the United States"—conveniently ignoring Green's 1906 team, Masko's 1908 Mikado's team, and its own short-lived 1909 squad.[52]

The games drew large crowds, but six years after Isoo Abe first brought his Waseda squad to California, Japanese teams in Los Angeles were no longer unusual. "The most peculiar thing about the Japanese team was that it was not peculiar," wrote Randall Henderson of the *Los Angeles Times*. "Except for the slant in his eyes and the deep guttural accent of his rooting, the Japanese player is as much like an American player as one pea is like another in a pod. He even wears his cap at the same rakish angle, and grabs handfuls of dust in the same way."[53]

On the field the JBBA impressed fans with its "general knowledge of inside baseball" and "clean playing and quite orderly conduct."[54] Spectators, however, seemed disappointed that the JBBA did not employ silent signals like the Waseda team but instead "kept up a constant chatter of Japanese." When asked if the players ever use silent signals, Saisho replied, "Use silent signals? No, we no use silent signals. What good use silent signals? No one understand Japanese talk. Only use them in Japan. No good in this country."[55]

The JBBA played well against Whittier and San Bernardino, losing tight games (3–2 and 3–1) behind the "nifty" pitching of Hikoji Mokuda, the twenty-two-year-old star of the Hayato team. Clyde Bruckman of the *San Bernardino Sun* noted, "Though very small he put considerable speed in his delivery and had a kink on the ball that fooled four of the locals' heavy hitters." Mokuda also starred at the plate in San Bernardino, stroking the JBBA's only hit, stealing three bases, and scoring the team's only run. For some unknown reason, however, Mokuda would not continue with the team.[56]

Lacking a quality Japanese pitcher, Saisho recruited Louis Lockhart, who had played for San Bernardino. Lockhart, a Native American, had attended the Sherman Institute in Riverside and had tried out for the Los Angeles Angels of the PCL. Harry also added A. S. Padilla, a Mexican American player from the amateur Pasadena squad, and Native American William Watkins. He renamed the trio

Fushima, Yama, and Naza (later changed to Naga) and attempted to pass them off as Japanese. A writer for the *Los Angeles Times* proclaimed, "All look the part and they will probably make a lot of the white trash stand for it." Fans, however, became suspicious during the May 10 game against the University of Southern California when the three "appeared strangely bewildered when the manager forgot and gave them some instructions in the Japanese language. In order to quiet the suspicions of the onlookers one of these players addressed the umpire with a string of gibberish that had a strong Spanish accent."[57]

On May 11 Saisho and ten players boarded an east-bound train for Needles, California. The tour had begun. Once again the young men were professional ballplayers living out their dreams.

12

Ballplayers and Diplomats

As the JBBA was about to go on tour in the spring of 1911, the Waseda team arrived in Chicago on May 5 to continue its goodwill series from the previous year in Japan. The teams would meet on the diamond just three times over a six-week period as Waseda would continue its travels and play other squads in between the games.

It was now the University of Chicago's turn to fete the Japanese. During Waseda's first stopover in Chicago the university planned nonstop entertainment. The first night featured a banquet; the next day included a band escort to the ball field, a formal tea party attended by city politicians and dignitaries, and a "smoker" with vaudeville entertainment at the Reynolds Club; the third day the team toured the city, watched a game between the Cubs and St. Louis Cardinals, and dined with Japanese consul Y. Shimizu; more receptions followed on the last day of the team's stay. Each event emphasized the friendship between the schools and the nations.[1]

The *Chicago Tribune*'s staff wit, Richard Henry Little, wrote a long satirical column poking fun at the university's efforts to promote international goodwill:

> All arrangements for the great politeness contest at Marshall Field tomorrow afternoon are complete. While nominally a baseball game . . . the real issue is not a vulgar matter of hits and scores but as to which side will prove the most truly polite. . . . The visitors will receive the most courteous treatment from the moment they arrive on the field. In their honor . . . a life-size photograph of Congressman Hobson will be dragged three times around the diamond and spoken to harshly by each member of the Chicago nine.

The ball that will be employed in the game has been soaked for three days in crushed rose petals, distilled essence of wild violet, and eau de cologne. After being carefully dried, it will be sprinkled with violet sachet powder and crushed geranium leaves. The bats to be used will be made of rosewood incrusted with diamonds and tied with pink satin ribbons. The young women of the university will preside at lovely floral booths to be placed at the bases for the convenience of the Japanese runners. At first base ice cream and cake will be served, at second base humming birds' tongues on toast, and at third base young orchids fried in honey.[2]

The game itself, however, was hard fought. Chicago went out to a comfortable 5–0 lead in the top of the third inning on four Waseda fielding errors and a costly mental mistake. It looked like a repeat of the one-sided games from the previous October, but Waseda had improved greatly since the fall. The Japanese settled down and held the home team to just one more run as they scored with a perfectly executed squeeze play in the bottom of the third inning. Down 6–1 in the bottom of the ninth, Waseda fought back with timely hits and aggressive base running. With one out Hitoshi Oi connected for a triple and moments later raced home on a weak grounder bobbled by the pitcher. Consecutive singles, a fielder's choice, a dropped fly ball, another single, and a stolen base brought left fielder Goro Mikami to the plate with runners on second and third, two outs, and Waseda down by two. A single would tie the game and make Mikami a hero. In the packed stands many Chicagoans switched allegiance, rooting for the visitors. But it would not be. Mikami swung hard but popped meekly to the pitcher to end the game.[3]

Mikami's destiny would change just a few days later. After leaving Chicago, Waseda headed southwest to play local college teams. It squeaked out a 2–1 victory in the fourteenth inning against Monmouth College before traveling down the road to Knox College, a small liberal arts school in rural Galesburg, Illinois.

Wednesday, May 10, was unseasonably hot—the local paper called it "a scorcher." By the time Goro Mikami stepped into the batter's box to lead off the first inning, the temperature hovered around 90 degrees. The heat may have drained Mikami and his teammates as both would have off days. Goro would go hitless in five at bats. The game fell apart for Waseda in the top of the second inning as a series of errors led to five runs and an eventual 8–4 Knox victory.[4]

Although we do not know what it was, something special caught Mikami's fancy that day at Knox College. Two years later, after he had graduated from Waseda, he returned to the United States and enrolled at Knox as a freshman. He stayed for three years, becoming the school's starting shortstop and team captain. The *Chicago Tribune* noted that he was "one of the fastest infielders in the middle west."[5]

In the summer of 1914, after completing his freshman year, Mikami joined the mixed-race All Nations barnstorming team. J. Leslie Wilkinson formed the famous club in 1912 in Des Moines, Iowa, and later moved its base to Kansas City, Missouri. As the name implied, the team contained players from various ethnicities or "nations." It fielded African Americans, Hispanics, Asians, Native Americans, Caucasians, and for a short time a woman called Carrie Nation. Although the club would entertain audiences with various diversions—dances, shadow ball, wrestlers—the baseball squad itself was top-notch and included several great Negro League players such as John Donaldson, Jose Mendez, and Cristobal Torriente. The team spent most of its time touring the Midwest until it disbanded for the first time in 1919. It re-formed in the early 1920s but never regained its previous popularity.

Box scores show that Mikami played both shortstop and outfield for the team in August 1914 and again in 1915. Nowhere is he listed as "Jap Mikado," a nickname erroneously assigned to him by historian Kazuo Sayama in 1996 and since reused by numerous writers.[6] Sayama and other historians have also mistakenly credited Mikami as Japan's first professional ballplayer.[7] Not only did Guy Green's Japanese Base Ball Team predate the All Nation's club by six years, but Mikami was not even the first Japanese to play for All Nations. From 1912 to 1914 a player identified only as "Naito" played right field for the squad. Little is known about Naito. The *Waterloo Evening Courier* calls him "the Jap from the University of Chicago," while the *Aurelia Sentinel* claims that he came "directly from the university at Tokio [sic], Japan, and is considered the best player on the team."[8] A 1912 article lists his first initial as "K," but no other source verifies this.[9] No "Naito" appears in University of Chicago yearbooks from the period, but a Naito did play on Guy Green's 1906 squad. Could this be the same person? Unfortunately the answer is currently unknown.

In September 1916 Mikami transferred to the University of Illinois at Urbana-Champaign and finished his degree in economics. During the summer of 1916 he played in Salt Lake City as his spot on All Nations was filled by Isamu Tashiro.[10] After graduating, he would join Mitsui Bussan, the large Japanese trading company, and work in New York City. Later he would head Mitsui's Shanghai office.[11]

Following the loss to Knox, Waseda played well in Illinois, beating Northwestern, 4–1, and taking the second game of the double-header against Ames College, 3–2, after narrowly losing the first game, 1–0, in ten innings. On May 22 the team arrived in Iowa City to tackle the University of Iowa. About three hundred students welcomed the Japanese visitors with a reception on the steps of the liberal arts building. Professors and local politicians gave welcoming speeches as a band played in their honor. The next day the two teams met at 4:30 on the diamond. Taking the mound for the Hawkeyes was their blue-eyed star, Burton A. Baird—the same young man who had defeated Guy Green's Japanese as a fourteen-year-old in 1906. Baird once again pitched well against the Japanese, holding them scoreless for five innings before giving up lone runs in the sixth and eighth innings. But this time he was outpitched by Sutekichi Matsuda, who limited the Iowa boys to just three hits and no runs for the win.[12]

Waseda spent the next three weeks playing schools in the Great Lakes region and finishing the series with the University of Chicago. On the diamond the Japanese rarely impressed opponents. After the win against Iowa they dropped nine straight, including a 13–1 beating by the University of Illinois and a second loss to Chicago (9–6).

Facing Chicago for the third time on June 17, Waseda nearly pulled off an upset. It was homecoming weekend, and an estimated one thousand alumni watched as the two teams pounded the ball in the early innings. Each had scored four when Chicago brought home six runs in the top of the third to build a seemingly insurmountable

10–4 lead entering the eighth inning. Then the Chicago got sloppy. A series of Chicago errors combined with timely Waseda hitting led to five runs and a 10–9 score as they entered the ninth. Both teams scored twice more in the final inning as Chicago salvaged a 12–11 victory. After the last out Chicago president Harry Pratt Judson presented the Waseda players with medals and a silver cup to commemorate the games and the friendship between the schools.[13]

Chicago Tribune satirist Richard Henry Little was partially correct when he had quipped "the real issue is not a vulgar matter of hits and scores but as to which side will prove the most truly polite." Although the primary reason for Waseda's visit to the United States was to improve the team's baseball skills, it was also an educational opportunity for the players and a chance to strengthen U.S.-Japanese relations.

Prior to the team's departure from Japan Count Shigenobu Okuma, the founder of Waseda University and former prime minister of Japan, told team manager Takizo Takasugi to impress upon the American people that rumors of war between the two counties had no foundation. As the players traveled to college campuses in the Midwest to play ball, they also acted as ambassadors, spreading goodwill toward Japan through their gentlemanly behavior and expressions of friendship. "This is a wonderful country," team captain Matsuda told reporters. "The more we see of it, the more we like it."[14] "These international matches . . . should be made an annual affair," added Takasugi. "It shows a friendly feeling between Japan and [the] United States. . . . The only battles will be on the baseball diamond."[15] A writer for the *Tipton Tribune* concluded:

> These young men have done a great deal to counteract the feeling propagated by alarmists that the Japanese are avowed enemies of this country and that they are only planning for a war with us. As a matter of fact, the Japs are trying to cultivate a friendly feeling for this country and are seeking a closer relation. . . . It is only regretted that there are not other ways in which this kindly feeling could be cultivated and that the American mind abused of the idea that the Japs are blood drinkers and that war is their profession and only diversion.[16]

Occasionally Takasugi addressed politics directly, openly attacking Richmond Pearson Hobson. In early May he told the press, "The war talk of Richmond Pearson Hobson and the yellow newspapers is all bosh. In Japan, when we speak of Hobson, we say: 'First hero, now fool.' When I was here before he was running around kissing and being kissed. And now he wants war."[17] A month later Takasugi, describing Hobson as a "double bonehead," spoke to a large audience at a Methodist Episcopal Church in Indianapolis. "Your man Hobson, who has been shouting War! War! War! Evidently lacks knowledge of our country or he would not talk as he does. Our people love the United States. . . . We regard your country as our greatest friend. . . . Talk of war between the two countries is nonsense."[18]

Most newspapers covering Waseda's tour praised the team for mastering the American pastime as well as the players' gentlemanly demeanor. Yet not all the midwestern newspapers ran flattering descriptions or supported Waseda's efforts to spread international goodwill. On May 18 the *Cincinnati Post* ran a large cartoon at the top of the sports section under the headline, "Yellow Peril in New Dress" (fig. 29). The illustration depicts the Japanese players in the yellow-face style reminiscent of the early cartoons from Waseda's 1905 tour. The cartoon is dominated by a caricature of an overweight grinning Asian in a baseball uniform with "Jap Ball Team" across his chest. A smaller, scrappy-looking Caucasian player, wielding a bat in one hand like a club and shaking his other fist at the Asian player, yells, "Bring on your Yellow Peril!!" The imagery paints the Americans as underdogs bravely facing down the menacing Asian hordes. To underscore the Japanese threat a vignette to the right of the large Asian player depicts a small, simian-looking Japanese ballplayer with a toothy grin flipping an American umpire with a jiujitsu move above the caption, "If the Japs should be handed a bunk decision."

Accompanying the cartoon was an article titled "Japanese Fans Need Lessons in Etiquette," in which Major League pitcher Bill Burns complained about his treatment by the Japanese fans. "Burns says the Jap fans have a great deal to learn about baseball etiquette; that they are the most unfair bugs he has ever run across," wrote By Ros. "I got a taste of Japanese unfairness when I played in Japan with the All-American team two years ago last fall," Burns told Ros. "I thought that as visitors to their country we would at least be treated courteously. But I was badly mistaken, for the Jap fans certainly gave us a raw deal. American fans support a man when he makes a sterling catch or a great stop. They do the same over in Japan, if a home player makes [a] brilliant play, but hiss an opposing player. Whenever we made an error that aided the Japanese team we were pitted against, the Jap fans applauded vigorously."[19]

The combination of the cartoon and article produced the powerful message that despite the baseball exchanges, the Japanese did not truly understand the game and were not completely trustworthy. The *Post*, although not vehemently anti-Japanese, was a pro-labor paper that routinely depicted the Japanese as both an international and a domestic threat.

No other newspaper was as openly anti-Japanese as that issue of the *Cincinnati Post*, but others belittled the Waseda team with the usual derogatory language, calling the players "little yellow men" and "tricky Orientals" or using stereotypical Japanese expressions, such as "honorable umpire."[20] Russell Brown of the *Bloomington Daily Student* poked fun at the goodwill tour by blatantly plagiarizing sections of Richard Henry Little's satirical article from the *Chicago Tribune*. *Sporting Life* even reprinted a lame racial joke first published in the *Philadelphia North American*: "How can the Waseda University baseball team of Japs, now touring America, expect to win? No matter how gamely they play, it will be impossible for them to keep from 'showing the yellow.'"[21]

Nonetheless, these were the exceptions. Most newspapers seemed to agree with the *Dubuque Telegraph-Herald*: "To promote peace . . . [one] can adopt no means better than to encourage baseball rivalry between Japanese and American teams. There remains through all of life a bond of attachment between boys who played 'two old cat' together, and between the members of rival teams there is mutual respect. Two nations each passionately fond of baseball, whatever their other differences might be, would find it difficult to go to war with each other."[22]

Promoting understanding and peace through baseball was also on Harry Saisho's mind. In March he wrote the *Albuquerque Morning Journal* (and probably other newspapers):

Dear Sir:

Please work at paper. If your town agree to use [*sic*] we want a game or more. Battle on the baseball [diamond between] two nations and peace and joy between two countr[ies].

Yours truly,

Harry A. Saisho[23]

Intrigued, Daniel Padilla, manager of the Albuquerque Grays, wrote back offering to play.

On May 10 Saisho and his JBBA boarded a train in Los Angeles and headed east toward Albuquerque, New Mexico. From there the team would follow the railroads north into Colorado, then east through Kansas to St. Louis. The club would then spend the entire summer barnstorming in Missouri, Illinois, and Iowa. Saisho had scheduled a few games before the team left California, but most games would be arranged only a few weeks in advance through letters, postcards, and telegrams sent to local teams each time the JBBA entered a new region. By October the team would cover almost four thousand miles, play about 130 games, and be the most successful Japanese-owned barnstorming team in history.

After stops for games at Needles, Holbrook, and Gallup, the JBBA arrived in Albuquerque on May 14 for the much-anticipated game against the Grays. As it was the first Japanese ball club to ever play in the city, a huge crowd was expected for the Sunday afternoon game. The *Albuquerque Morning Journal* gushed with excitement under the headline, "Dan Padilla's Men Tackle Minions of Mikado, Struggle Likely to Live in Fan History":

> Let everybody go to the ball game! And let everybody whoop 'em up for the Grays, while the locals wallop the Japs. The big international battle of the diamond comes off at Traction Park this afternoon when the only professional Jap baseball team in the United States, a team that is accorded to be stronger than the University teams that are at present visiting the country and taking all the fast colleges into camp, cross bats with the Albuquerque Grays. It is authoritatively stated that the Jap baseball teams are drawing like a circus everywhere they go. The interesting spectacle of the little brown men, playing the big

American game, and coaching and signaling in their own language is said to be a sight for the gods and fans.[24]

The game would start at 3 p.m., but first the team needed to find a drug store. One of the hotels on the trip from Los Angeles had been infested with fleas. Some of the players were covered with little red welts that itched! The twenty-five cents for flea powder was fairly expensive, more than a player's meal, but well worth the money for the suffering men.[25]

Unfortunately "the game was rotten," complained the *Morning Journal*. The Grays had unleashed a secret weapon—Traction Park. Located at the county fairgrounds on the infield of the race track, the ball field had a notorious reputation for difficult conditions. During wet spells poor drainage created "a much better place for ducks than for ball players." During dry spells "swirling clouds of alkali dust" blinded players.[26] It was a dry day. "The wind was blowing a gale and the sand would engulf both bleachers, grandstand and players during critical points of the game. The little Japs, not used to such treatment on the part of the elements, could not see, and under the influence of the sharp gusts of wind the ball didn't net naturally to them." The JBBA committed six errors and allowed other balls to fall untouched for hits as the Grays romped to an easy 10–5 victory. Nevertheless, the crowd seemed pleased with the spectacle and praised the determination of the Japanese, who did not let the lopsided score "deter them from going back up to the slaughter willingly and making a good effort."[27] Ken Kitsuse and Toyo Fujita had outstanding days at the plate, each gaining three hits in four at bats. On the base paths Kitsuse stole four bases while Fujita swiped two.

Despite the loss the JBBA made a killing at the gate. With the preparations for the barnstorming tour—purchasing equipment, advertising, and sundries—the team had left Los Angeles in the hole by sixty-five cents. The gate receipts from the games en route to Albuquerque refilled the coffers. Receiving 50 percent of ticket sales, Saisho's team earned $59.80 at Needles, $24.75 at Holbrook, $89.20 at Gallup, and a glorious $125 at Albuquerque. Daily expenses included about $8 for hotels, $10 for meals, and a few dollars for miscellaneous items. By the time the team left Albuquerque, just a week after the start of the tour, it was $206.40 in the black.

On May 15 the team headed northeast toward Colorado. It stopped along the way, playing at Santa Fe, Las Vegas, and Raton, New Mexico, before arriving at Trinidad, Colorado, on May 20. Today Trinidad is a small town of nine thousand, but in 1911 it was a booming commercial center for the surrounding coal mines, a railroad hub, and a stop along the Santa Fe Trail. Mine operators, merchants, and professionals lived in stately houses, while workers crowded rickety boarding houses and flocked to the town's many saloons and notorious brothels.

Trinidad also became a baseball hub. The mines, railroad, and larger businesses all fielded teams. The town team, known as the Big Six, recruited the area's top players and won the state championship in 1907. For a time famed journalist Damon Runyon managed the Bix Six, while pioneer female sportswriter Ina Eloise Young covered the team for the local *Chronicle News*. Both writers had moved on by the time the JBBA came to town.[28]

Southern Colorado's mining region was not known for its tolerance of Japanese immigrants. When the first group arrived to work the mines in 1902, local miners boycotted the new workers, forcing them from their jobs. A couple of years later, during a period of labor strife, mining companies brought in Issei and Mexicans as strikebreakers. Hostility toward Japanese became intense.[29] In early 1911 anti-Japanese sentiment was on the rise throughout Colorado, fueled both by white concern over cheap Japanese labor and by Richmond Pearson Hobson's war mongering. In late March a series of random attacks occurred throughout the state. On March 17 in Greeley, scores of local men and boys attacked the home of merchant George Ikeda, smashing windows as Ikeda and his wife hid in the basement. Police arrived and dispersed the mob before it could enter the house. Six days later eight white men attacked Japanese agricultural laborers in the western part of the state, forcing the immigrants to leave the area. That same night a Japanese cleaning establishment in Denver was pelted with stones and bricks. The city ordered police to protect Japanese inhabitants and their property.[30]

The JBBA played a doubleheader at Trinidad, with Harry Saisho making a rare appearance behind the plate. Kitsuse pitched the opener while William Watkins, the Native American renamed "Naga," pitched the second. Neither game went well for the Japanese. The Trinidad team pounded both pitchers, winning 11–1 and 8–0. In keeping with the recent wave of bigotry the *Chronicle News* mocked the visitors and all Japanese with an insulting account of the games, supposedly written by "Dr. Katsuma Kiyo, Special Japanese Korrespondent to Hon. Kronickle News." Titled "Honorable Trinidads Bingo Honorable Cork Center Very Much Japanese Boys No Can Hit Same," the article is written in fake Japanese pidgin English, emphasizing the Issei's foreignness, supposed inability to assimilate, and the superiority of the white opponents:

> The Hon. Jap ball team, him one fine class aggravation—play twice ball game with Hon. Trinidad 'Mericans, and two times lose to classified bunch of local maps by big scorings. First game played in bitterness cold weather, and Hon. Japs get long row of nothingness and Hon. Trinidads cross home plate by grand stand yelling, eight times. Hon. Japs work hard like fat mans to crank automobile but can no find Hon. Jack Nash [the pitcher], so game lose. . . .
>
> Hon. Carpenter, him umps what fan swear at, just like rotten—start game beginnings by sayings: "Batteries: honorable Japs, Katsusa and Suzurki."—sound like big sneeze and Hon. peoples in grand stand laughter and remark: "What is it—Something to eat?"—and Hon. Carpenter say some more to peoples and then slaughter commencement, just like at stock yards. . . .
>
> Both games show honorable white mans more superior over honorable Japs. Little fellows no match for Hon. Trinidad, but never kick like hell when Hon. umpire make bad decision. Japs quiet bunch, just like mother-in-law that never was. Play clean game, do Japs—just like Gentleman. Indians in honorable Jap team wear false names like stage actresses and nobody knows difference on score cards.[31]

After the game at Trinidad, Harry Saisho made a decision. The team had secured some games through letters and telegrams, but to play every day would need an advance man—somebody to travel ahead of the team, schedule games, and distribute advertising. Saisho's skills behind the plate had been deteriorating, and he had already spent more time managing than on the diamond. He would give up playing the game he loved and become the advance man. In his absence Arthur Shiomichi would manage the team. On May 21 Saisho took $16.25 of the team's cash and left on a train to Kansas City.[32]

The rest of the players also headed east on the Atchison, Topeka and Santa Fe Railroad, but instead of continuing straight to Kansas City, they made daily stops to play games. The series started off well with their first recorded win—beating Garden City, 5–3, on May 22. Three years earlier the small town had hosted Tozan Masko's Mikado's for two games, topping the visitors twice. This time, excited by the exotic visitors, Garden City closed all the businesses and shops on Main Street during game time so that its 1,500 residents could watch the game. A "fairly good crowd" showed up to witness a "nifty" game.[33] After besting Garden City, the team lost close games to Dodge City and the African American semi-pro Hutchinson Sunflowers; was trounced, 19–2, by Halstead; and beat Strong City, 8–6. Despite the close game the reporter for the *Hutchinson Daily Gazette* was unimpressed by the quality of play. "If the delegation of Japanese, representing the baseball team in Hutchinson yesterday are considered high class Japanese baseball players, the Americans need to have no fear that the Orientals will rob us of the glory and excitement of our national pastime. . . . Owing to their small stature they are unable to cover as much ground as the Yankee, can't throw nor can they think fast enough."[34]

On the morning of May 27 the players arrived at Kansas City after an all-night train ride. Putting their luggage into storage at the train station, they grabbed a quick breakfast and the trolley to the Old Soldiers Home, officially called the Western Branch, National Home for Disabled Volunteer Soldiers, in Leavenworth, just north of the city. Residents were looking forward to the game, and a large crowd was expected. The *Leavenworth Times* ran a long article previewing the game and, befitting the game's location, made liberal use of military metaphors. The favorable article noted, "The little brown men are quick on their feet and are cunning in baseball as well as in warfare and for this reason they are well adapted to the game." The writer, however, was not up to Japanese names. "[I] was given the lineup . . . over the telephone yesterday but as the names of some of the players can only be spelled and not pronounced a lineup will not be published."[35]

The game began at 2:45 p.m. with a hiccup, as umpire "Red" Conlin announced, "Batteries for today's game: Schineer and Gardner for the Home and . . ." He paused uncomfortably, struggled to pronounce the pitcher's name, and then, thinking quickly, spelled out, "S-c-h-i-r-a and S-u-z-u-k-i for the visitors."[36]

Right away it looked like the JBBA would run away with the game with its predicted speed and cunningly played "scientific baseball." Tokutaro Tachiyama began with a clean hit to right field but instead of stopping at first, aggressively stretched it into a double. Kitsuse then laid down a perfect bunt single that advanced Tachiyama to third. A wild pitch scored Tachiyama and moved Kitsuse to second. Fujita next drove a hit over the shortstop's head to score Kitsuse. After Minori Sohara hit into a fielder's choice, Naga singled home Sohara as the throw to nab him at third went wild. By the end of the inning the sharp-looking JBBA led, 3–0.

But the lead would not last long. Unable to start its best pitcher, Naga, who had pitched the day before, the JBBA put Sohara on the mound. By the end of the fourth Sohara had surrendered a dozen hits and ten runs. Playing on little sleep, the JBBA's offense stumbled, gaining only two hits after the first inning in the eventual 13–6 loss. Once again spectators left unimpressed with the Japanese playing. "The game yesterday," concluded a writer for the *Leavenworth Times*, "showed that baseball is a game which belongs to Americans."[37]

Following the game the team took the trolley back to Kansas City, retrieved bags at the train station, and checked into the Morgan Hotel. The next day, Sunday, May 28, it would play the famed Kansas City Giants in the second game of a doubleheader at Association Park. Founded in 1907 by Tobe Smith, the Giants of Kansas City, Kansas, were one of the premier African American teams in the Midwest. In 1909 they won fifty-four straight games and topped the Chicago Leland Giants in a best-of-three series to determine "the colored championship of the United States and a purse of $1,000."[38] The team was strong again in 1911. Led by playing manager Topeka Jack Johnson, it would go 18-7 against other black professional teams. Johnson, a former professional boxer, had played with the Chicago Union Giants from 1903 to 1905. The Giants also featured Bingo DeMoss, one of the top second basemen in Negro League history.[39] A huge crowd was expected at Association Park, partly because the JBBA was mistakenly billed as Keio University.[40]

The mix-up was not surprising, as Keio had been in Kansas City just two weeks earlier. After leaving California, the Keio team had traveled through Colorado and Kansas, playing well against the top universities and drawing accolades at each stop. The team's "orderly conduct, their clever inside baseball, and antics on the field have kept the crowds in splendid good humor out of admiration for them," wrote the *Wisconsin Rapids Daily Tribune*.[41] On May 12 Keio had arrived in the city to face a semi-professional team organized by future Hall of Famer Charles "Kid" Nichols. Nichols had retired to Kansas City a few years earlier after a sixteen-year pitching career in the Major Leagues, where he had won 361 games between 1890 and 1906. In 1911 he was forty-one years old and active in the city's baseball and bowling leagues. To the surprise, and even delight, of the spectators, Keio rallied from behind, scoring four runs off the great pitcher in the eighth inning to win, 7–6. The *Kansas City Star* praised the visitors' play and seemed particularly impressed when ace Kazuma Sugase defied the stereotype of the polite Japanese by hurling his glove to the ground and barking at the umpire in Japanese after a missed third-strike call.[42] Although Keio moved on to Missouri the following day, it remained in the Midwest for several weeks, making it possible that it had returned to Kansas City to play the Giants. It would not be the first time, nor the last, that the JBBA would be confused with the collegiate teams. Perhaps Saisho encouraged the confusion to increase attendance.

About "1,600 fans . . . wild with excitement, screaming for the game to start" packed Association Park for the Sunday matchup. The JBBA decided to bill itself for the day as the Tokio Japanese University. The Giants had already defeated the Kansas City Cyclones with their usual starting pitcher, Chick Harper, in the opening game, so they gave the mound to a non-roster pitcher listed only as "Chambers." Chambers held the Japanese in check, not allowing a single tally as the Giants won easily, 7–0.[43] Despite the outcome the team did well, as its share of the gate receipts totaled $66.30.

The loss to the Giants marked the end of the first stage of JBBA's barnstorming tour. The following day, May 29, the team would board a train to St. Louis to begin a tour of the Midwest. On the diamond this first stage had been rough. The team had lost nine of the eleven recorded games (the results of four games are unknown), often by lopsided scores. Although it could play competitively with small-town teams, it was no match for other independent or stronger amateur squads.

Financially, however, the tour so far had been a great success. Gate receipts for the fifteen games had brought in $809.15, for an average of $54 per game. The larger towns of Albuquerque, Trinidad, Gallup, and Kansas City were the most lucrative, while the game at Halstead (with a population of one thousand) brought in a measly $11.40. Operating expenses, including hotels, food, train tickets, and player salaries, came to $469.75, giving the team a surplus of nearly $350.[44] Perhaps the players' choice to give up their day jobs and become professional ballplayers would pay off.

1. Atsuyoshi "Harry" Saisho, 1903. Author's collection. Courtesy of Taro Saisho.

2. Ken Kitsuse, ca. 1913. Ken Kitsuse Collection.

3. Tozan Masko, 1908. Author's collection.

4. Shin Hashido, 1905. National Baseball Hall of Fame and Museum.

5. Waseda University Baseball Team, 1905. Author's collection.

6. Detail of cartoon depicting Japanese fans from *San Francisco Chronicle*, May 3, 1905.

7. Cartoon of Waseda players from *Los Angeles Examiner*, May 16, 1905.

8. Illustration of Waseda and Sherman Indians from *Los Angeles Examiner*, May 21, 1905.

9. Nebraska Indians Team, 1907, with Guy Green (#10), Kissell (#4), Tobey (#6), and Seguin (#11). Author's collection.

10. Uyeda brothers. From left to right: Junjiro, Takatomo (Bob), and Tetsusaburo (Tom). Courtesy of Tom Tucker and the Ueda family.

11. Dan Tobey, ca. 1908.
Author's collection.

12. Green's Japanese Base
Ball Team advertising card.
Ken Kitsuse Collection.

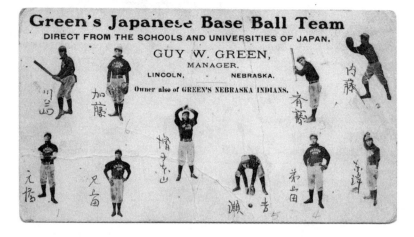

13. Tom Uyeda, 1906.
Courtesy of Tom Tucker
and the Ueda family.

14. Umekichi "Kitty"
Kawashima, 1906. Ken
Kitsuse Collection.

15. Toyo Fujita, 1911. Ken Kitsuse Collection.

16. Ken Kitsuse, 1906. Courtesy of Jesse Loving, Ars Longa Art Cards.

ANNUAL TOUR OF

Mikado's Japanese Base Ball Team

DIRECT FROM THE SCHOOLS AND UNIVERSITIES OF JAPAN

*THE MOST MARVELOUS TEAM OF GENUINE JAPANESE BALL
PLAYERS ON EARTH, AND THE ONLY ONE IN AMERICA*

TOZAN T. MASKO, Proprietor, Denver, Colo.

Telephone Purple 306   **1232 Twenty-First Street**

17. Mikado's Japanese Base Ball Team letterhead, 1908. Author's collection.

18. Cartoon from *Denver Times*, February 21, 1908.

19. Mikado's Base Ball Team, 1908. Courtesy of Tom Tucker.

20. Richmond Pearson Hobson, 1898. Library of Congress Prints and Photographs Division, Washington DC.

21. Kiichi Suzuki, 1911. Ken Kitsuse Collection.

22. Nanka players, ca. 1908. Author's collection.

23. Atsuyoshi "Harry" Saisho, ca. 1908. Ken Kitsuse Collection.

24. The Nanka team practicing behind 636 S. Maple Avenue, Los Angeles. Author's collection.

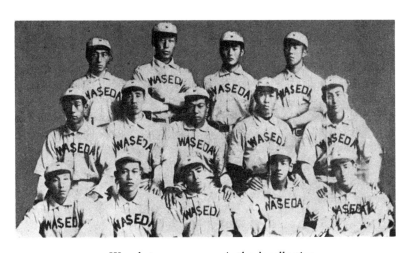

25. Waseda team, 1910–11. Author's collection.

26. Keio team, 1910–11. Author's collection.

27. JBBA team, 1911. Front row (left to right): Toyo Fujita, Atsuyoshi "Harry" Saisho, Kiichi Suzuki, Tokutaro Tachiyama, and Ken Kitsuse. Back row: Kesaichi "Arthur" Shiomichi, Umekichi "Kitty" Kawashima, Minori Sohara, Takaji Kubo, Shoichi Motohashi, Riichiro Shiraishi, and Naga (William Watkins). Ken Kitsuse Collection.

28. Goro Mikami of Waseda University, 1911. Courtesy of Robert Klevens.

29. Cartoon from *Cincinnati Post*, May 18, 1911.

30. JBBA game action, 1911. Ken Kitsuse Collection.

31. JBBA game action, 1911. Ken Kitsuse Collection.

32. Tetsusaburo "Tom" Uyeda, ca. 1940. Courtesy of Tom Tucker and the Ueda family.

33. Atsuyoshi "Harry" Saisho, Ken Kitsuse, and Kiichi Suzuki, 1956.
Ken Kitsuse Collection.

13

Barnstorming across America

With Harry Saisho traveling ahead setting up games, the JBBA entered Illinois on June 4 to begin a six-week stay before heading to Iowa. But in some areas of these states, Japanese may not have been welcome.

Rural parts of Iowa and Illinois contained numerous "Sundown Towns"—places where only whites could stay after dark. Immediately after the Civil War sympathy toward the newly emancipated African Americans was strong. Northern Republicans passed legislation protecting black civil rights, as specified in the Fourteenth and Fifteenth Amendments, ensuring citizenship and extending the right to vote to Africa Americans. Blacks moving north into midwestern communities were often welcome, although they were rarely truly integrated, usually settling in clusters on the edge of town.[1] From the mid-1870s to early 1880s this idealism faded as Darwinian theories of racial supremacy took hold. By the late 1880s the Jim Crow era had replaced this brief window of racial inclusion. African Americans were denied access to public places such as restaurants, hotels, schools, and barbershops and excluded from certain occupations, including professional baseball.

In the midst of this strengthening racism many northern towns in the 1890s became all white. Sociologist James W. Loewen, an authority on Sundown Towns, argues that this shift happened in two stages. The first attack was against Chinese. By 1884 about one hundred thousand Chinese immigrants lived in the western United States, spread throughout the region. As anti-Chinese sentiment grew during the 1880s and 1890s, towns across the West drove out Chinese residents, forcing them into the urban enclaves known as Chinatowns. The second stage began in the 1890s, when rural whites began forcing black residents from towns across the Midwest. In some places Hispanics, Native Americans, Asians, and Jews were also expelled. After the purges minorities were allowed in town to work and complete tasks but were required to leave before dark. Many of these towns posted signs reading, "Whites Only after Dark," leading to the term "Sundown Towns." Loewen concludes that there were hundreds of such communities, including entire counties, across Illinois and Iowa— the very region where the JBBA was traveling.

The JBBA seems to have avoided many Sundown Towns. The area in Illinois south of present-day Route 70 was notorious for the high number of white-only towns. The JBBA dodged the area altogether, entering Illinois north of St. Louis and traveling northeast as far as Earlville before returning southwest through central Illinois and crossing into Iowa at Fort Madison. We do not know if the team purposely avoided this area, if Saisho tried but was unable to arrange games there, or if the team entered Illinois to the north by chance.

A plotting of the JBBA's route through central Illinois, along with known and suspected Sundown Towns, shows that the team bypassed many white-only communities to play in more welcoming places. But with over 360 suspected Sundown Towns in Illinois, they were difficult to avoid. Of the JBBA's forty-three games in Illinois, twelve were in Sundown Towns. How this affected the Japanese ballplayers is unclear. In some towns the ban may not have extended to Asians, or citizens may not have objected to the ball team staying one night in a hotel. The team's account book shows that it spent the night in nine of the twelve Sundown Towns, including Beardstown, which a few decades later would contain a strong KKK contingent and a sign warning African Americans to keep out.

The data for Sundown Towns in Iowa are not as complete as those for Illinois, so comparing the JBBA's schedule with Sundown Towns is not fruitful. Yet in at least one instance the team played, but did not sleep in, a Sundown Town. On August 12 the players woke up in Pella, took a bus and then a train twenty-one miles to Bussey, played the game, had supper in town, and then took another train fifteen miles to Albia, where they stayed the night at the Monroe Hotel.

The JBBA's Illinois tour began with an altercation. On the first day the team arrived by train at Greenfield, a town of just one thousand inhabitants, sixty miles north of St. Louis. Residents were excited to host the unusual visitors and canceled a game with the Jacksonville Printers to accommodate the Japanese team's schedule. A crowd of about two hundred, a quarter of the town, watched the home team grab an early 7–0 lead. The visitors impressed the spectators with their slick fielding and daring base running, but the JBBA had trouble hitting pitcher Roy Hedgecock's screwball—then known as a fadeaway—as he struck out sixteen. Hedgecock was also not afraid to throw inside, hitting three batters. The Japanese calmly took their bases without comment. Late in the game Naga, who had been struggling with his control throughout the game, hit Hedgecock with a pitch. Believing that he had been struck on purpose, Hedgecock and his brother Ira charged Naga, and "for a time it looked like there might be a race war between the Hedgecock family and the Japanese nation." Spectators stormed onto the field but instead of escalating the ruckus, separated the players and restored order. Perhaps to the Japanese players' surprise, the hometown fans blamed the Hedgecocks for the "unwarranted attack [which] took all pleasure out of the contest."[2]

The defeat at Greenfield kicked off a losing streak as the team headed northeast through central Illinois. From June 4 to 15 the JBBA played twelve games, dropping at least eleven (the result of one is unknown). Opponents were mostly town teams drawn from municipalities with fewer than three thousand residents—hardly the state's top ball clubs. At Lewistown the JBBA lost to "a scrub team made up of the younger ballists and a few has-beens" who were playing together for the first time.[3]

With the losing streak the team realized that it had to bolster its lineup. It was already relying on William Watkins (Naga) as its primary pitcher, but it also needed a better catcher. For the first month the Japanese players took turns filling the position. Saisho had proved inadequate, and the *Hutchinson Daily Gazette* noted that although Kitsuse was "a nice receiver . . . his throwing is a joke." On June 11 they sent a telegram from Bloomington to Kansas City requesting help and soon afterward transferred money to purchase train tickets for two men identified only as Hobart and Shields.[4]

Hobart, a Native American, debuted behind the plate on June 14 at Minonk, using the stage name Oyama, while Shields, a Caucasian, took the mound using his own name. Both men gave a jolt to the lineup—Oyama gained three hits and Shields two—but Shields was less than stellar on the mound, surrendering nine runs for the loss.[5] The two players stayed with the team for about two weeks before returning to Kansas City. Their presence helped but did not turn the JBBA into a winning squad—the team went 3-8, with the results of four games unknown. At times the team still looked embarrassingly weak. "The Japanese may be great fighters," complained a reporter for the *Earlville Leader*, "but the little brown men who came to Earlville last Tuesday could not play ball a little bit—at least they put up such a tame article that the crowd sort of kicked itself for having believed that it was to see a ball game."[6]

Yet in most towns, spectators left the ballparks thrilled by the home team's victory in an interesting, close game. "A great game," "greatly enjoyed by the crowd," and "one of the most brilliant games of the season," concluded some reporters.[7] Often after the visitors had been upset by the locals, newspapers praised them, making the victory seem even more impressive. "The Japanese were in excellent condition and gave our boys one of the best contests of the season," exclaimed the *Henry Times*. "They are lively little fellows and good natured and play the game like professionals."[8]

After Hobart's departure on June 26 the JBBA decided to hire another "Oyama." On June 28 James G. Blain, described as a big, powerful, full-blooded Oklahoma Indian and a corking good ballplayer, joined the team using the name Oyama.[9] Blain stayed for three weeks and hit in the third spot with a .350 average in his twenty recorded at bats, but the team's record remained roughly the same—just four wins out of the twelve recorded games. During this time the team often called itself the "Tokio Japanese Base Ball team." The new name was both more elegant than "the Japanese Base Ball Association" and made the team sound more exotic. It also created a tie to the more talented and celebrated Tokyo-based Waseda and Keio teams touring the country.

No matter the name, the team had little trouble drawing an audience. Newspapers repeatedly note large crowds in the stands. The ledger book, however, shows that a big turnout in a small town was barely enough to cover expenses. On June 10 as eight-inch hail pelted nearby Bloomington, the team played in front of a "large enthusi-astic crowd" at Minier, but with a town population of only 746, the game brought in just $15.95.[10] Railroad tickets to town, room and board at the local hotel, and a round of beer for the players cost $18.16, leaving the team $2.21 in the hole for the day's work. During the month of June, gate receipts fell under $20 eight times, and only five games brought in more than $50. With the low income the sur-plus gained during the first leg of the tour dwindled. After a poor turn out in Chenoa on June 12 that brought in just $7.80, the team had only $11.39 to its name. Luckily $52.50 of gate receipts from the following day's game at Pontiac replenished the coffers. Rain could be devastating, as the team would have no income but would still need to pay the daily expenses of room, board, train tickets, and sundries. Two days of rain on June 23 and 24 reduced the team's cash from $71.37 to just $27.27, but once again the JBBA bounced back with a few well-attended games and began the month of July with a $122 balance.

On the Fourth of July the team arrived in Versailles, a village of about 550 people, to play in the annual holiday game. Independence Day and baseball have been intertwined since the mid-nineteenth century. Earlier celebrations featured readings of the Declaration of Independence, patriotic speeches, marching bands, and, of course, fireworks, but after the Civil War the holiday became recognized as a day of leisure and sport. About the same time, baseball emerged as the national pastime—explicitly linked to the American national character. The game was believed to both display and teach the Amer-ican values needed for democracy—the combination of individual-istic thinking and teamwork. Love of the sport also helped unify the country, cutting across regional, class, and ethnic lines. For many Americans watching, or playing, baseball on the Fourth became an enjoyable patriotic act. By the early twentieth century no Indepen-dence Day celebration would be complete without a ball game.[11]

But in Versailles the holiday's usual excitement was missing. It was unbearably hot. The temperature would hit 104 degrees at noon and rise to 106 by 4 p.m. Suffering in their heavy wool-flannel uniforms, the JBBA players, advertising themselves as "the only professional baseball team of Japs in the world," lost a morning game, 17–8, to a team of young men from Versailles and nearby Mt. Sterling. After lunch the two teams packed into buggies for the nine-mile trip to Mt. Sterling—a larger town of nearly two thousand inhabitants.[12]

The *Mt. Sterling Democrat Message* had advertised the game earlier in the week: "What is claimed to be the only team of Japanese professional ball players in the world is announced for a game with our local nine at the fairgrounds next Tuesday afternoon at 3 o'clock. The visitors are credited with being experts at baseball and use their native language and signals during the contest. Their opponents will be selected from well-known ball players from the city, with perhaps one or two more from Versailles."[13]

The heat, however, stifled the festivities. It was "the quietest Fourth of July in the history of Mt. Sterling," lamented the *Democrat Message*. "Business was practically suspended and very few people from the country were in town. The weather was intensely hot and everybody sought the shade. . . . The traditional small boy[s] and youth inclined to be rowdyish [*sic*] were mostly quiet, no accidents occurred and the streets this morning showed none of the littered condition usually following a Fourth of July celebration."[14] Nevertheless, two or three hundred fans came to watch the ball game. Tired from the earlier game and the rising heat, the teams played listless ball that ended with a 10–4 Japanese victory.

A week later the local newspaper ran an article on the team. Although it contained several inaccuracies, it was based on a rare interview with Harry Saisho conducted by a reporter for the African American *Iowa State Bystander*.

> During their stay at Macomb last week a *Bystander* reporter had a talk with Saisho, the manager of the Japanese baseball club that visited this city, July 4. His home is at Los Angeles, and he has been in this country long enough to speak fairly good English and become somewhat familiar with American ways. He told the newspaperman that but six of his players are actual residents of Japan, while the others of his countrymen make their homes in California. They are all educated young men, having completed their schoolwork and are touring the country mostly for recreation, but are also making some money. The two Indian players, Oyama, the catcher, and Naga, the pitcher,

are from Kansas City and they were joined at Golden last Wednesday by another of their men. There is a vast deal of difference between the red and brown men on the ball field. The Indians do not hesitate to "chew the rag" and volubly express their dissent when dissatisfied with an umpire's ruling and are prone to say things from the bench. Nothing seems to worry the little brown men. They smile at a good play and merely look somewhat more serious than usual when the tide is going against them, but do not say a word when a close decision deprives their side of an advantage. So far during their tour they have won the greater part of the games, thereby walking off with the big end of receipts. Those played at Versailles and Mt. Sterling last week netted them about $65 for the day's work. Their tour is to end October 1, when the Indian players will go home and most of the Japs are to return to their native country. Saisho says baseball is very popular in Japan, but they do not have it reduced to the science it is in the United States.[15]

With the heat lingering after nightfall, Mt. Sterling's citizens toned down their usual fireworks display. "A few firecrackers, hot air balloon or two, a dozen or so sky rockets and a small number of Roman candles constituted about all the pyrotechnic display visible after nightfall," noted the *Democrat Message*.[16] The Japanese players, however, decided to celebrate on their own, having bought firecrackers and American flags earlier in Versailles that morning.

In New York City the Waseda University team was also celebrating the Fourth of July. The metaphor of the country as a melting pot—the idea that the different customs and beliefs of immigrant groups would be combined and melded to form a stronger culture—had been used since the 1780s but had become increasingly popular in the early twentieth century. Mayor William Gaynor had declared it the theme of New York's 1911 Independence Day celebration and had organized a grand "Parade of All Nations" to celebrate and promote the inclusion of diverse ethnic groups into the United States.

The parade down Broadway began with a contingent of Native Americans—"braves . . . in feathered headpieces and buffalo robes . . . attended by squaws and papooses with beaded moccasins and painted faces"—followed by the Sons of the Revolution marching in colonial dress to the sounds of fife and drum.[17] The firemen came next, dressed in mid-nineteenth-century uniforms of red shirts and buff pants. "Then began a series of newcomers from all parts of earth": Dominicans; Norwegians; Finns; Irish; Swiss; Tyroleans wearing short velvet jackets, tight-fitting knee breeches, and feathered felt hats; Italians "in the garb of gondoliers"; and Greeks dressed in both classical and modern costumes.

The Chinese came next. They were led by Sam Ping Lee, an attorney and prominent community member, dressed in the colorful robes of a Mandarin noble, followed by "several merchants from Chinatown in tall hats and frock coats, perspiring to show how the race had become Americanized." The Merchants Association of Chinatown brought a dragon; operated by forty-five men, "its great body had a sinuous movement as though it were alive." Toward the end of the parade marched the Japanese Waseda baseball team, dressed in team uniforms; a contingent from the Hebrew Orphan Asylum; and Hungarians dressed as hussars.

During the speeches that followed, Mayor Gaynor concluded, "It remain[s] to Americans of this day and generation to continue the amalgamation and unification of the people represented by the procession," while City Comptroller William Prendergast noted "the lesson to be drawn from the Parade of Nations was that never should the bars be raised against immigration." The celebration ended with a benediction from Archdeacon G. F. Nelson and a performance by the police department band. The crowd dispersed, and the Waseda baseball team traveled twenty miles north to play in the Yonkers Field Club's Fourth of July ball game.

After leaving Chicago on June 18, the Waseda team had gone east, playing ball and spreading international goodwill. The squad traveled through Ohio, dropping games to Oberlin College and a Cleveland semi-pro club, before heading to Buffalo, New York, whose fans anxiously awaited the chance to see how Waseda would compare to Keio.

The Keio squad had headed east a month earlier, passing though Indiana, Ohio, West Virginia, Pennsylvania, Washington DC, and New York before heading back to the Great Lakes region. On the diamond Keio did better than Waseda. It would finish its U.S. tour at the end of June with a 21-21-2 record, while Waseda at that point would have an 8-25 record. Visiting Buffalo on May 28, Keio lost, 7–1, to the amateur Pullman team. The fans, however, cheered the Japanese for every good play and went home happy with "a splendid game."[18]

In the week prior to the two scheduled games between Waseda and the Simon Pures—Buffalo's top amateur team—the local papers introduced the Japanese to local fans. The *Buffalo Courier* wrote:

> The Waseda University baseball team is a most noteworthy aggregation. Every one of the players, and there are 14 of them on the roster, is the son of a wealthy and influential subject of the Mikado, and this trip to the New World was approved by them on account of the experience their sons would gain by travel. The Wasedas can play baseball, too. . . . The most peculiar feature of the team is their smallness of stature, which is accentuated by the American baseball uniform. But their very size lends speed to their play and accounts of their games in other cities indicate that the little brown men have nothing to learn of the great American game.[19]

When the players arrived on June 21, prominent locals threw a reception in their honor at the University Club the evening before the first game. The next day about three thousand fans watched the locals top Waseda in "the most interesting amateur games played in this city in a long while." The packed grandstands, "holding many people prominent in the business and social life of Buffalo," supported the Japanese, applauding "every clever play." Despite the losses the papers praised the visitors for "surely master[ing] the national game" and being "a brainy, hard-working and sportsmanlike team."[20]

After a day in Hartford, Connecticut, where the Waseda players toured the city in open-top luxury automobiles, were treated to lunch, and lost to Trinity College, 5–4, they arrived in New York City.[21] Their royal treatment continued in the Big Apple. They attended a Major League game between the Giants and Boston Braves at the Polo Grounds before visiting the Japanese consulate. On July 1 Mayor Gaynor threw out the ceremonial pitch prior to their first game in the city. Over 2,500 spectators, including the Japanese minister to the

United States and hundreds of New York's Japanese, came to Dyckman Oval in northern Manhattan to watch Waseda beat Manhattan College by scoring seven runs in the top of the tenth inning. It would be the only game the Waseda players would win in New York as they lost the Independence Day game to the Yonkers Field Club, 6–2; were out hit by the semi-pro Metropolitans, 6–1; and were held hitless for eight innings as the New York City Fire Department walloped them, 10–0.[22]

Once again, however, Keio had been the first Japanese team to play in the city. It had arrived in the Big Apple on May 26 and stayed just long enough to beat Fordham University, 11–7, at the Bronx Oval before boarding a train for the long trip to Buffalo. The five thousand fans had anticipated "that the Japanese collegians would play a distinctly Oriental brand of the national game, but before the first inning was over it was evident that the Keio nine was putting up a much more American sort of game than the Fordhamites." As soon as they took the field, the players began "to talk it up . . . and the jargon of English and Japanese that drifted across the diamond from the coaching boxes was probably as disconcerting to the Bronx collegians as the fusillade of hits and runs that the Orientals directed at their Yankee opponents." The Keio batters "hit the ball hard . . . plant[ing] themselves firmly, and when they swung on the ball they put every ounce of energy in their bats. But they did not always try to hit it out, for when they had men on bases, they switched over to bunting and put them down where they were most bothersome to the Fordhamites." On the mound Sugase surprised the Americans with his speed and "a puzzling underhand ball that completely fooled the hard-hitting Fordham nine."[23] It was a great showing for the Japanese that was featured in the following season's *Spalding's Official Base Ball Guide* to illustrate how far Japanese baseball had progressed since Waseda's 1905 visit.[24]

On July 7 Waseda traveled to Maryland, where the *Baltimore Sun* had been covering the team's tour and touting its skills since April. But again Keio had set a high bar with its May 26 game against nearby Georgetown. A week before Keio arrived in Washington, the *Washington Post* extolled the team's record against top U.S. colleges and its daring on the base paths. In keeping with the science of the time,

the paper argued that part of Keio's success was due to Japanese natural traits. "True to the oriental trait of shrewdness and powers of
observation, the Japs have a facility of arriving at their opponents'
methods of play. On the other hand, their own marvelous cunning
and intricate signs and foreign expressions mystify even the veterans on the American diamonds."[25]

On game day the *Post* previewed the meeting under the headline,
"Jap Invasion at Last: Keio's Warriors Will Engage Georgetown Nine
Today." "The long-heralded Japanese invasion is scheduled. This,
however, is not the one which Mr. Hobson has viewed with alarm. . . .
These Japanese come carrying bats as war clubs, and using as missiles the five-ounce spheroids that Messrs. Reach or Spalding furnish for such occasions. Keio University is the enemy that must be
repelled, and the Georgetown nine will act as the army of defense."[26]

A huge crowd filled Georgetown Field—"the largest gathering
that has witnessed an athletic exhibition" since the previous year's
Georgetown-Virginia football game. Nearly the entire Japanese delegation came to cheer on its countrymen. Understanding the diplomatic importance of the event, the American fans supported the
Japanese at every turn. "Plays made by them which would have
hardly received more than passing notice had it been an American
team playing, were applauded long and loud."[27] Keio played well,
"putting up a good article of ball from every standpoint" but lost,
3–2, as Georgetown came from behind to win in the top of the ninth
inning. The Keio players "look to be in a class with the college nines
in this country," concluded the *Washington Evening Star*, but "[they]
know baseball a great deal better than the average American college
team," added the *Post*.[28] From Washington the Keio players head back
west, traveling through the Great Lakes region, the Dakotas, and
the Northwest before ending their tour in San Francisco on June 27.

Following Keio's performance, reporters and fans in Baltimore
expected a close game when Waseda met the Maryland Athletic
Club on July 7, and they were quite upset when the Japanese "were
unmercifully beaten," 13–2. "It must be announced right here that
half of the things said about their ability have been exaggerated,"
a reporter complained. "It is safe to go even further than that and
say that they have been poorly coached or that they are not quite

such good imitators as they have been given credit for being. . . . The teams of this country that have been beaten by Waseda College must be pretty weak."[29]

It was the first time since the team had come east that a reporter explicitly questioned the Japanese players' knowledge of the game. In an editorial titled "No Yellow Peril in Baseball," the *Baltimore Evening Sun*, linking the ability to play baseball with general cultural capabilities, used the one-sided loss to attack Richmond Pearson Hobson's irrational fear of Japan:

> A vigorous investigation of the question by members of the Maryland Athletic Club yesterday seems to have demonstrated the fact that the Japanese are not necessarily preeminent in all lines of human endeavor. The baseball team from Waseda College was not only beaten by the local players; it was overwhelmed. This must be somewhat discouraging to Mr. Hobson and other proponents of the Yellow Peril doctrine. We have been told that their vices exceed description and that they are capable of any infamy. . . . When the truth is known it will be found that . . . the little yellow-skinned men . . . are pretty much like ourselves, with good and bad, intelligent and ignorant, forceful and weakling individuals among them in about the same proportions. . . . At any rate, American supremacy in the game of baseball is not yet threatened.[30]

That same week the *Reporter* in Logansport, Indiana, also used Waseda's visit to rebuke Hobson, this time in the form of a joke: "Captain Hobson, attention! The Japanese ball players from Waseda University are inspecting American batteries, thus warns the *Marion Star* [a newspaper from a rival town]. But the *Star* forgets that the Japs inspected the Cub batteries, which belong to the National, not the American."[31]

Waseda followed the loss in Maryland with an 11–8 win over the University of Pennsylvania before spending a few days in Washington DC sightseeing and visiting Japanese and American dignitaries. On July 11 the team headed west, traveling for a week without playing until it reached Butte, Montana.[32] A city of thirty-nine thousand on the Continental Divide, Butte was a copper-mining town straight out of Western dime novels, with hundreds of saloons, gambling dens, and an infamous red-light district. Morgan Earp had been on the police force in the 1870s, and the city would be rocked by labor riots in 1914. But in July 1911 the inhabitants were fixated on baseball.

Butte's citizens were ecstatic that Waseda would play in their city. "The game has been the sole sporting topic in Butte and Anaconda for the last two days," wrote the *Anaconda Standard*. "Everyone in the city is taking a great interest in the exhibition," added the *Butte Daily Post*. "This will be the first opportunity, and possibly the last, that the devotees of this sport have to see a Jap team on the Butte field. . . . This is unquestionably the greatest baseball attraction ever given the residents of this city, and if they really care for something unique, original and interesting in the great pastime, they should turn out at least 3,000 strong tomorrow afternoon." Butte's two hundred or so Japanese residents made plans to meet the players at the train station and give them "a welcome they will not soon forget." The Waseda colors of maroon and white were "prominently displayed in all Japanese quarters of the city, and a special flag [was] made for the occasion."[33]

The game was everything the fans had hoped for—"one of the fastest and most interesting games seen in this city in some time." The Boston and Montana Club, considered one of the strongest semi-pro teams in Montana, went out to a quick lead, scoring in the bottom of the first and again in the fourth and sixth innings. Down 5–0, in the top of the seventh Waseda scored three "by clean hitting, clever base running, waiting patiently at the plate and getting in front of the ball."[34]

Goro Mikami, the future All Nations barnstormer, began the top of the ninth inning with a hard line drive to right field that should have been a single, but as right fielder Bill Jackson went to glove the ball, it struck a rock and darted past him. By the time Jackson retrieved it, Mikami was on third. The next batter, Katashi Iseda, hit a clean triple over the center fielder's head, scoring Mikami. After an unproductive out, first baseman Hitoshi Oi came to the plate. With only one out, a hit, a slow ground ball, or a deep fly would tie the game. Oi worked the count full. Just as the pitcher started his windup, Iseda dashed toward home with "both the runner and the catcher shouting shrilly in their native tongue." Oi dropped a perfect bunt down the line, catching the third baseman by surprise, as Iseda streaked home with the tying run. "All in the stands applauded the brilliant play."[35]

Eight outs later, in the bottom of the tenth inning with a runner on first, Bert "Hans Wagner" Schils, the captain of the Boston and Montana Club, captured the victory for the home team with "a low line to deep left field, traveling with the speed of a bullet [that] after it struck the ground continued . . . through the weeds in the out-field . . . until it almost reached the fence," and the crowd of 1,500 "left the park well pleased with the exhibition."[36]

The spectators and the reporters left with a favorable impression of the Japanese as both individuals and players. "They are quiet, gen-tlemanly players, never argue with an umpire, and play the game for all that there is in it," noted the *Butte Daily Post*; by the end of the game "the big crowd . . . was pulling for them to win." "They play the game from a scientific standpoint, know all the strategy of the sport, and use it when occasion demands," continued the *Daily Post*. "They never kick at a decision and never quit. . . . They have the best batting eyes of any team that ever played here. They watch the ball closely, and if it misses the plate by an inch, they do not offer at it. They can be fooled by a curveball, but even then, they make the pitcher curve it over the plate, and rarely ever offer at a waste ball. This makes the opposing twirler work from start to finish, and gives [them] a good chance to get hits when they count the most." Indeed they "put up a fairly good article of our national game," added the *Anaconda Standard*.[37]

From Butte, Waseda continued west, stopping to play in Mis-soula, Montana; Spokane, Seattle, and Tacoma, Washington; and Vancouver. Playing mostly semi-pro teams and no colleges, Waseda did well, winning seven of the eleven contests. The players' mas-tery of "scientific baseball" and their daring led to several victo-ries. In Spokane Waseda played a three-game series against C. M. Payne, the top team in the city league. After splitting the first two games, the teams battled "tooth and nail" in the third. "With the score tied [2–2] in the eleventh inning, the crowd biting its finger-nails and holding its breath with expectancy and suppressed excite-ment, [Goro] Mikami placed a pretty single over the Payne infield."

Katashi Iseda, who had tripled in the ninth inning comeback against Butte, did it again, "plastering the ball on a line to the right field corner of the lot for three bases." Mikami scored with the go-ahead run. But "the tumult and shouting had scarcely died away when, with two strikes on [Inasahuro] Matsuda, Iseda suddenly broke for the plate." Startled, the pitcher threw high and Iseda slid under the tag with a steal of home."[38]

Waseda ended its fifteen-week-long tour with a win. On July 31 at 4 p.m. it met the Mainlands at Vancouver's Recreation Park. About 1,200 fans, including hundreds of Japanese, watched what "was easily the best amateur exhibition seen in Vancouver for a number of moons." The game was scoreless until Goro Mikami homered in the top of the eighth inning. The Japanese fans chanted, "'Banzai! Banzai! Banzai!" as Mikami crossed the plate. Waseda added three insurance runs in the top of the ninth to win, 4–0. The next morning the team boarded the *Inaba Maru* at Vancouver's docks and steamed home.[39]

Both Keio and Waseda had accomplished their goals. The Keio players had improved their baseball skills, learning the secrets of inside baseball, and, by winning twenty-one of their forty-four games (with two ties), showed that they were equal to American collegiate teams. The lessons learned during the tour would help them dominate Japanese baseball for decades. The Waseda players also improved their game, but baseball was not their sole focus. With their gentlemanly behavior, protestations of goodwill, and the shared love of the sport, the team provided a tonic to the rantings of Richmond Pearson Hobson and the hostile depictions of Japanese in the press. "Our national game . . . has become part of Japanese recreative [*sic*] life," concluded J. J. Pegues. "It is significant in the way of building mutual friendship and respect . . . [and] will accomplish much toward furthering the friendship already existing between the United States and Japan."[40]

14

End of a Dream

With the departure of the Waseda and Keio university teams, the
JBBA was now the only Japanese squad touring the United States.
On July 16 it left Illinois to begin an eight-week stint in Iowa at Fort
Madison, a town of nine thousand located on the banks of the Mississippi River. A week earlier Harry Saisho had arrived to arrange
a game, while the club continued to play across the river in western Illinois. Harry told the local newspaper that the team members
had been together for about fifty days and were "a fine lot of players [who] have been winning most of their games." Trying to capitalize on the public's fascination with Waseda and Keio, he correctly
explained that Kubo had graduated from Keio but also fabricated
that three of his players (Sohara, Motohashi, and Tachiyama) had
graduated from Waseda. Local manager Pete Kern readily agreed
to play the Japanese the following Sunday at 2 p.m. at the amusement park field.[1]

Five years earlier Guy Green's Japanese, with Ken Kitsuse and
Toyo Fujita, had squeaked by Fort Madison's squad, 1–0, but this
time the Japanese dominated the locals. With a barrage of 17 hits, 5
walks, and 9 stolen bases, the JBBA racked up 16 runs in a lopsided
victory—its first recorded win since the Fourth of July. Kitsuse led
the assault by swiping 6 bases.[2] Although called "practically a midget"
by the *Hutchinson Daily Gazette*, Kitsuse had been leading the team
all season.[3] Twelve box scores survive for games played before July
17; in these recorded games Ken led the squad with 11 stolen bases
and 11 runs scored. Toyo Fujita topped the team with a .366 batting
average (15 for 45) as Ken placed second with .302 (13 for 43). No
other Japanese player hit over .200, while the two Native Americans
playing under the stage name Oyama had a combined .231 average.

For the remainder of July the players traveled through eastern Iowa, drawing large crowds. In thirteen games they earned less than twenty dollars only once and brought in over forty dollars seven times. A few days before the July 30 game the *Oelwan Daily Register* announced:

> The Japs have been playing around Illinois and Iowa for the past two weeks and are cleaning up everything and the local management was indeed fortunate in securing them for this date. This is the only Japanese team in the country now and are a great attraction everywhere as the little brown boys are very fast and the way they run the bases is a sight to watch. . . . On shortstop for the foreigners will be Kitsuse, who some time ago captured the 26-mile Marathon race held in Los Angeles, California [which was untrue]. He is one of the best athletes that Japan has ever had. He will be here Sunday with the Japs and seeing this great athlete in action will be worth the price of admission.[4]

The plea worked, and a packed grandstand watched the locals win, 9–2, as Kitsuse and his team brought in $90.15.

In early July Admiral Heihachiro Togo, the hero of the Russo-Japanese War, announced that he would visit the United States in August. For a month newspapers throughout the country covered the impending visit. Some printed exposés of the admiral's achievements, from his education in England to his great naval victories. Others expressed outrage that Congress had allocated $10,000 to entertain the visiting Japanese admiral.

Togo's upcoming visit also brought Richmond Pearson Hobson back into the news. The congressman was uncharacteristically silent about the visit, but that did not stop the press from printing snide comments on what Hobson might be thinking. "Congressman Hobson should volunteer as a special detective to watch Admiral Togo," declared Kansas City's *Gazette Globe*.[5]

On August 4 Togo disembarked from the RMS *Lusitania* in New York. Four years later the ship's destruction by a German U-boat would push the United States into World War I, but on that day it carried an admiral "bearing a message of peace and good will."[6] Togo stayed in the country for just fifteen days, visiting New York, Washington DC, Baltimore, Philadelphia, Boston, and Niagara Falls. At each stop he received thunderous applause as he stressed the friendly ties between Japan and the United States and reiterated his country's desire for peace. A confrontation with Hobson never occurred as the congressman avoided the admiral by visiting Maine, Buffalo, and, finally, the southern states. "Since Admiral Togo arrived in America, Capt. Hobson like 'Ber rabbit' is lying low," exclaimed the *News Dispatch* from Clinton, North Carolina.[7] During the visit Hobson also refrained from giving his usual anti-Japanese speeches, instead focusing on his next cause—prohibition. Although he would continue with his Yellow Peril rants for years, the prohibition movement would take up most of Hobson's energy until the implementation of the Eighteenth Amendment in 1920.

With Togo and Hobson on the front pages, jingoist and racist language appeared in the Iowan sports columns. For example, the *Oelwan Daily Register*'s July 28 headline read, "Japs vs. U.S.A. The Oelwan Team Will Have a Battle with the Japanese Ball Team." The article continued the military metaphors. "War is declared between the Oelwan baseball team and the Japanese professionals who will invade the city Sunday afternoon at 2:30 p.m. and try to capture the game of baseball from the locals. The Japs are coming here under the command of General Saisho." "Japanese vs. Americans. The War is On. We'll Tan Their Hides," bragged the *Audubon County Journal*. The *Mt. Pleasant Daily News* was even more nationalistic with racist overtones: "The men from the Land of the Rising Sun demonstrated once more their inability to win out over American nerve and skilled and 'bluff' and despite their artistic performances and jiujitsu stunts for which the race is noted, were beaten fairly and squarely by a pick-up aggregation of town and college players who have never played together before."[8]

Other Iowa newspapers emphasized racial differences in their game accounts, often with derogatory descriptions. "Little brown boys," "a bunch of chocolate-colored sons of the island empire of Nippon," and "little yellow fellows from the flower kingdom" were typical examples.[9] The *Williamsburg Journal-Tribune* coverage of the local team's exciting come-from-behind 3–2 victory in the bottom of the tenth inning went further, undercutting the Japanese players' humanity by evoking themes common in Yellow Peril literature. Throughout the long, column-and-a-half article, no Japanese is referred to by name, as the writer "did not try to get the names of the Jap players; just fill your mouth with k's and s's and w's, chew once and then spit out a Jap name." Instead the players are referred to as "the first Jap," "the Jap at bat," "the Jap up with a sullen grin." Much like the yellowface cartoons common in anti-Japanese propaganda, the writer also gives the players animalistic attributes. "The little brown fellows emitted emphatic grunts and began to move with cat-like rapidity on the diamond and in the field."[10]

But in most towns the JBBA players' behavior earned them respect, undercutting negative stereotypes, forcing reporters to revise their jingoistic tones. At Oelwan, where the game was advertised as a war, the locals found that "the Japanese team were a gentle lot of fellows and never kicked and were smiling all the time."[11] After the game at Exira the *Audubon County Journal* proclaimed that the "war with the Japanese is over. . . . Both sides were intent on winning the game and they struggled for every point of vantage. . . . The Japanese were gentle, quiet and inoffensive, and good sports."[12] The *County Journal* went further, praising each member of the JBBA in turn:

> Togo [Toyo] on first did not let any balls past him, Tachiyama on second did fine work until his guns were accidentally spiked by Stafford. . . . Suzuki on third was a clown as well as a good ball player. Kitsuse the shortstop was as active as a cat in his work in supporting others and was always in evidence. Sohara in right field, Kubo and Saisho in center field, and Kawashima in left field were on the job at all times and took in some pretty flies. Kayama [Shiraishi] as pitcher was playing ball for the true sport.[13]

Even the overtly nationalistic reporter for the *Mt. Pleasant Daily News* had to admit that the Japanese "conducted themselves as gentlemen on the field and impressed the crowd as a clean, sportsman like bunch."[14] After the JBBA dropped a close game, 6–4, to the town team from Webster, Iowa, a reporter for the *Webster City Freeman* could not resist a reference: "The little brown men from the Orient were not the big 'yellow peril' of which Lieut. Hobson USN has preached so much . . . but they were pretty good ball players."[15]

As the team traveled through Iowa, finding an adequate catcher continued to be a problem. James Blain, the second player called "Oyama," left the team a couple of days after it entered the Hawkeye State. On July 17 Katow, described as "a white man with a Japanese nom de plume" by the *Webster City Freeman*, joined the team as the new catcher.[16] The next day's box score listed the backstop as Kenton, suggesting that this may have been Katow's real name. Katow, although a fine hitter, was not a true catcher, and on July 22 the team sent a telegram to a Caucasian catcher named Wheeler (first name unknown) to offer him the job. He arrived the following day.

A hulking man, Wheeler came with an abrasive personality. "Wheeler, the catcher, was a big bunch of beef and did not take at all with the crowd," exclaimed the *Boone News Republican*. A reporter for the *Humeston New Era* also complained, "It would have been a great event except for the wrangles the catcher for the Japs caused. He seemed to have a perpetual grouch and even went so far as to try [to] pick a fight."[17] After praising the Japanese players, the *Audubon County Journal* singled out Wheeler for disdain. "The dirty white conglomeration . . . introduced the offensive, rotten, fetid methods that were not conceived when the game of baseball was originally launched.[18] The man, however, could hit. He moved straight into the team's cleanup spot, providing a legitimate power threat to the otherwise light-hitting lineup. On August 9 he won the game in Jefferson with a long home run.[19] Wheeler and Katow would both remain with the team for the remainder of the season.

With the new recruits the JBBA began to win—maybe not a lot but more than before. During August the team played .500 ball, with eleven wins, eleven loses, and two ties. The results of eight games, however, are unknown. Even so, prior to August the team had only ten recorded wins in the first three months of the tour (a 10-40 record with the scores of twenty-three games unknown).

Almost fifty years later Kiichi Suzuki remembered the August 18 matchup against Centerville as one of the team's best games. A coal-mining town in south Iowa containing over seven thousand people, Centerville could field a strong team. The JBBA put Naga on the mound while Centreville countered with local star Pete Morris. Both pitchers were on their game, with Naga showing "tremendous speed." For the first six innings each pitcher held the opposition to just one hit and no runs. In the top of the sixth with two outs Suzuki doubled to right field and dashed to third as the right fielder bobbled the ball. Kitsuse then slashed a pitch down the left-field line. The fans in the packed bleachers and home team saw it land two feet foul, but the umpire saw it otherwise and called it fair. Suzuki scampered home with the game's only run as Naga continued to shut down the Centerville batters, striking out a total of eleven. "Kitsuse's hit was priceless," Suzuki recalled.[20]

As the team improved, Saisho began to exaggerate its abilities in his advertising. Previously he had emphasized the team's uniqueness as the only professional Japanese squad and just claimed that they were a fast group of ballplayers. Now he bragged that the team was winning most of its games. On August 5 the *Boone News Republican* announced, "The Jap baseball team, composed entirely of genuine Japanese, is the only professional Japanese team in the world and is composed of the nation's best players. They can justly be proud of their record in this country as they have played the strongest of the fast semi-professional teams on their tour and won about two-thirds of the games played. Their fast base running and fielding game is said to be unsurpassed."[21]

To help draw spectators the JBBA created a baseball card. In July or early August the team posed for a photograph (fig. 27). The eleven players, plus Arthur Shiomichi dressed in street clothes, formed two rows. Fujita, Saisho, Suzuki, Tachiyama, and Kitsuse sat with crossed legs in the first row, while Shiomichi, Kawashima, Sohara, Kubo, Motohashi, Shiraishi, and Naga stood behind. Wheeler and Katow were not included. On August 23 the team spent $2.75 to "cut" the picture, which they mailed to a printer in Des Moines along with $13. The printer reproduced the team's picture on three-by-four-inch heavy cardboard stock. The card was probably distributed by Saisho as he searched for opponents and tried to drum up attendance. A surviving card has "Admit three ladies to the ball game and grand stand, Japs Ball Team, J.B.B. Mgr." written on its back.[22]

The team continued to draw well in August as it covered west central Iowa. Newspapers routinely mention large crowds and enthusiastic fans as many towns treated the squad's visit as a special event. At Pella a band "rendered a few lively selections" as the teams warmed up prior to the game. At Neola the large crowd, to the surprise of the local newspaper, contained "a number of ladies of the city."[23] Gate receipts varied from a pitiful $3.30 on August 31 in Ripley to $79.75 on August 13, when the JBBA topped the African American Buxton Wanderers, 6–4, but they averaged $34.78 a game. As expenses were low in rural Iowa (room and board often came to about $15 a day for the entire team), the team's accounts showed a healthy balance. Once the surplus topped $150, the players began to treat themselves for the first time during the long season. They purchased beer on August 13, five pies on August 15, cigars on August 20, and on August 16, for an unknown reason, the team sent $10 back to California to Shichiji Kikuchi, Saisho's and Kitsuse's childhood friend from Miyakonojo. On August 25 the balance reached $202.25, the highest since the team had entered Kansas City three months earlier. But the good fortune would not continue.[24]

By late August the team had been on the road for sixteen weeks, playing nearly every day. The players were tired, and injuries began to mount. On August 20 at Creston, Kitsuse sustained an unknown injury. He stayed in the lineup but moved to third base, allowing Suzuki to take over shortstop. About a week later at Exira, Tachiyama's leg "was accidently spiked . . . which caused his retirement from the game for several days, perhaps weeks."[25] The wound seemed serious, and after the game the team called in a doctor. A few days later it purchased iodine for Toyo Fujita to help prevent an infection. Both Tachiyama and Fujita would be out of the lineup for about two weeks. The night before the September 3 game in Des Moines, Saisho told the *Des Moines Register* that the team would be unable to perform the pregame athletic exhibition as advertised, as the fencing expert and Kitsuse, the jiujitsu wrestler, remained injured. "We are still playing good baseball," he added, "but we don't want to mislead people, we will be unable to put on the fencing and wrestling, and we wish everyone to know it."[26] Even without the exhibition a good crowd, numbering about three hundred, turned up to watch the local All Stars beat the JBBA, 3–0.

After Des Moines the team headed southeast, covering territory it had already traversed in late July and early August. Financially it was a mistake. The JBBA's main draw was as a curiosity. Most rural

Iowans had never seen a Japanese; just thirty-six were living in the entire state in 1910, so watching an entire team play the American pastime was worth the price of a ticket.[27] But as the squad was not particularly talented, few were willing to pay to watch it a second time.

On September 11, for example, the team returned to Centerville. The locals were eager for a rematch after losing, 1–0, on the umpire's blown call of Kitsuse's winning hit, and the JBBA was hoping for another strong turnout; it had made $62.60 at the earlier game. Once again the game was tight. Neither team had scored as Flactiff, the Centerville shortstop, led off the seventh inning with a triple and came home on a wild pitch. Two outs later the right fielder, Bowie, also tripled. The next batter, Harris, pounded the ball deep to center field. Takaji Kubo raced back, focusing on the ball—and only the ball. The crowd hollered and cheered as the ball seemed destined to clear the fence. Kubo continued to sprint, his back to the plate. As the ball reached the fence, Kubo extended his arm, catching it as his body slammed through the cheap wooden outfield fence. But he held on, recording the third out. The JBBA struck back the next inning, scoring four to take the lead and eventually the game, 5–1. The thrilling victory, however, was tempered by the mediocre turn out. The gate receipts brought the team just $25. The teams decided to meet again the following day, and this time Centerville got its revenge, winning easily, 12–2. Once again the midweek turnout was low, and the JBBA earned just $25.[28] Other games in the area brought in similar returns. The team played ten games between September 4 and 14, bringing in just $270.75 (or $24.61 per day)—not enough to cover daily expenses. The account balance slowly dropped, reaching $60.04 on September 15, when the team left Iowa for Missouri.

The final stint of the barnstorming tour began with two days of rain. With no income the team's savings dropped to $31.04 as it arrived in Macon on September 17. The town's three newspapers had been touting the game with "the well-known Tokyo Japanese baseball team" for over a week. "The Japs have a fast team, having played in Chicago, Kansas City, and St. Louis," the *Times-Democrat* exaggerated. "Just before the game a novelty will be introduced in the form of Japanese fencing and wrestling. One of the Japs, Kitsuse, has made an enviable record for himself in amateur athletics, having recently won a 26-mile marathon race at Los Angeles, Cal," added the *Daily Chronicle*. Four days later the *Daily Chronicle* reminded its readers with a one-line advertisement: "Don't fail to see Shortstop Kitsuse at Macon-Jap game on Sunday." Although Macon's population was over 3,500, only about 150 people came out to watch Sunday's game, bringing in $22.40. The teams decided to play again the following day, but few fans attended as the game brought in a pitiful $4.80. Despite all the pregame advertising, the three local newspapers did not even bother to report the results of either game.[29]

As the team wound its way southeast toward St. Louis, rain seemed to follow. Local farmers reveled in it. "It has been raining for several days. The constant monotorious [sic] dripping from the wet leaves of the maples still breaks the silence when all other sounds are hushed," mused a writer for the *Macon Daily Chronicle*.[30]

But for the JBBA the turn in weather was devastating. After a poor turnout on the muddy fields of Paris, Missouri, the game at Auxvasse was rained out. Already low on funds, the missed game sent the account balance to a negative $4.06. Luckily Harry Saisho had cash on him and put $50 into the team accounts so the players could continue the tour.

The team played a few games on the northwest outskirts of St. Louis before entering the city on the evening of September 23. The Japanese planned to stay for a week, playing the city's many semipro and top amateur squads, before ending the tour on October 1. Saisho had arranged a strong opponent, sure to draw fans, for the first game.

At 3:30 on Sunday, September 24, the JBBA would face the St. Louis Giants. Founded in 1906–7, the Giants were one of the top African American ball clubs in the country. Run by Charlie Mills, they were having a strong season, with a 26-17 record against other midwestern independent teams. The lineup included future Hall of Famer Ben Taylor, his brothers "Steel Arm" Johnny and "Candy" Jim Taylor, captain Dick Wallace, and Tullie McAdoo, who had played with the Salt Lake City Occidentals. On October 8 they would capture the city championship by blowing out the white Trolley League winners, 12–4.[31]

A tremendous crowd came out to Athletic Park, expecting the

locals to demolish the visiting Japanese. To everyone's surprise Naga baffled the Giants, and the two teams were locked at two after nine innings. In the eleventh the Giants squeaked out a 3–2 victory. Perhaps even better than the strong performance was the $92.40 the team collected from the gate receipts. With the windfall it prepaid the hotel for three nights, paid William Watkins (Naga) $15 of owed salary, and paid back $30 of the $50 owed to Harry Saisho.[32]

The next day the rain came again. The team was unable to play for two days, and the savings dropped to $31.52. On Wednesday, September 27, it met the St. Louis Giants in a rematch at Athletic Park.[33] Unfortunately the weekday game did not generate much excitement—the St. Louis newspapers did not even report the game's outcome. The poor turnout brought in just $7.60, reducing the team's balance to $18.02. That evening the players ate chop suey to save money.

The second game with the Giants would be the JBBA's last. For most of the players it was the end of a lifelong dream. For a season they had been professional ballplayers, minor celebrities playing in front of tens of thousands of people and featured in hundreds of newspapers across seven states. They had played 128 games in 143 days. Admittedly they had amassed a mediocre 25-60-2 record (with the results of another 41 games unknown). But many of their losses had been in close, hard-fought games that could have gone either way. They had held their own against the independent African American Hutchinson Sunflowers, St. Louis Giants, and Buxton Wanderers, as well as the white independent Des Moines All Stars.

The team's downfall had been poor hitting. In the eighty-seven games where results survive, they were outscored 448–601. In the twenty-two found box scores the team picked up 133 hits in 702 at bats, for a .190 batting average. Toyo Fujita led the regulars with a .288 average (19 for 66); Kitsuse came in second with a .269 average (21 for 78); Wheeler finished third by hitting .261 (6 for 26); while the pair of Oyamas hit .258 (8 for 31). No other player batted above .183.

Throughout the season the JBBA had earned $4,556.88 in gate receipts. Newspapers note that the Japanese kept between 60 and 75 percent of tickets sales, and in most towns tickets cost twenty-five cents for regular admission and ten cents for the grandstand. Assuming that the team received 75 percent of the proceeds at all games and that the average ticket price was a quarter, then over twenty-four thousand people came to watch it play that summer. With lower ticket prices at some ballparks, as well as a lower revenue share in some towns, the actual number of spectators must have been higher. Yet both the attendance at JBBA games and the team's income were about a third of the estimated numbers from Guy Green's 1906 Japanese tour (60,000–70,000 spectators and $12,000 in gate receipts; see chapter 8).

On Thursday, September 28, the team paid off Wheeler's outstanding salary of $15, leaving a balance of just $2.27. The Japanese players stayed another two days in St. Louis, living on twenty-five cents each and searching with no luck for an opponent. Broke, on September 30 they borrowed money from acquaintances and headed back to Los Angeles.[34]

15

Japanese American Baseball Comes of Age

"I returned to Los Angeles flat broke," Harry Saisho recalled in a 1970 interview.[1] Having given up their jobs to barnstorm, the JBBA players were also unemployed. The team members spent the fall picking olives on the farms in Spring Valley, just outside of San Diego, and playing local ball clubs on their days off. As the low wages were not enough for Saisho to pay the mortgage on his investment properties, he lost his land in Lancaster and the San Fernando Valley. In 1912 Harry moved to the Imperial Valley with five other Japanese men, leased four hundred acres of land, and raised lettuce.

Most of the other players returned to Los Angeles and re-formed the Nanka Base Ball team. On weekends they played the city's other Japanese teams (the Sanshu, Nippon, Asahi, and Hayato) and non-Japanese amateur squads. The results of these games, however, rarely entered the city's mainstream newspapers.

Between 1912 and 1914 Japanese ball clubs sprang up throughout the West Coast. Nearly every Japanese community soon boasted at least one amateur team. Most teams played pickup games with nearby Japanese nines and local white amateur teams, but a few wanted to play in more competitive, organized leagues. Seeking an edge, these teams reached out to the former members of the JBBA—the most experienced and only professional Issei ballplayers. By 1914 nearly all of the players had left Los Angeles to play for other teams, breaking up the club for good.

During the winter of 1913–14 Ken Kitsuse received an intriguing request from Mitomi "Frank" Miyasaka, the captain of Seattle's Nippon baseball team. Miyasaka planned to take his team to Japan; it would be the first time a Japanese American ball club would tour the homeland. To build the best squad possible he asked Ken to join the team and bring along one or two of his professional teammates. Kiichi Suzuki agreed to accompany Kitsuse on the adventure.

Founded between 1904 and 1906, the Nippon was the oldest Issei team in the Northwest.[2] In July 1908 the *Seattle Daily Times* featured the team when it took on the all-female Merry Widows. Mistakenly referring to the Nippons as "the only Japanese baseball club in America," the newspaper reported, "Seattle boasts the only Japanese baseball aggregation in America, so that when these sons of Nippon went up against the daughters of Columbia, viz., the Merry Widow Baseball Club, it is a safe assumption that the game played at Athletic Park yesterday afternoon was the most unique affair in the annals of the national game." Over a thousand fans, including a "great crowd" of Japanese, watched the Nippons win, 14–8. Relying on stereotypes, the *Daily Times*' reporter concluded, "It is a national characteristic of the Nipponese to be short on respect for the abilities of the weaker sex and . . . the little fellows did everything but pull the girls by the hair in order to win that game by as large a margin as possible."[3]

Soon afterward the Nippons' second baseman, Tokichi "Frank" Fukuda, left the team and join the newly founded Mikado. Although modern historians often confuse the Seattle Mikado with Tozan Masko's Mikado's from Denver, there was no affiliation between the two clubs. Seattle's Mikado soon rivaled the Nippons as the city's top Japanese team. In September 1910, for example, the University of Chicago chose to play the Mikado in a warmup game prior to its tour of Japan. Chicago won comfortably, 15–1.[4] As Fukuda's love for baseball grew, he realized the game's importance for Seattle's Japanese. The games brought the immigrants together physically and provided a shared interest to help strengthen community ties. They also acted as a bridge between the city's Japanese and non-Japanese population, showing a common bond that he hoped would undermine the anti-Japanese bigotry in the city.

In 1909 Fukuda created a youth baseball team called the Cherry team—the West Coast's first Nisei (Japanese born outside of Japan) squad. Under Fukuda's guidance the club was more than just a baseball team. Kakuei Nakamura, one of the early members, explained, "The purpose of this club was to contact American people and understand each other through various activities."[5] As the boys matured, the team became stronger on the diamond and in 1912 changed its name to the Asahi and began playing adult teams.

Between 1907 and 1910 the Japanese in other Northwest cities were also organizing baseball clubs. Tacoma, Washington, had at least two Issei teams. A surviving photograph taken in front of the Union Steam Laundry between 1907 and 1910 depicts a dozen men and women dressed in street clothes and nine ball players dressed in spiffy dark uniforms emblazoned with "Union Laundry." A second photograph of the Union Laundry team is tentatively dated to 1911.[6] No information on the team has been located in the Tacoma newspapers. Tacoma's top Japanese team, the Columbians, was organized before 1910 as that May they faced the Seattle Mikado to determine the Japanese champion of the Northwest. The Mikado won. The following year the Columbians, Mikado, and Nippons held a tournament to decide the champion. A 1911 team photograph of the Mikado displaying a trophy with a banner reading "Nippon Baseball Championship" suggests that it had won again.[7] That summer, when Waseda University visited the region, it played both the Columbians and Nippons. The visitors took both games easily, 21–0 against Tacoma and 10–0 against Seattle.

In June 1907 English-language newspapers reported that Youshi K. Nakamura, the publisher and editor of the Japanese-language *Spokane Times* and secretary of the Japanese Commercial Club, had organized a ball team in the city known as the Keis Gijiku Club. According to the report, Nakamura claimed the team included eight former members of the 1905 Waseda University team—impossible, as no Waseda player, besides Shin Hashido, had returned to the United States. Nakamura also stated that Issei teams would soon be organized in the nearby towns of Cheney, Waverly, and Espanola. The four clubs planned to form a league, playing a twenty-game schedule starting July 4, 1907, with games each subsequent Sunday. The league champion would play a champion from the white Spokane leagues. This plan probably never came to fruition. No record of such a league exists in the English-language newspapers (no copies of Nakamura's *Spokane Times* survive), and a September 1908 article in the *Spokane Press* called the Seattle Nippons "the only Japanese team in the United States" and noted "a Japanese team may soon be formed in Spokane to meet the Seattle sons of the island kingdom."[8]

Nakamura also lectured on the differences between Japanese and American baseball:

> It is not generally known that the Japanese play more scientific ball than their American brothers, but they do, and judging from the way the game is being taken up, I should say that in a few years we will be able to pick a team from among our people to give battle to any nine on the diamond.
>
> While it is true we may never be able to develop hitters like Lajoie, Wagner and Keeler, we are learning to play a faster and more strategic game, which, experts tell me, accounts for more than the hit-and-run play. I do not mean to imply that we think quicker, but the knowledge I have gained from the American national game in a few years play leads me to believe that our people will study out the finer points now almost entirely overlooked even by the star players in the big leagues. We are patient and cool, two important elements of success in this most excellent past time and sport.[9]

Newspapers across the United States republished Nakamura's comments, causing a visceral reaction. Under the headline "Boastful Jap Ball Manager," the syndicated sports columnist Charles E. Edwardes responded:

> The Japanese baseball team in Spokane, Washington, has a manager, a native Jap, who talks as though he habitually partook of the seductive fruit of the poppy. Mr. Namkura [sic] is his name and he has a prestidigitated out of his think tank a few observations that would be merely foolish if, unfortunately, they are not utterly ridiculous. He says the Japanese play a more brainy game, a better strategic game; in fact, a more scientific game, really a better game, than do any Americans. One reason for this alleged Jap superiority is that Japs "keep cool, don't lose their heads or temper in the game, no matter how exciting it may become."
>
> There is only one thing the matter with Mr. Namkura. He doesn't know what he is talking about. The Jap team in Spokane would have about as much to show to win a single game against the tail enders

in any one of the six or seven or eight or nine best leagues in America as a California jack rabbit would have to dictate terms of surrender to a convention of coursing greyhounds. After all, must we go to war with Japan and blow the measly little dirt pile off the left hind leg of the earth in order to show the bunch of yellows that they should recognize the voice of the boss when they hear it?[10]

It seems that the tension between the United States and Japan over immigration and military dominance in the Pacific could be overcome, but a Japanese claiming to be better at baseball was a cause for war.

When Ken Kitsuse and Kiichi Suzuki arrived in Seattle in March 1914, they found that they were not the only recruits on the Nippon. Manager Miyasaka had also brought over Masashi Takimoto from San Francisco. Not much is known about the history of Issei baseball in the Bay City after the 1906 earthquake until the mid-1910s. Because San Francisco was the headquarters of the anti-Japanese immigration movement, the local newspapers rarely discussed Issei baseball, and when they did, the reporting was often derogatory. The first mention of a Japanese team in the *San Francisco Call*, for example, reports on the June 28, 1908, game between the Asahi Athletic Club of Alameda and a Chinese team from San Francisco. Under the headline "Chinese Lose Ball Game Because of Chop Suey Penchant," the article began:

A tuft of fresh grass out in left field looked so much like well matured chop suey that the left fielder forgot the game for a few minutes and let a home run pass him while there were three on base. That briefly explains the defeat in Alameda yesterday of the Chinese Athletic Club's baseball nine of this city by the Banzai Japanese team of Alameda. The score was 17 to 9 and the game was particularly noteworthy, as it was the first to be played by the Asiatic Inclusion league. There was a large gathering at the baseball race riot.[11]

Scattered newspaper references show that by 1911 there were several Issei teams in the Bay Area.[12]

To train the Nippons in the finer points of the game, Miyasaka hired thirty-eight-year-old George Engel as a manager/coach. Although Engel had never made the Majors, he had spent fourteen seasons in the Minor Leagues, mostly in the Western and Northwest Leagues, as a pitcher and utility player. Miyasaka had also created a challenging schedule for his players. They began their season with games against the area's two professional teams from the Northwest League. On Sunday, March 22, they lost, 5–1, to the Tacoma Tigers, led by player/manager and future Hall of Famer Joe "Iron Man" McGinnity. The Nippons played well in the field, turning three double plays, but garnered just one hit off the professional pitchers. The following Sunday the Seattle Giants, a team that included eight men who would play in the Major Leagues, beat them, 5–1. This time the Nippons collected two hits—one by Kiichi Suzuki and one by the San Franciscan Takimoto. Once on base, Takimoto advanced to third and tried a straight steal of home with two out in the ninth and two strikes on the batter. The pitch beat Takimoto, who was tagged out just as the umpire signaled strike three on the batter. Despite the one-sided loss, the *Seattle Daily Times* noted, "The Nippons . . . walked off Dugdale Field yesterday afternoon feeling well satisfied with themselves for they had tackled a professional team and had made a run."[13]

In April 1914 Keio University returned for a second tour of North America. After dropping two games in Vancouver and a third to the University of Washington, Keio met the Nippons on April 9 at Dugdale Park in what the *Seattle Daily Times* called "the world's series for the baseball championship of Japan."[14] On the mound for Keio was the great Kazuma Sugase, the half-German "Christy Mathewson of Japan," who had starred during the school's 1911 tour. The team also included future Japanese Hall of Famer Daisuke Miyake, who would manage the All Nippon team against Babe Ruth's All Americans in 1934, and Hisashi Koshimoto, a Hawaiian-born Nisei who would later manage Keio.

Nippons manager George Engel was in a quandary. His usual ace, Sadaye Takano, was not available, and as Keio would host his team during its upcoming tour of Japan, he needed the Nippons to prove they could challenge the visitors. An apocryphal (and racially insensitive by today's standards) story in the *Seattle Star* explained:

> George Engel . . . was stuck for a pitcher to use against the Keio University boys. While struggling with the problem he ran across [Wil-

liam] Cadreau. Cadreau is copper skinned, his hair is black, and, comparatively, he is short of stature.

"Wanta be a Jap for a day, Cad?" George asked.

"Name your terms. I'd be a wooden Indian for a cigar store at the right price."

Engel unfolded his proposition, and the redskin acquiesced. The game started. Engel was very careful to let the Keio boys know that Kato, his pitcher, was deaf and dumb. But later in the game Kato became enthused, as ball players will, and the jig was up when he began to root in good English.[15]

Cadreau, also known as Chief Chouneau, had pitched for Spokane and Vancouver in the Northwestern League and one game for the 1910 Chicago White Sox. Later he would pitch a season for the African American Chicago Union Giants. He handled Keio relatively easily, striking out thirteen en route to a 6–3 victory. Both Kitsuse and Suzuki went hitless in the game, although Ken did steal a base.[16]

In late May an unusual telegram arrived at the Nippons' office. Each year the town of Cumberland on Vancouver Island in British Columbia held a baseball tournament to celebrate Victoria Day. Cumberland was a rough coal-mining town of about three thousand, mostly young male miners of various ethnicities—whites, Chinese, blacks, and some Japanese. Baseball was a popular pastime among the miners, but the Japanese team was weak and usually lost. According to an unnamed source, republished in 1954, "The white people despised the Japanese, often saying, 'Japanese are not good enough to play baseball.' This grated on the Japanese's nerves. So, they had decided to invite some players from Seattle" for the tournament.[17]

Kitsuse, Suzuki, pitcher Sadaye Takano, and catcher Yohizo Shimada traveled to Cumberland to help their countrymen. There would be three teams in the tournament, two Caucasian—Cumberland and Bevan—and the Japanese. The draw pitted the two white teams against each other in the first round, with the Japanese playing the winner. Even so Suzuki was nervous. "We had a few days with the team and no player was good. I thought that the four of us [from Seattle] had to play a central role in the game and somehow come through."[18]

Cumberland beat Bevan, 13–9, in the opener, and no doubt expecting an easy victory in the final, kept the same pitcher on the mound. But the tired amateur was no match for the Japanese ringers. "His pitches were weak and he gave us a lot of walks and we hit a lot," remembered Suzuki. The *Cumberland News* summed it up nicely: "The little brown men from the Far East, knocked the stuffing and conceit out of the Cumberland boys at baseball by a score of 8–4. The little men were as proud of their victory over the boasted Anglo-Saxons as they were at the taking of Port Arthur from the Russians."[19]

"We had a big party in the evening," Suzuki continued. "We were relieved because we won the game by luck, but I was very nervous in the beginning. I was afraid we would not come home in one piece if we had lost the game! On the next day, when we were supposed to go back to Seattle, they asked us to coach the team for two more days. We could not refuse the request having received a large honorarium. Even now, when I remember the game that only four of us had to play, I still get nervous."[20]

Throughout the spring and summer the Nippons continued to face the area's top teams, including the African American Keystone Giants, to prepare for the trip to Japan. Yet in their minds the most important matchup was the three-game series against the Asahi for the Japanese championship. The Nippons took the first game, 4–2, on July 12 at Dugdale Park, but there is no evidence that they finished the series. In each of the following few weeks both teams play non-Japanese opponents.

Not to be outdone by their rivals, the Asahi also announced that they would tour Japan later that year. But for Frank Fukuda the trip to the home country was about more than baseball. He "thought that seeing and understanding their old country was indispensable for his Nisei players to become better citizens and to establish a better Japanese community in Seattle." These players would form a cultural bridge between the United States and Japan, reducing misunderstandings and bigotry.[21] Sponsored by the *Yomiuri* and *Chunichi* newspapers, the Asahi would begin their trip about a month after the Nippons left Seattle on August 25.

The Nippons stayed in Japan for almost four months. The players spent most of that time touring their homeland and visiting family. The baseball tour itself consisted of just eight games—all played during September against Tokyo's top universities. Engel decided not to let Sadaye Takano, his usual starting pitcher, face the Japanese colleges. Instead Engel would take the mound himself.

Engel had not pitched professionally for two years. Although he had gone 7-4 in eighty-seven innings with Vancouver of the Northwestern League, now, at thirty-eight years old, he was no longer as effective. He won his first game, scattering four hits, as the Nippons beat Waseda University, 6–4. But three days later Keio pounded him for seven runs while Kazuma Sugase shut out the Nippons on four hits. Later in the week the two pitchers dueled again. This time Engel held Keio to three runs as the Nippons scored four off Sugase to win. That, however, would be Seattle's last win in Japan. The next day Engel let Takano start against Waseda. It did not go well. Waseda scored twenty-three times as Takano gave up sixteen hits and walked ten, and the Nippons made nine errors. Engel returned to the mound for the deciding games against Waseda and Keio but lost both. The tour ended with a 6–6 tie after ten innings with Keio alumni's Mita Club. Neither Ken Kitsuse nor Kiichi Suzuki did well on the tour. Kitsuse gained only three hits in twenty-one at bats, scoring four times, while Suzuki went hitless in nineteen at bats.[22]

On the diamond the Seattle Asahi fared no better in Japan. Playing mostly against high schools, Asahi won two, lost three, and tied two before meeting Waseda and Keio. The two universities dominated Fukuda's team, as Waseda held them to a single hit and Keio won, 7–4. Yet as a cultural exchange the Asahis' trip was a resounding success. The players learned about their parents' homeland, attended receptions, and created ties with Japanese ballplayers. Frank Fukuda and the Asahi would return to Japan twice more—in 1918 and 1921—each time strengthening cultural and economic bridges between Japan and Seattle.

The Asahi were not the only ones who had success off the field. On November 30, 1914, Ken Kitsuse married sixteen-year-old Suye Hoshiyama in Tokyo. Suye would stay in Japan for another year, as Ken and his teammates returned to the United States on ss *Aki Maru* on February 5, 1915. In September she joined Ken in Los Angeles, and they started a family. The Kitsuses had two sons, James (born

July 13, 1917) and Paul (born April 5, 1919), while living in Los Angeles. Ken worked as an elevator operator but spent most of his free time with Kiichi Suzuki, playing and coaching the city's Japanese ball clubs. In late 1919 or early 1920 the Kitsuses moved to the Imperial Valley and became farmers. They had two more children, Alice Toshiko (born October 13, 1921) and John Itsuro (born August 24, 1923), before returning to the city in the mid- to late 1920s. Although their skills had deteriorated, Ken and Kiichi continued to play ball. Suzuki recalled in 1956:

> Slowly we were getting old, and the time for retirement was coming. One year [around 1930], . . . [Kitsuse said,] "Hey Suzuki, we will play baseball until we get to 50," and we joined the league of white people. However, both of us were nearly 50-year-old "old soldiers." We could not contribute with our weak shoulders, lower backs or legs, but somehow managed to use our brains instead to survive. [In one game] Kitsuse got on first base by a walk or something, and I hit the ball into right field, but Kitsuse stopped at second base. I asked him, "What are you doing? Why don't you go to third base?" And he replied, "I am too old to run." The old king of base-running had finally gone bad. We retired after that. We were probably 50 or 51 at that time. I could not help feeling how much we had changed.[23]

After helping the JBBA with its abortive 1909 tour, Tozan Masko had returned to Denver to focus on his job as editor of the *Denver Shimpo*. Published semi-weekly, the paper's circulation had risen to about 1,500 in 1911. As the editor of the city's first Japanese newspaper, Masko became a leader in the Japanese community, helping fellow immigrants and championing their causes. The paper, for example, helped protest Commissioner of Property Otto F. Thum's decision to ban Japanese from bathing in the Washington and Berkeley city park ponds. "If Japanese go to the beaches it would be necessary for them to use the lockers and dressing rooms and showers," explained Thum. "To this, white patrons would object and we must observe the wishes of the majority for whom the beaches are constructed. We must keep out objectionable things. Snakes and crocodiles would be objectionable and we would keep them out." The protests were unsuccessful, and Japanese, along with African Americans, were excluded from the public bathing areas.[24]

A few years later, in July 1914, Masko and the *Denver Shimpo* spearheaded an attack on Kamataro Itow, accused of collecting bribes in the Japanese community on behalf of Chief Deputy F. F. Graves of the city's license department. Unable to touch the powerful Graves, they focused on his henchman Itow, revealing his shakedowns in a series of articles and culminating with Masko's personal appeal to the Japanese community that either the community drive Itow out of the neighborhood or Tozan would cease editing the newspaper. The Japanese Business Men's Association told Itow to leave town.[25]

Tozan still remained active in baseball. Scattered newspaper references, including a black-and-white picture in *Leslie's Weekly*, indicate his Mikado's team still existed in 1911, although it was now a local amateur club and not a semi-pro barnstorming team.[26] During the 1906 Guy Green tour, Masko had acted as an umpire in several games, receiving praise from the *Stark County News* and the *Covington Friend* as "exceptional[ly] good" and "one of the fairest umpires in the state."[27] Having turned thirty years old in 1911 and having never been a good player, Tozan decided to become an umpire in the city's amateur leagues. By 1914 he had become a regular umpire for Denver's Senior Amateur Division.[28]

In early 1913 the Nippon Club, "an aggregation of prominent Japanese residents" located at 2049 Champa Street, decided to sponsor a baseball team in the Senior Amateur Division.[29] Although newspaper articles do not mention Masko, it is likely that he managed, or at least directed, the team, as Toyo Fujita and Kitty Kawashima left Los Angeles to join the squad.[30]

The season began poorly for the Nippons, and by August 3 they were in last place with a 1-8 record. Pitching was once again a problem for the Japanese until they recruited an ex-Minor League pitcher identified only as Thum, who turned the Nippon club from "a consistent loser into a good bet against any team."[31] Fujita also excelled, batting .385 in fifty-two at bats.[32] The team would win its final three games and end up tied for seventh place with a 6-10 record.

In 1914 with Thum on the mound from the beginning of the season and Fujita playing first and batting third, the team gelled. To the surprise of the local papers, the Japanese were pounding the ball. After an initial loss they won the next three games with forty-four combined hits and thirty-eight runs. By the beginning of September in the last published Senior Amateur Division standings, the Nippons were in first place with a 5-1 record.

Despite their success, the team disbanded after the season. "The members of the Nippon club have scattered throughout the country," reported the *Denver Rocky Mountain News*, "much to the disappointment of their admirers."[33] Toyo Fujita relocated to Salt Lake City, while Kitty Kawashima went to Chicago. In January 1916 Masko, now thirty-four years old, traveled to Japan to marry eighteen-year-old Haruko Kimura. The newlyweds returned to Denver in April but moved to Salt Lake City within the year, where Tozan became an editor at the *Utah Nippo*, the city's daily Japanese newspaper.

Masko soon became involved in the local Japanese baseball scene. The city's first Japanese team, the Salt Lake Nippons, was organized in 1915 as an independent amateur nine. The squad is first mentioned in the *Salt Lake Telegram* on July 19 of that year, when it lost to the Paris Military ball club. From that date on the Nippons routinely enter the local sports pages playing non-Japanese amateur teams. During the summer of 1916 the club recruited Goro Mikami, the former Waseda and All Nations player, as their captain, along with first baseman Toyo Fujita. In April 1916 a second Japanese team, known as the Magna Nippons, joined the newly formed Salt Lake Amateur Baseball Association. The league had only four teams, and the Magna finished second.

The following year, 1917, the Salt Lake Nippons and Magna Nippons joined with four new teams, Tooele, Arthur, Smelter, and Magna Junior, to form the Utah Nippon Baseball League. Masko acted as one of the league's umpires. Captained by Fujita, the Magna club finished on top with an undefeated record. At the end of the season an all-star team from the league played a Japanese team from Pocatello, Idaho, to raise money for the tobacco fund for American troops in France.[34]

Tozan and Haruko would have two children while in Salt Lake City. Their daughter, Shigeko, was born in 1917 and their son, Takahiko, in 1918. Before 1920, however, the Masko family had moved to

Yokohama, Japan. Drawing on his past experience promoting the Mikado's and JBBA baseball teams, Tozan decided to become a sports promoter. The endeavor did not go well—his tendency to exaggerate and his lack of scruples getting in the way.

Masko began his new career by bringing Ad Santel and Henry Weber to Japan to "test the relative merits of American wrestling with Japanese jiujitsu." Santel, who is still considered one of the greatest "catch wrestlers" of all time, was the reigning world light heavyweight champion. Since 1914 he had been wrestling Japan's top Judo champions—often defeating them easily. As a result, he was well known in Japan, although he had never been to the country. Weber, a 6-foot, 200-pound blond who "looked like a Greek god," was not Santel's equal on the mat but was nonetheless a renowned wrestler and Santel's manager.[35]

A large crowd met Santel and Weber on the pier as they arrived in Yokohama on February 26, 1921. Beneath banners bearing the wrestlers' names in both English and Japanese, kimono-clad girls presented the visitors with wreaths of flowers and bouquets as the crowd cheered, "Banzai!" Tozan accompanied the wrestlers to Tokyo, where they would spend the next week preparing for a match against Japan's experts from the Kodokan Judo Institute—the school created by the sport's founder Jigoro Kano.[36]

An advertisement, probably submitted by Masko, in Japan's English-language newspapers stated, "The Greatest Wrestling Match Ever Held in Japan will start at 1 p.m., Sunday, March 6. Santel and Weber in matches with Experts from the Kodokan." Although Masko had arranged for a prominent judo expert to provide opponents for Santel and Weber, he had never contacted the Kodokan itself. Members of the school were outraged when they heard of Masko's plans and the use of their name "without any notice or consent of the officials of the school." At a special meeting Kodokan representatives decreed that any student who took part in the match would be expelled as "the spirit of Bushido prevents . . . taking part in any professional show of judo."[37]

Despite the edict several judo experts accepted the challenge and wrestled Santel and Weber on March 5 and 6 at Yoshikuni Shrine. Sellout crowds of 6,000–8,000 attended each day, bringing in over

¥20,000. After the matches the wrestlers asked for their 35 percent cut of the gate receipts plus reimbursements for their travel expenses. Masko, however, claimed that the two days at Yoshikuni Shrine had produced a profit of only ¥196 and promised to pay when cash became available. They next went to Nagoya, where Tozan had arranged two more matches. Despite strong attendance the wrestlers still did not receive their money. A few days later in Osaka, Santel and Weber refused to enter the ring unless they were paid up front. For two days Masko coughed up ¥300, and the matches took place. Noting the large crowds, the wrestlers demanded ¥1,000 prior to the third match. After much wrangling, they eventually accepted a check from a local promoter.[38]

The next morning, when Santel presented the check at the bank, he was told that the promoter had no account, making the check worthless. Returning to the Osaka promoter's office, Santel learned that Masko and the local promoter "had drawn on the money due to them until there was nothing left." The American wrestlers searched in vain for Tozan, who had left Osaka and gone into hiding.[39]

A sympathetic judo expert stepped forward and arranged bouts to raise enough money for Santel and Weber to return to the United States. As he left, Santel told reporters, "Our stay in Japan has been very pleasant in some ways, and we will not carry away the impression that everyone here is bad. . . . There are swindlers everywhere and we just happen to become connected with two in Japan." Santel and Weber declined to bring charges against Masko as legal fees and further time in Japan would have been prohibitively expensive.[40]

A few months later Tozan once again brought athletes to Japan. This time he returned to the sport he loved and arranged a tour for the Suquamish Indians and the Canadian Stars baseball teams. The Suquamish, a group of Native Americans from the western shores of Puget Sound, had been playing baseball since the late nineteenth century. How Masko learned of the Suquamish team or organized the tour is unknown, but the *Bremerton Searchlight* reported, "In their efforts to secure an all-Indian ball team for the trip, the promoters have tried out practically every Indian ball team on the coast and the fact that the Suquamish team was finally chosen is a considerable boost for the local players." Accompanying the Suquamish was a semi-pro team from Ballard, Washington, that had been renamed the Canadian Stars for the Japanese visit.[41]

The two clubs arrived in Yokohama on the steamer *Alabama* at noon on August 22, 1921, and immediately went to Yokohama Park to practice. "A big gathering of Japanese fans" waited at the park "to give the invading teams an enthusiastic welcome . . . and to watch their every movement with bat and glove." The clubs were expected to stay in Japan for two months, playing collegiate teams in Tokyo and touring the country.[42]

The Suquamish team's tour began poorly as it was crushed by Meiji University, 10–0, in a game that featured "all around poor playing" by the visitors. Because it was the first Native American ball club to tour Japan, Masko expected it to draw huge crowds and extensive media coverage. But neither happened. The results of most of the games are unknown as Japan's numerous sports newspapers did not cover the tour. The few surviving scores show that the Suquamish team was not strong. After losing to Meiji, it was embarrassed by Keio, 16–0, and even by the Canadian team, 20–0. By November Tozan decided to abandon the project. Once again he simply disappeared, leaving the teams to fend for themselves. The Tokyo-area universities volunteered to play a series of benefit games to raise enough money to pay for the teams' passage back to the United States. Masko dodged criminal charges again, but it was the end to his brief career as a sports promoter. At this point he disappears from the historical record. Oral tradition, however, notes that he briefly returned to the place of his birth, the rural village of Niida in Fukushima, during World War II to escape the Allied bombing of Tokyo and Yokohama.[43]

In late September 1921, as Masko was still touring Japan with the Suquamish Indians, Harry Saisho arrived in Yokohama with his own Native American baseball team. Since retiring from the JBBA and moving to the Imperial Valley in 1912, Saisho had made and lost a small fortune. He and his partners had begun by growing melons and lettuce on four hundred acres. The business boomed, and "the dream of becoming a big tycoon was practically at [my] fingertips."[44] In 1919 they decided to diversify, leased another thousand acres, and planted cotton. An economic crisis in 1920, however, caused the price of cotton to plummet. Saisho and his partners went broke. Harry then decided to work as a produce buyer, purchasing small farmers' crops and reselling them at regional markets. During his travels in 1920 he met Kiyo Minami in Sacramento. It was "love at first sight." They married within a few months and traveled to Japan for a traditional ceremony in December. While in Japan, Harry visited with his old JBBA teammate Shin Hashido. Hashido had become a famous sportswriter and had recently helped organize Japan's first professional baseball club, Nihon Undo Kyokai, featuring many of his former Waseda teammates. With the Nihon Undo Kyokai's backing, Saisho decided to bring to Japan a team of Native Americans from the Sherman Institute—the school that had played Hashido's Waseda team in 1905.

Unable to use students enrolled at the Sherman Institute, Saisho recruited ten recent graduates, led by James Alexander, to make the trip in September 1921. The team arrived in Yokohama on September 29 and immediately ran into trouble. According to the *Japan Advertiser*, "The Indians . . . were so anxious to embark that they neglected to obtain passports or other papers which would gain them admittance to Japan." Unable to enter the country, the players remained aboard ship for several days as the American consulate-general pleaded their case to the Japanese government.[45] After gaining permission to disembark, the team spent a week practicing at the Nihon Undo Kyokai's ballpark before starting its tour in Osaka.[46]

The Sherman Indians were the eighth of nine American baseball clubs to tour Japan in 1921. When the team arrived, seven of these squads were in the country: the University of Washington, the Seattle Asahi, the Vancouver Asahi, the Hawaiian Nippon, the Hawaiian Hilo, and Masko's Suquamish and "Canadian" teams. The University of California had visited that spring, and the Hawaii All-Stars would arrive on October 22.

With Nihon Undo Kyokai's support, Saisho's Sherman Indians received the media attention Masko's Suquamish had lacked. The *Osaka Mainichi Newspaper* sponsored the team's games in western Japan and covered them in print. On October 8 the newspaper previewed the first game under the headline "A Major Baseball Game,

Black People vs. Stars, at 3 p.m. This Afternoon at Toyonaka Athletic Field—The Attack by the Black Troop, Looking Gruesome—Shiny Eyes and Extremely Strong!" The article began, "The black troop, the Sherman Indians, who arrived yesterday in Osaka, will have their first game against the Star Club. Let's see how strong they are and how powerful they are as the black troop is known to be fierce."

The team, however, was not as strong or fierce as advertised. It lost to the Star Club, 3–1. The Nihon Undo Kyokai tried to bolster the Indians by loaning them several of their junior players, but they still lost their next two games in Osaka. The following week the Sherman Indians traveled to Tokyo. On October 15 they played Frank Fukuda's Seattle Asahi, losing a close game, 6–5. The next day they beat Rikkyo University, 2–1, before losing on the October 17 to the Keio alumni Mita Club, 7–6. And then Saisho's old enemy—rain— struck again, canceling a number of games. Saisho also had trouble finding opponents. As the Sherman players were no longer students and were being paid to make the trip, many considered them to be professionals. Heavily influenced by an idealized version of the "Bushido code," most Japanese believed that being paid to play sports, including baseball, was immoral.[47] Schools worried that playing the Shermans would sully their reputations. The team's next recorded game was not until October 28, when it lost to Waseda, 2–1. Unable to find further opponents, Saisho and his team packed their bags and returned to California on November 22.[48]

Despite the lack of games and victories, the players returned happy. They had been paid to visit Japan and thoroughly enjoyed the experience. The team's pitcher, Kruse, told the Japanese-language *Nichi Bei Times*, "We are happy because in addition to Nihon Undo Club paying for all the costs as it had been agreed, they gave each of us $200. This trip to Japan was so wonderful that I would like to go back there again in the future." But for Harry Saisho the trip was a financial disaster, wiping out his savings. "Saisho," recalled his friend Masaru Akahori, "would never talk about this bitter experience."[49]

By the time Saisho returned home, Japanese American baseball had transformed from a game played by a handful of immigrants to the passion of thousands of American-born Japanese. "Now it seems football is considered the national sport," Harry Saisho remembered in 1956, "but back then baseball was the American sport. Baseball was in its golden age among Japanese people as the young Nisei became active." Leagues thrived in nearly every Japanese community—urban and rural. The *Rafu Shimpo*, the newspaper that had given birth to Japanese baseball in Southern California, reported that in 1926 "twelve Nisei teams with 120 to 130 players were playing baseball every Sunday in the Los Angeles area."[50] The top teams routinely traveled across the western states to play each other and compete for the official Japanese American championship.

Baseball brought Japanese American communities together—literally and figuratively. Thousands of fans came to watch important games. The ballparks could be like parties—a place to socialize with neighbors, discuss local concerns, meet new people, and cheer for a common cause. Love for the game also brought the generations together. Many Issei felt alienated from their Nisei children, who spoke English fluently, dressed and acted like white Americans, and openly questioned Japanese traditions and values. Baseball created a common bond between them. "The Issei men," writes Kerry Yo Nakagawa in *Japanese American Baseball in California*, "were fanatical in their support of Nisei baseball. Not only were the Issei the loudest and most numerous fans, but they also built baseball fields, provided financial backing for the equipment, sponsored most of the tournaments and even drove their sons to games in distant towns." Baseball was simultaneously an American symbol of assimilation embraced by both generations and for the Issei a game from the old country that promoted the Japanese values of respect, perseverance, harmony, and teamwork.[51]

Ironically, as Japanese American baseball grew, it became a less effective tool for building bridges with mainstream white American society. Many Japanese Americans believed that seeing Japanese embrace the national pastime would help white Americans overcome their prejudices. To show their loyalty the Japanese leagues routinely enacted patriotic displays at their games—Fourth of July celebrations, Boy Scout events, flag ceremonies, patriotic music. But by the late 1930s few non-Japanese witnessed these displays of patriotism as most Nisei played in all–Japanese American leagues.

Historian Samuel O. Regalado concludes, "Unfortunately, only [Japanese Americans] saw these displays and fully grasped the[ir] meaning and purpose. . . . Apart from a few teams and players, the entire structure of Nikkei baseball existed in virtual isolation from the very group with whom they hope to someday fuse. . . . And, sadly for them, it could not have come at a worse time."[52]

16

Incarceration

December 7, 1941, the day that would live in infamy, would change the lives of every Japanese American. It would force many to question their loyalty and most fundamental beliefs. For some it would tear their lives apart, stripping them of their personal possessions, communities, and dignity.

Members of Guy Green's Japanese Ball Club and the JBBA had different experiences. Kitty Kawashima and Minori Sohara had moved to the Midwest and were not forced to leave their homes during the war. Kawashima ran the Tokio Cafe in Chicago until his death in 1967. Sohara worked as a waiter in St. Louis before also moving to Chicago. He died in June 1946. Tom Uyeda, Harry Saisho, Ken Kitsuse, and Kiichi Suzuki, however, spent the war in captivity.

On December 3, 1941, Tom Uyeda, who had recently become the manager of the posh Bridlespur Hunt Club in St. Louis, purchased a block of tickets to "Fun to be Free," a patriotic show featuring a historical pageant and performances by leading entertainers produced by the Fight for Freedom Committee to Defend America.[1] He would never have a chance to attend.

After the Mikado's disbanded in 1908, Uyeda spent two years as a construction foreman for the Union Pacific Railroad in Wyoming before trying sugar beet farming for another two years. He was working as a waiter at the Colorado Springs Country Club in 1912 when Togo Hamamoto, the man who was supposed to have attended spring training with the New York Giants, invited him to come to St. Louis to help organize a baseball club.[2]

Although there is no evidence that the team was ever created, Tom moved to St. Louis and began working as a waiter at the St.

Louis Country Club, the playground for the city's elite. His younger brother, Takatomo, now known as Bob, soon joined him. Ambitious and smart, within two years Tom became the club's head waiter. "While I worked in the dining room, I found it uninteresting," he later recalled. But "I was anxious to find how I could best develop my personality. So, I watched the guests at the club and patterned myself accordingly, for I too wanted to be cultured and considerate. I have had the pleasure of serving President Theodore Roosevelt, President Taft, the Queen of Romania . . . and noted professional men and women." He learned well and was promoted to the club's assistant manager, a surprising position at the time for a Japanese.[3]

On April 11, 1917, Tom defied convention by marrying Lulu Lamb, a thirty-year-old American-born Caucasian woman of Irish-English descent. At the time, Japanese-white marriages were rare and illegal in ten states, including California and—more important for Tom— Missouri.[4] In 1909 the state had revised Section 8280 of its marriage laws so that it now declared, "All marriages between . . . white persons and Mongolians [i.e. Asians] are prohibited and declared absolutely void."[5] The statute, which also outlawed black-white marriages, would remain in place until the U.S. Supreme Court declared it unconstitutional in 1967. To circumvent the law Tom and Lulu married in Springfield, Illinois, on their way to their honeymoon in Chicago. By marrying an unnaturalized foreigner, Lulu forfeited her American citizenship, as prior to 1921 a woman took the citizenship of her husband. The couple would remain happily married for almost thirty-nine years, having a daughter named Vivian in 1922.[6]

In 1926 Tom was promoted again, this time to manager of the St. Louis Country Club, and brother Bob became the club's steward. But Tom did not stay long. In 1927 August A. Busch Sr. founded the Bridlespur Hunt Club and asked Tom to become its first manager. He would stay in the position until the start of World War II.

In the fall of 1937 the Japanese Board of Tourist Industry appointed Uyeda as its honorary representative in Missouri "to promote a better understanding and friendship between the Unites States and Japan and to furnish travel information to those traveling to the Orient."[7] To accomplish this Uyeda was expected to do the following:

1. To answer letters of inquiry about Japan.

2. To offer editors of newspapers and magazines material on Japan.

3. To distribute suitable printed matter for publication purposes.

4. To lend out pictures, films, and lantern slides.

5. To deliverer lectures on Japan as opportunity presents itself.

6. In all other ways possible to introduce Japan to the public.[8]

A few months later Tom received a letter requesting that he speak at a meeting of the Pacific Movement of the Eastern World (PMEW) on the conflict between Japan and China. Uyeda balked, claiming that he was a poor public speaker and knew little about the topic but that he could talk about "the Japanese country, our history, our habits or customs." On February 4 he addressed 200–300 people, nearly all African Americans, at Pythian Hall, at 3137 Pine St. in East St. Louis. "I just told a few things about how our children are raised, our education, our culture [and] our history." He then passed out brochures printed by the Japanese Board of Tourist Industry. He returned home, probably thinking that it had been an uneventful albeit unusual evening. Tom did not know that the FBI had categorized the PMEW as a dangerous insurgent group.[9]

Founded in 1932 in Chicago by Satokata Takahashi, the group advocated the worldwide unification of non-white races under the leadership of Japan. The following year Filipino con man Policarpio Manansala assumed the organization's' presidency, posing as a Japanese named Ashima Takis. Manansala moved the PMEW headquarters to St. Louis, recruited disenfranchised African Americans, and charged them membership dues, which he pocketed. Manansala claimed that the organization had thousands of members, an exaggeration that prompted the FBI to scrutinize the group.

By 1940 Tom Uyeda had become a respected member of St. Louis society and the most successful of the city's forty-six Japanese residents. As the managing director of the elite Bridlespur Hunt Club, he had an annual salary of $4,000 and owned a luxurious $25,000 home designed by the architectural firm of Marita, Young and Dusard, which had been featured in the *St. Louis Post-Dispatch*. His daughter Vivian had married Albert Tucker, a well-known musician. Later in her life Vivian would marry Walter Reisinger, the great-grandson of Adolphus Busch, co-founder of the Anheuser-Busch brewery. Yet Tom's success would be his undoing.[10]

As the likelihood of war between the United States and Japan grew, the FBI began gathering information on Japanese living in America. Using the federal census, newspaper articles, and other public resources, the bureau made a list of Japanese American community leaders, dubbing them "Suspect Enemy Aliens." The group included business leaders, clergymen, educators, and newspaper editors. The FBI made no effort to assess these individuals' loyalty or their potential threat to the country. Immediately following the attack at Pearl Harbor, federal agents arrested more than 1,200 Japanese on the list.[11]

At 8:55 p.m. on the evening of December 7, 1941, Special Agents D. C. Limprecht, W. H. Cole, and S. A. Amdur barged into the Bridlespur Hunt Club and arrested Tom Uyeda. His affiliation with the Japanese Board of Tourist Industry and lecture to the PMEW had placed him on the FBI's list. That night agents searched Uyeda's home, confiscating Japanese-language pamphlets and letters. These were sent to Washington for translation. Uyeda was the only Japanese arrested in St. Louis.[12]

Tom would spend almost three months in the city jail before facing charges. At 2 p.m. on February 26, 1942, at a closed-door hearing in the grand jury room on the fourth floor of the Federal Building, the Enemy Alien Hearing Board reviewed his case.[13] U.S. Attorney Harry C. Blanton presented the case against Uyeda. Basing his statements on documents seized from Tom's home, including the letter inviting Uyeda to address the PMEW, Blanton argued that Tom was either an active Japanese agent or was in a position to aid his former country. After just a few hours the board concluded:

> [Uyeda] has a wide acquaintance among the Japanese as well as whites in the country; . . . he is in close contact with officials of the Board of Tourist Industry of the Japanese Government Railways, and with many important Japanese, and therefore he is in a position to give information and aid to a hostile nation at war with the United States. Moreover, his testimony, demeanor and conduct while on the wit-

ness stand gave the Board the decided impression that he is unreliable [and] untrustworthy and these circumstances compel the conclusion that he is dangerous to the safety of the United States. It is therefore recommended that he is interned.[14]

As the most visible and integrated Japanese man in the city, Uyeda made a tempting target for the politically ambitious and overzealous Blanton. According to the *St. Louis Post-Dispatch*, "Numerous patrons of the hunt club intervened on Uyeda's behalf, but Harry C. Blanton, then United States Attorney, and the Enemy Alien Hearing Board disregarded all pleas."[15] The board sentenced Uyeda to prison as an enemy of the state, sending him temporarily to Camp McCoy in Wisconsin before transferring him to the Camp Livingston Detention Facility in Louisiana.

While Uyeda was incarcerated and unable to testify, he became a scapegoat during the trial of members of the PMEW. Before a grand jury on September 22, 1942, Blanton contended that Uyeda had conspired with Ashima Takis (a.k.a. Policarpio Manansala) to create a "Fifth Column" to aid a Japanese invasion of the United States. Blanton testified that the organization believed "in reality there were only two races—white and colored—and that all colored persons, no matter what degree of color or race, belong to the dark race and should join [together] when the Japanese invaded America."[16] Speaking at the organization's 1932 national meeting in St. Louis, Takis had supposedly urged African Americans "to store firearms against the day when the Japanese invaded America." At that time "members . . . would be given a secret counter sign and furnished with special banners to put in their windows so that they would be safe from the attacking Japanese who could identify them as friends in this manner. The stored firearms could then be brought out and used against the white race."[17] There was, of course, no evidence that Uyeda was involved in the organization.

During the summer of 1943 Uyeda was transferred from the Livingston detention camp to the Santa Fe Detention Camp. In both centers Tom ran the camps' athletic departments and received accolades for his cooperation. He "has been a model internee . . . prefers to see the United States victorious in the war with Japan, [and] is willing to work to help the war effort," noted a November 1944 internal report.[18] Several federal officials attempted to parole Tom but to no avail. Ivan Williams, the commander of the Santa Fe camp "has come to know Mr. Uyeda very well and he is absolutely convinced that this man does not belong in an internment camp," wrote W. F. Kelly, the assistant commissioner for alien control, to his superior, Edward J. Ennis.[19] Each time Blanton blocked Tom's early release.

The U.S. government finally released Tom Uyeda in December 1945, with "a clean bill by the Washington authorities."[20] Despite his unjust incarceration Tom proclaimed, "I can honestly say that I have always been loyal to this country, and my love for this country shall remain the same until my death."[21] On May 7, 1954, he became an American citizen. Tom returned to managing clubs and restaurants before dying from a heart attack on March 11, 1956. His younger brother, Bob, lived until 1971, dying during a visit to Japan.[22]

Since returning from Japan in 1921, Harry and Kiyo Saisho had moved around California, leasing land and farming as opportunities presented themselves. Issei, such as the Saishos, were unable to own agricultural land or lease a property for more than three years since California's 1913 Webb-Haney Act had denied these rights to "aliens ineligible for citizenship" (i.e., Asians). Times were difficult, but their family grew; the couple would have seven healthy children. "[We] saw many days of poverty and there were times when [we] had only soup and dumplings between [our]selves and starvation."[23]

Although he no longer played at a high level, Harry continued to be crazy about baseball. He even named his first daughter Mariko—*mari* means "ball" in Japanese. When Mariko was a toddler, Harry took her to a pickup ball game but became so engrossed in the game that he forgot she was there and left the field without her.[24]

In 1935 the Saishos settled down in Hilmar, a small town about a hundred miles southwest of Oakland. Harry leased forty acres and grew melons, strawberries, and vegetables. Once the children were old enough, they helped on the farm—working before and after school and on weekends. It was hard work, and money was always tight. Harry was, by his own admission, "a rather easygoing farmer." During his trips to the market he would often stop by local coffee shops and spend hours in conversation instead of returning to work on the farm. His "philosophy was to enjoy life, good or bad, . . . and to make the most of it." His son Giro recalled, "My father . . . was not a typical Japanese father. He was very gentle. I don't think he ever spanked me or [did] anything [violent] in my whole life. It's a wonder that we didn't grow up more spoiled. But he was essentially a dreamer. He had a lot of good ideas but he wasn't a very good executioner. He couldn't really carry out his good ideas. So, my mother took the burden of raising the family and looking after all the kids and everything."[25]

Sunday, December 7, 1941, was market day. Harry, now fifty-nine-years-old, and his sixteen-year-old son Taro packed their Chevy truck before dawn and drove to Oakland to sell the week's produce. The morning trip was uneventful, and they returned home, filled the truck a second time, and headed back to Oakland.

Japan attacked Pearl Harbor in two waves, first at 7:53 a.m., Hawaii Standard Time, and again sixty-two minutes later. The Associated Press first announced the attack at 11:22 a.m. PST; radio reports began a few minutes later. Within hours the FBI began rounding up Japanese and Germans believed to be a threat to the United States.

When Harry and Taro arrived at the Oakland produce market in the afternoon, the FBI was waiting. Father and son were whisked to a nearby military office and questioned. Determined that they would not be a threat, the bureau agents "marched [them] through town" to their truck and escorted them home—a hundred miles away. At the farm the "agents acted courteous but suspicious, canvassing the home, and warning a child not to play with a toy model airplane" before leaving.[26]

In the days following Pearl Harbor, Californians panicked. Rumors spread of imminent Japanese invasions, the bombing of major cities, and the sabotage of local installations by spies. Throughout the West Coast Japanese Americans were verbally and physically harassed. "Carloads of people from other areas of the city descended on the streets of Little Tokyo and attacked the Japanese stores and stands. The vigilante 'patriots' overturned carts and tables and threw tomatoes and potatoes at anyone with an Asian face."[27]

The sinking of the oil tanker USS *Montebello* off the coast of Cal-

ifornia by a Japanese submarine on December 23 kicked off a new
wave of hysteria. FBI agents, police, and the military raided Japanese American homes, seizing 1,458 radios, binoculars, 2,592 guns,
and 2,015 cameras. The government imposed an 8 p.m. to 6 a.m.
curfew on Japanese Americans and forbade travel of more than five
miles from their homes.

On New Year's Day 1942 Harry Saisho received shocking news.
His old friend from Miyakonojo and former JBBA teammate Shichiji
Kikuchi had been murdered. Kikuchi, now sixty years old, was living peacefully with his wife Mitsuko and five children on a ranch in
Brawley, California. They were established members of the community and active in the local Methodist church. In the early morning
of January 1, a man described as "a Filipino wearing a hat" knocked
on the Kikuchis' door. As Mitsuko answered it, he drew a .32-calibre
revolver, shot her, and fired at her son Katake, narrowly missing
the eighteen-year-old. The assailant then went to an adjacent building and shot the sleeping Shichiji in the face, killing him instantly.
The shooter escaped in a waiting automobile. Mitsuko died of her
wounds later that morning.[28]

The murder outraged the local community. A few days later the
Women's Christian Temperance Union passed a resolution proclaim-
ing, "We . . . have been deeply shocked by the outrages committed
against our Japanese people, citizens and not citizens alike, who for
years have been law-abiding Christian residents of our community. . . . We denounce such action as un-American and a violation
of the principles of justice, tolerance, and freedom, for the preservation of which we are now engaged in war. If we are defeated on
the home front, there is no object in waging war across the sea."[29]

The murderer was never identified. Authorities concluded that
the Kikuchis were chosen at random by a Filipino retaliating for the
Japanese Army's brutal invasion of the Philippines in December 1941.

By January 1942 government officials, the military, the press, and
most white Americans viewed Japanese Americans as a threat. Karl
Bendesten, adviser to Gen. John L. DeWitt of the Western Defense
Command, summed up the prevailing belief: "A substantial majority
of the Nisei bear allegiance to Japan, are well controlled and disci-
plined by the enemy, and at the proper time will engage in orga-

nized sabotage, particularly should a raid along the Pacific Coast be attempted by the Japanese."[30] A *Fresno Bee* editorial argued, "The possibility of a Japanese attack on the coast has loomed ever larger. . . . Californians never can feel secure until all enemy aliens and Fifth Column citizens, too—are put in place and surrounded with conditions which will make it utterly impossible for them to serve superiors in any totalitarian capital whose deadly purpose is to destroy the United States of America."[31]

In response Los Angeles mayor Fletcher Bowron dismissed all city employees of Japanese descent, declaring, "Right here in our own city are those who may spring to action at an appointed time in accordance with a prearranged plan wherein each of our little Japanese friends will know his part in the event of any possible attempted invasion or air raid. . . . We cannot run the risk of another Pearl Harbor episode in Southern California."[32] Bendesten and others wanted to go further, devising a plan to remove all Japanese Americans from the West Coast.

On February 19, 1942, President Franklin D. Roosevelt signed Executive Order 9066 authorizing the secretary of war to designate areas within the United States as military zones and to remove any inhabitants deemed a threat to national security. Ten days later General DeWitt declared the entire West Coast from the shore to two hundred miles inland as Military Area One and announced plans to relocate all people of Japanese descent from the area. Initially residents were encouraged to leave voluntarily.

Wanting to control their own fate, members of the Saisho family prepared to leave. They sold their crops and farming equipment at near give-away prices and began packing their truck with the necessary supplies and tools to move east. Just days before the Saishos planned to leave, DeWitt changed his mind. Japanese Americans were now forbidden from leaving Area One on their own. Instead they would be rounded up and escorted to government-run detention camps, euphemistically called relocation centers.[33]

Despite the dubious legality of detaining American citizens without a trial, there was little outcry against DeWitt's plan. Using many of the same racist arguments contrived by the Asiatic Exclusion League in the early twentieth century, DeWitt and others viewed all Japanese as a danger. "Racial affinities are not severed by migration," argued DeWitt. "The Japanese race is an enemy race and while many second and third generation Japanese born on United States soil, possessed of American citizenship, have become 'Americanized,' the racial strains are undiluted. [And there] is no ground for assuming that any Japanese . . . will not turn against this nation when final test of loyalty comes."[34]

In March 1942 the U.S. military began removing Japanese Americans from their homes and placing them in twelve "assembly centers" while it finished building the more permanent relocation centers. Each person was allowed to bring only what he or she could carry—the equivalent of two suitcases. Pets were forbidden and had to be left behind. Families across the West Coast were forced to sell their businesses and personal items they could not pack in as little as a week; most received just pennies on the dollar. The Saishos had already sold most of their farming equipment. Valued possessions that did not fit in their suitcases—such as Kiyo's Japanese kimonos—they left in the care of non-Japanese friends.

Avoiding the indignity of being forced from their home, in early April the Saishos—Harry and Kiyo; their sons—Taro (sixteen years old), Giro (fifteen years old), Takayoshi (ten years old), Kiyoto (five years old); their daughters—Emiko (nineteen years old), Mataye (eighteen years old); and their wards—Harry Akune (twenty-two years old) and Ken Akune (eighteen years old)—loaded their truck and drove themselves to Merced Assembly Center.

Located at the county fairgrounds, the center consisted of 286 buildings—200 barracks, 11 mess halls, 5 laundries, 40 communal showers, and 30 toilet houses—surrounded by a barbed wire fence. The 4,669 Japanese American prisoners, including about 1,000 children, were guarded by 160 soldiers. Families were assigned to 100-x-20-foot barracks, cheaply built of rough pine boards covered with tar paper. Many of the less fortunate bachelors were forced into the hastily cleaned cattle barns and stables that already stood on the fairgrounds. Despite the cleaning, the barns still reeked of horse urine and manure. "The barracks were very plain," remembered Harry's daughter Mataye Saisho Nishi, "but we came from a plain background, so it was not such a shock for us as it was for people from the city."[35]

Harry Akune, one of the Saishos' wards, recalled:

We went to the Merced Assembly Center. . . . [There were] fences all around you, and MPs around you. . . . I really resented that a great deal. So . . . I thought to myself, "Okay; you put me in here; you'll take care of me. . . . I'm not gonna lift a finger to do anything."

[But] other people, Isseis and Niseis, were working in the kitchen . . . so they could feed each other. . . . That . . . lasted maybe about a week. Then Mr. Saisho said to me . . . "You know, Harry, if everybody did what you did, we wouldn't even eat here. There would be no way for you to even have food. So, you can't just not do anything, because you're affecting your own kind." Then I thought "That's right; that makes very good sense [but] . . . being that I'm so angry . . . how could I . . . kind of work it out?" . . . So, I joined them, and I became a dishwasher. And that was really, really hot work, and I sweated a lot. And eventually I worked that hostility away—you know, through myself, by just forcing myself to suffer a little bit, physically. So that helped me join the group as one of the members.[36]

The inmates did their best to transform Merced into a community. They set up schools, churches, theater groups, a newspaper, and athletic leagues. Baseball and softball were the most popular sports. Two of the six pages in the bi-weekly newspaper were dedicated to game results, and complete batting averages for all participates were calculated and published. At fifty-nine years old, Harry did not play, but with his love for the sport he probably helped organize the games.

By September 1942 construction of the relocation camps had been completed. Most of the inmates at Merced were loaded onto trains bound for the Amache Relocation Camp in the small town of Granada in the southeastern Colorado desert.

"The trip to Amache took two days by train," remembered Mataye Saisho Nishi. "As we went east, we saw trains full of young soldiers going west. Sometimes the trains would stop next to each other, and we would open our windows and talk. We wondered where they were going, and they wondered where we were going. The young soldiers weren't aware what was happening to us—that we were being evacuated from our homes and taken to another place. When we told them, they felt so bad that they passed food and fruit to us through the open windows."[37]

On September 16, 1942, the Saishos saw their new home. Amache consisted of 550 hastily constructed wooden buildings surrounded by a barbed wire fence with eight machine gun towers; the guns faced inward. It would house 7,597 people. The camp enclosed 640 acres and stood on a low hill in the midst of the Colorado prairie. Strong winds pummeled the buildings. Blinding dust storms blew frequently across the region. "There was really nothing there at the time," Giro Saisho remembered. "It was barren, just barracks, and it was a desolate place."[38]

The family was assigned two rooms in one of the twelve 20-x-120-foot barracks. Like at Merced, the barracks were built with cheap, rough-cut pine boards. Although it was only September, it was cold in the desert—especially for Californians, most of whom owned no winter clothes. The icy winds rushed through gaps between the pine boards, often bringing in sand. Harry and his fellow inmates went immediately to work to make the quarters inhabitable. They obtained tar paper from the quartermaster and covered the interior walls as best they could, blocking the wind and sand. As the thin insulation did little to keep out the cold, families huddled in their rooms by the central potbellied stove.

Ken Kitsuse's and Kiichi Suzuki's experiences after Pearl Harbor were probably similar to Harry's, but neither recorded details of their incarcerations. After retiring as active ballplayers, both Kitsuse and Suzuki remained in the Los Angeles area working as gardeners. In April 1942 Ken, his wife Suye, and eighteen-year-old son, John, were interred at Manzanar, located in the desert at the foot of the Sierra Nevada Mountains. The climate was harsh, with daytime temperatures soaring to 100 degrees Fahrenheit and falling to below freezing at night. Although also living in Los Angeles, Suzuki was relocated first to the Turlock Assembly Area and in July 1942 removed to the Gila River camp in the Arizona desert.

The interred in the "relocation centers" did their best to make their incarceration as bearable as possible by transforming their environments and creating communities. Families fixed up their shoddy barracks as best they could, planted gardens, and built structures for entertainment and athletics. They created churches, Buddhist temples, schools, and medical clinics, and they ran farms. They also formed their own council to govern their fellow internees. At Amache Harry Saisho served as a block manager and representative on the council.

Ironically for many, internment brought a respite from a lifetime of backbreaking work and struggle. This was especially true for farmers such as the Saishos. Giro Saisho recalled, "My mom, all she did was work, work, work, work, and it was the first time in her life that she had some idle time . . . she could do things there."[39] The Saisho children also enjoyed the break from farm life. Mataye remembers, "For me it was not a bad experience. We came from the farm, where we had to work every day and do chores. At the camp we had a lot of playmates, and we didn't have to do work. We just had to play and go to school. I had a great time."[40] Giro added:

> As for us kids, when we went into camp we thought, "God, gee, I don't have to do any work anymore." So, all we did was play baseball, football, basketball, and so in that sense it was good, but I look back on it and I really, really have a big resentment against the fact that I was placed in camp. I really feel it was a great injustice . . . just the idea behind the whole thing was so terrible. . . . There were some pluses but the big negative was [that our] life was taken away from [us]. . . . [I] can hardly imagine how that affected my parents. But as young kids we didn't know any better.[41]

Athletics, and in particular baseball, helped fill this newly found leisure time and create a sense of community. Soon after their arrival internees began laying out diamonds and building ballparks. At the Gila River camp Kiichi Suzuki would have watched and perhaps helped the famous player and manager Kenichi Zenimura build his ball field. Zenimura's wife, Kiyoko, recalled, "One day, I saw [Kenichi] . . . cutting down the sagebrush and clearing rocks by hand. He decided that he was going to build a baseball field. At first, it was just with our sons." Zenimura's son Kenso added, "Guys from the other blocks asked, 'What are you doing?' Pretty soon all these people were coming with shovels, helping to clear the area. We piled up the brush and burned it, and my dad somehow got a bulldozer to level the ground. We flooded it to pack the ground down." With picks and shovels they created dugouts and covered them with wood stolen from the camp's lumber yard. Eventually they built a small wooden grandstand. At first they used scrap wood for home plate and the pitcher's rubber. The bases were bags filled with rice, and the foul lines were "painted" with flour, but soon they raised enough money to purchase regulation items. "Building the ballpark really saved us, concluded Kiyoko Zenimura. "It kept the spirits of the people up and helped everyone to stay positive and not become angry and short tempered."[42]

Most camps had a variety of baseball leagues, including a top circuit filled with experienced adult players, recreational adult leagues, teenage leagues, youth leagues, a block league (pitting residences against each other), and girls' softball leagues. The games were well attended, becoming a place for the community to gather. Pat Morita, costar of *The Karate Kid* and a Gila River internee, recalled, "The teenagers and the adults would gather every night to watch the games. I had never seen a live baseball game before, so this was my introduction to baseball—sitting and cheering with a couple of thousand rabid fans."[43]

Harry Saisho, Ken Kitsuse, and Kiichi Suzuki turned sixty years old in the camps and were too old to play in a league. Their children played, however, and it is possible that the old professionals coached or helped organize teams. They were certainly among the crowds of "rabid fans" watching.

Japanese American baseball expert Kerry Yo Nakagawa concluded, "At the start of interment, conditions in the assembly centers and camps were dismal, and morale was low. It was natural for the internees to turn to baseball as a way to bring a sense of normalcy to daily life. Playing and watching baseball created a positive social atmosphere, encouraged physical conditioning and maintained self-esteem despite the harsh conditions of incarceration in remote and desolate camps. Ironically, America's national game helped to sustain the people singled out as 'enemy aliens.'"[44]

On June 4–7, 1942, the U.S. Navy destroyed the Japanese fleet at the Battle of Midway, eliminating the threat of an invasion of California. The relocation centers were now superfluous—even before most were occupied. California governor Earl Warren, however, was emphatic that he did not wish the evacuated Japanese to return to his state. "I firmly believe there is positive danger attached to the presence of so many of these admittedly American-hating Japanese in an area where sabotage or any other civil disorders would be so detrimental to the war effort," he told a press conference the day after his election in November 1942.[45] Despite the continued widespread bigotry toward Japanese Americans, the War Relocation Authority began creating programs to gradually release the incarcerated as students, soldiers, and laborers. Neither the Saisho nor the Kitsuse families would stay long in the camps.

Nisei students were allowed to leave the relocation centers if they enrolled in schools outside the declared military areas. The American Friends Service Committee (AFSC) began sponsoring students and placing them in midwestern and eastern colleges. Oberlin College in Ohio, for example, enrolled forty Japanese American students.[46] By the end of the war over four thousand youth had left the camps to pursue their education. Among these was John Itsuro Kitsuse, Ken's youngest son. On March 30, 1943, after a year's incarceration, AFSC placed the nineteen-year-old at Boston University. His parents would soon join him in Massachusetts. After graduation John earned a PhD from UCLA and would become one of the preeminent sociologists of his time.

In February 1943 the U.S. Army formed the famed 442nd Regimental Combat Team, a unit consisting of Nisei soldiers and Caucasian officers. The military expected 3,000 volunteers from the internment camps. To its surprise few enlisted. Many eligible Nisei openly questioned why they should fight and risk their lives for a government that had shattered their dreams and imprisoned them without due process. Only 1,256 volunteered. But these included Ken Kitsuse's sons James and Paul, as well as Harry Saisho's son Taro.

The 442nd shipped out to Italy in May 1944, seeing heavy action. Using the rallying cry, "Go for Broke," it became the most decorated unit in American military history with outlandish casualty rates. Purple Hearts were awarded to 9,486 of the 14,000 men who served in the unit. Twenty-one received the Congressional Medal of Honor, including future senator Daniel Inouye. In October and November

1944 the 442nd formed the spearhead as the Fifth Army drove the Germans from the Vosges Mountains. On November 3, during the assault on Saint-Dié-des-Vosges, Paul Kitsuse was killed in action. Both James Kitsuse and Taro Saisho returned safely from the war.

With over sixteen million Americans serving in the military, the country faced severe labor shortages both in factories and in the fields. Realizing that many incarcerated Japanese were farmers, the War Relocation Authority authorized furloughs and even complete discharges for people willing to work on midwestern and eastern farms. In mid-1943 Harry Saisho joined a committee to locate places in the Midwest for Amache internees to farm. The committee visited several sites, but Harry found a farm owned by Dr. T. A. Petersen in Holdrege, Nebraska, particularly appealing. The soil was a black sandy loam, and Petersen wanted a Japanese family to work the land. On October 8, 1943, Harry was released from Amache and relocated to Holdrege to prepare the farm. His son Taro joined him in May 1944, while his wife Kiyo and younger sons Takayoshi and Kiyoto arrived in June. His daughter Mataye had already left the camp in October 1943 to work as a domestic in Colorado Springs. The Saishos spent nearly three years raising potatoes and sugar beets on Petersen's farm in Holdrege. They made ends meet, but with Nebraska's short growing season they were unable to make much profit. Although the locals "treated them with kindness," "[we] knew that California was the most prosperous place for [us], in all respects. [We] could not restrain [our] longing for [our] home state—by mutual agreement [we] decided to return to California."[47]

In 1946 the Saishos returned to the West Coast with a plan. Each adult family member would find work, and they would pool their earnings. In just over a year they had saved enough to buy a farm. In late 1947 Harry and Kiyo fulfilled their lifelong dream by purchasing a two-acre lot in Baldwin Park, to the east of Los Angeles. As the 1913 Webb-Haney Act (forbidding real estate sales to immigrant Asians) was still in effect, they put the land in their children's names. (The act would be declared unconstitutional in 1952.) They bought an old army barrack, moved it to the lot, and transformed it into a home. Soon after Harry leased ten acres to grow fruits and vegetables. The small farm prospered.

Ken and Suye Kitsuse were frequent visitors. At the end of the war the couple had returned from Massachusetts, and Ken resumed his career as a gardener. Kiichi Suzuki would also stop by. He had remained at the Gila River camp for the duration of the war before returning to Los Angeles in October 1945. "Weekends were happy times," Harry remembered; "the house was besieged with visitors from Los Angeles. Men helped with the farm work while the women were busy cooking delicacies. Everyone sat around in a happy circle in the evening—eating, drinking, and having a pleasant chat. The house was filled with many people. Saying, 'See you again,' people from town left . . . late at night."[48]

On June 27, 1952, the Immigration and Nationality Act abolished racial restrictions for citizenship. Issei were now eligible to become American citizens. Despite the bigotry Harry had faced since his first day in the United States, despite the forced evacuation and the incarceration at Amachi, Harry and Kiyo immediately filled out their applications for naturalization and became "American citizens in the sight of the world."[49] It was one of the proudest moments of their lives. Two years later Ken Kitsuse also became an American citizen.

When the families sat around the kitchen table talking late into the night, Harry and Ken rarely mentioned their past. Both were quiet, modest men. To talk about their exploits on the diamond would have seemed like bragging. Mataye Saisho Nishi noted, "That generation didn't talk about themselves or their past. It's a shame. All of their knowledge, their stories are lost." Her brother Taro believed there might have been another reason. "My father didn't really talk much about baseball. Life was hard and my mother had trouble making ends meet. He may have been a little embarrassed that it [his baseball career] wasn't a success."[50] Looking back on his life, Kitsuse noted, "I am not good at anything else but baseball. People claim that I am crazy about it. . . . I think if I had invested the money on property or thought about the future, I could have been a great capitalist. . . . But I was happy to spend all my money on my beloved baseball. Nothing can cure stupidity. I loved baseball so much!"[51]

In 1956 Harry and Ken's friend Masaru Akahori decided to document what he could. "It is written that Japanese moved to the U.S. 100 years ago, but there is no literature about baseball. . . . Not many records, such as group pictures and newspaper scraps, survived the war. . . . I was afraid that the history would be forgotten."[52]

Akahori scoured newspapers for game accounts and Harry, Ken, and Kiichi shared their stories and old photographs. Later that year Akahori privately published a thirty-eight-page booklet—written in Japanese—titled *Nanka Nihonjin yakyushi* (History of Japanese baseball in Southern California). Unfortunately it did not circulate far beyond the former players' friends and families.

In early March 1958 Ken Kitsuse decided to visit Japan. He was now seventy-five years old and had not seen his extended family or birthplace since 1915. While in Tokyo on April 17, Ken died of a heart attack. No obituary noted the passing of the greatest Issei ball player of the early twentieth century. Within three years Suzuki would also pass in relative obscurity.

Harry Saisho would live to the ripe old age of ninety-four. His belief in his fellow man and commitment to racial equality stayed true until the end. Interviewed in 1970, six years before his death in October 1976, he said, "Life has been hard but good. Money is necessary but not the most important thing. We have been in good health and are very happy. For this . . . [I] give most of the credit to [my] wife of 50 years. It was she who worked the hardest on the farm, in the home, I think keeping up the spirits of the family."[53]

Harry tried to live by several principles. First, "We should realize that our society owes us nothing but what we owe to society is unfathomable." And, "Everyone is equal. If you think one race is superior to the other races and has priority in this world, that idea is nothing but one of prejudice. . . . That is the cause of war. All races are equal." "People with different cultures will live together amicably in the future."[54] For Harry Saisho, Ken Kitsuse, Tom Uyeda, Isoo Abe, and many other Japanese, baseball was an avenue to achieve this lofty goal—the shared love of the game acting as a bridge between people from different sides of the globe.

"Battle on the baseball [diamond between] two nations and peace and joy between two countr[ies]."—Harry Saisho, 1911.[55]

Acknowledgments

The idea for this book came from an eBay purchase. In July 2003 I bought an unusual baseball card that depicted a team of Asian players with "J.B.B. Association" stretched across their chests. On the reverse somebody had written, "Admit three Ladies to the Ball game and Grand Stand Japs Ball team J.B.B. Mgr." The seller wrote that the card had come from a scrapbook from Iowa made between 1900 and 1915. Realizing this was one of the earliest baseball cards of any Japanese team in the United States, I contacted Japanese American baseball expert Kerry Yo Nakagawa to help identify the team. Kerry Yo sent me a photocopy of a page from Masaru Akahori's book *Nanka Nihonjin yakyushi* identifying the team as the Japanese Base Ball Association of 1911. Prominent players included Harry Saisho, Ken Kitsuse, and Kiichi Suzuki. Kerry Yo also sent me a photocopy of the team's account book. "Interesting," I thought. "Someday I'll look into this."

Ten years later I was researching Japanese ballplayers who played professionally in the United States as background for *Mashi*, my biography of Masanori Murakami—the first Japanese in the Major Leagues—when I came across a player on the All Nations barnstorming team named Naito. Further research showed that a Naito had played on Guy Green's 1906 Japanese Base Ball Club with Ken Kitsuse and several other members of the 1911 Japanese Base Ball Association! Despite the numerous examinations of Japanese American baseball between the world wars, nobody had focused on these early teams. Before I had even started writing *Mashi*, I had identified the topic of my next book.

Issei Baseball took four years of research, and along the way many people have generously shared their expertise and time. First and foremost, I would like to thank Kerry Yo Nakagawa and Bill Staples Jr. for helping me from day one. Both freely shared their impressive knowledge of Japanese American baseball, guided me to sources, provided me with introductions, and encouraged me to undertake the project.

This book would not have been possible without the enthusiastic support of the Saisho, Kitsuse, and Uyeda families, who shared with me documents, photographs, and their memories of their parents and grandparents. I especially want to thank Harry Saisho's children Taro, Giro, and Mataye, as well as his grandson Sam Nishi; Ken Kitsuse's grandchildren Alicia Kitsuse, Paulette Watanabe, Ed Kitsuse, and Suzanne Kuwano; and Tom Uyeda's daughter Vivian Reisinger, grandson Tom Tucker, and Japanese cousins Fujio Ueda and Yooichi Ueda.

Five friends helped throughout this project, answering numerous questions, conducting research on my behalf, and helping to translate. Keiko Nishi Komei has been my Japanese research assistant for over a decade. She translated most of the Japanese-language documents and retrieved sources at Tokyo libraries. Without her I would be lost. Yoichi Nagata is always there to share his extensive knowledge on Japanese baseball and provide important sources. Masanori "Max" Ninomiya is my expert on Japanese culture and quick translator. It helps that he is *always* on Facebook. In an impressive bit of sleuthing Akiko Osaki tracked down Tozan Masko's Japanese relatives and provided most of the information on his family. Tsuneo Yoshioka, my wife's former high school teacher, spent days researching early baseball in Miyazaki, translated his findings, and showed me around the town during my 2016 visit.

Beverly Fitts, Jonathan Greenberg, Rick Huhn, Bill Lamb, Andy McCue, Sam Regalado, Dennis Snelling, Bill Staples Jr., and Myrna Watkins read drafts of the book. Their insightful comments and critiques made the book stronger. The encouragement of the other members of the Baseball Historians Writers Group—Jean Ardell, David Block, Rob Garratt, Steve Gietschier, Dan Levitt, Mitchell Nathanson, Roberta Newman, and Lyle Spatz—kept me going during the difficult periods when I nearly gave up the project.

I would like to thank the staff of the University of Nebraska Press, especially Robert Taylor, Courtney Ochsner, Sara Springsteen, and my superb copy editor Bojana Ristich, for their hard work and diligence.

As I delved into topics for the first time, many scholars generously responded to my requests for guidance. I would like to thank Rebecca Allen, Gary Ashwill, Larry Baldassaro, Thomas Crist, Takako Day, Brent Dickerson, Phil Dixon, Susanna Fessler, Mike Galbreath, Masako Gavin, Sayuri Guthrie-Shimizu, Donna Halper, Leslie Heaphy, Naomi Hirahara, Santaro Kawakami, James Loewen, Jim McKee, Brian Niiya, Gary Otake, Ann-Lee Switzer, Bob Whiting, and Ryan Whirty.

This book is based upon detailed research in Japan, California, and the American Midwest. I greatly appreciated the help of the staff at the Japan Baseball Hall of Fame, Tom Shieber of the National Baseball Hall of Fame in Cooperstown, the UCLA Charles E. Young Research Library Special Collections, the C. V. Starr East Asian Library, Columbia University, and Special Collections at the University of Washington Library. As I was unable to visit all of the repositories myself, many local researchers helped obtain newspaper articles, genealogical references, and primary documents. I would like to thank Adam Berenbak for the National Archives, Washington DC; Wendi Bevitt for the Kansas State Historical Society; Daniel Clausen for the Nebraska Historical Society; Keitaro Hamada for Kagoshima high schools; Javierrey Katzenstein for Brawley, California; Molly Kennedy for the Lincoln Presidential Library; Yohei Kitazumi at UCLA; Mary Logsdon of the Versailles Genealogical and Historical Society; Belinda Luke for the State Historical Society of Missouri; Alexandra Margolin at UCLA; Maryjo McAndrew of Knox College; Mallory Pillard at the Trinidad, Colorado, Library; Josiah Schmidt for the Iowa State Historical Library; Dennis Snelling for the California State Library; LaVern Velau for Garner, Iowa; Tom Willman for Riverside, California; and Claude Zachary of the University of Southern California Archives. Mieko Erber, Carla Grace, and Jonathan Hall helped with translating various documents.

Many others helped along the way but do not fit into the above categories. They are Miki Crawford, Doug Erber, Scott Forrest, Izumi Ishii, Robert Klevens, Chris Komai, Mickey Komai, Mary Logsdon, Lynn Miyauchi, Yoko Nishimura, Yuriko Romer, Jill Shiraki, Hanako Yamagata, Pam Yoshida, and Lauren Zuchowski.

Finally, the greatest debt of gratitude goes to my wife, Sarah, for unfailing support and endless hours of listening to my yammering about Harry Saisho and his baseball teams.

More information on Issei baseball, including unpublished photographs, can be found on my website: www.RobFitts.com.

Appendix A

Schedules and Game Results

Table 1. 1905 Waseda University American Tour

Date	Opponent	Result
April 29	Stanford University	Loss, 9–1
May 2	Stanford University	Loss, 3–1
May 3	Yerba Buena Navy School	Loss, 11–8
May 4	Encina Club of Stanford University	Win, 5–3
May 5	Stanford University Faculty	Win, 8–2
May 9	St. Mary's College	Loss, 16–0
May 13	Presidio Army Team	Loss, 7–5
May 14	Vallejo Semi-Pro	Loss, 14–3
May 15	University of California, Berkeley	Loss, 5–0
May 17	Los Angeles High School	Win, 5–3
May 18	Occidental College	Loss, 6–5
May 20	Sherman Indian Institute	Win, 12–7
May 21	Los Angeles Pacific Railroad	Loss, 5–4
May 22	St. Vincent's College	Loss, 6–4
May 23	Pomona College	Loss, 12–4
May 24	University of Southern California	Win, 13–6
May 27	Bakersfield High School	Loss, 6–5
May 28	Bakersfield High School	Loss, 5–2
May 30	Fresno CA State League	Loss, 10–3
May 31	Fresno CA State League	Loss, 13–0
June 6	University of Oregon	Loss, 3–0
June 7	Multnomah Athletic Club	Loss, 3–2
June 9	University of Washington	Loss, 9–2
June 10	University of Washington	Loss, 4–0

| June 11 | Seattle Rainiers | Win, 2–1 |
| June 12 | Whitworth College | Win, 2–0 |

Table 2. 1906 Guy Green's Japanese Barnstorming Season

Date	Place	Result
April 15	Frankfort KS	Win, 11–8
April 16	Irving KS	Win, 8–5, 12 innings
April 19	Topeka KS	Win, 3–1
April 20	Topeka KS	Loss, 10–0
April 20	Hoyt KS	Win, 8–7
April 21	Clay Center KS	Win, 30–12
April 22	Ft. Riley KS	Loss, 22–5
April 24	Minneapolis KS	Win, 10–5
April 25	Marquette KS	Loss, 10–3
April 26	Salina KS	Win, 9–5
April 27	Haven KS	Win, 7–5
April 30	Altamont KS	Win, 3–0
May 1	Oswego KS	Win, 5–0
May 2	McCune KS	Win, 10–3
May 3	Vinita IT	Win, 9–3
May 5	Stroud OK	Win, 23–3
May 6	Luthers OK	Win, 11–3
May 7	Yukon OK	Win, 4–0
May 8	Mustang OK	Win, 17–3
May 9	Comanche OK	Loss, 2–0
May 10	Bowie TX	Loss, 6–3
May 11	Whitesboro TX	Win, 9–1
May 14	Leonard TX	Win, 4–1
May 16	Bonham TX	Win, 3–1
May 17	Dodd City TX	Win, 9–7
May 17	Bonham TX	Win, 6–0
May 18	Sherman TX	Win, 1–0
May 19	Mt. Vernon TX	Win, 14–8
May 20	Texarkana TX	Win, 3–0

May 21	Prescott AR	Win, 10–1
May 22	Camden AR	Loss, 5–4
May 23	Camden AR	Win, 11–10
May 26	New Madrid MO	Win, 4–2
abt May 26	Blytheville MO	Win, 9–4
May 29	Benton IL	Rainout
June 3	Marion IL	Win, 9–7, 10 innings
June 5	Marissa IL	Win, 7–0
June 8	Belle Rive IL	Win, 15–6
June 9	Shawnee IL	Win, 11–8
June 9	Enfield IL	Win, 13–5
June 11	Mt. Vernon IL	Loss, forfeit, 9–0
June 12	Poseyville IN	Win, 6–4
June 16	Toledo IL	Win, 7–5
June 17	Neoga IL	Win, 12–6
June 18	Stewardson IL	Win, 10–1
June 19	Windsor IL	Win, 11–7
June 21	Ridge Farm IL	Win, 4–3
June 22	Newport IN	Win, 3–1 or 5–1
June 23	Covington IN	Win, 9–3
June 24	Danville IL	Loss, 5–3
June 25	Mansfield IL	Win, 12–0
June 26	Potomac IL	Win, 19–2
June 27	Cissna Park IL	Win, 8–5
June 28	Martinton IL	Win, 4–1
June 30	Melvin IL	Win, 15–2
July 3	Cropsey IL	Win, unknown score
July 4	Colfax IL	Win, 5–0
July 4	Bloomington IL	Win, 10–3
July 5	Wapella IL	Win, 3–2
July 6	Maroa IL	Win, 1–0
July 8	Roanoke IL	Win, 5–1
July 9	Gridley IL	Win, 10–3
July 10	Flanagan IL	Loss, 8–2 or 9–3
July 11	Cornell IL	Win, 5–1

July 12	Dwight IL	Loss, 3–2
July 15	Varna IL	Win, 5–0
July 16	Wyanet IL	Loss, 4–2
July 18	Neponset IL	Win, 9–3
July 19	Orion IL	Win, 5–4
July 20	Toulon IL	Loss, 1–0, 13 innings
July 23	Elmwood IL	Win, 10–7
July 25	Cuba IL	Win, 5–3
July 26	Table Grove IL	Win, 10–6
July 27	Table Grove IL	Win, 10–2
July 29	Tallula IL	Win, 15–4
July 30	Waverly IL	Win, 9–8
July 31	Bluffs IL	Win, 11–4
August 1	Versailles IL	Win, 11–3
August 2	Mt. Sterling IL	Loss, 9–3
August 3	Clayton IL	Win, 5–0
August 4	Carthage IL	Win, 15–4
August 5	Quincy IL	Loss, 10–3
August 6	Mendon IL	Win, 21–7
August 7	Loraine IL	Win, 11–7
August 8	Bowen IL	Win, 8–0
August 9	Augusta IL	Win, 11–0
August 10	Plymouth IL	Win, 5–2
August 11	Avon IL	Win, 9–2
August 12	Muscatine IA	Loss, 5–1
August 14	Viola IL	Win, 10–3
August 15	Alexis IL	Win, 4–1
August 16	Keithsburg IL	Win, 8–3
August 17	Wapello IA	Win, 4–1
August 18	Morning Sun IA	Win, 3–1
August 19	Ft. Madison IA	Win, 1–0
August 20	New London IA	Win, 8–2
August 21	Batavia IL	Win, 4–0
August 22	Pella IA	Win, 6–0
August 23	Monroe IA	Win, 7–6

August 23	Prairie City IA	Loss, 9–8
August 24	Adel IA	Win, 5–0
August 25	Granger IA	Win, 3–2
August 26	Perry IA	Win, 5–1
August 27	Ripley IA	Unknown
August 28	Gilmore City IA	Win, 8–3
August 29	Pocahontas IA	Win, 8–0
August 30	Rolfe IA	Win, 14–1 or 19–1
August 31	Eagle Grove IA	Win, 8–1
September 1	Belmond IA	Win, 6–0
September 2	Dougherty IA	Win, 9–1
September 3	Garner IA	Win, 5–3
September 4	Dows IA	Win, 15–0
September 5	Grundy Center IA	Win, 9–1
September 7	Dysart IA	Win, 7–0
September 8	Shellburg IA	Win, 9–3
September 9	Lowden IA	Win, 7–3
September 10	Wheatland IA	Win, 14–9
September 11	West Liberty IA	Win, 6–0
September 12	Oxford IA	Win, 11–2
September 13	Marengo IA	Win, 13–1
September 14	Gladbrook IA	Loss, forfeit
September 15	Jewell Junction IA	Win, 6–5
September 16	Dayton IA	Win, 4–1
September 17	Livermore IA	Win, 26–12
September 18	Forest City IA	Win, 3–0
September 19	Thompson IA	Win, 11–4
September 20	Corwith IA	Win, 6–1
September 21	Cherokee IA	Win, 11–2
September 22	Alta IA	Win, 5–2
September 26	Manilla IA	Win, 6–5
September 27	Audubon IA	Win, 9–2
September 28	Anita IA	Win, 12–1 or 11–1
September 29	Exira IA	Win, 10–3
September 30	Atlantic IA	Doubleheader: Win, 5–3; Win, 5–0

October 1	Cumberland IA	Win, 9–1
October 3	Nodaway IA	Win, 11–9, 12 innings
October 4	Clarinda IA	Doubleheader:
		Loss, 4–2; Loss, 2–1
October 5	Essex IA	Win, 13–8
October 7	Craig MO	Win, 6–0
October 8	Darlington MO	Win, 8–3
October 9	Albany MO	Loss, 9–4
October 10	King City MO	Win, 20–2

Table 3. 1908 Denver Mikado's Barnstorming Season

Date	Place	Opponent	Result
April 19	Denver CO	Cottrells Clothiers	Win, 5–4
April 20	Denver CO	Denver University	Loss, 7–3
April 21	Denver CO	Sacred Heart College	Loss, 12–4
April 22	Denver CO	All Stars	Unknown
April 23	Colorado Springs CO	Colorado Springs High	Win, 7–5
April 24	La Junta CO	La Junta High	Win, 8–4
April 26	Garden City KS	Garden City	Loss, 6–5
April 27	Garden City KS	Garden City	Loss, unknown score
April 28	Dodge City KS	Dodge City	Win, 15–1
April 29	Dodge City KS	Dodge City	Win, 6–5
April 30	Larned KS	Larned Maroons	Loss, 10–1
May 1	Larned KS	Larned Maroons	Loss, 6–2
May 2	Great Bend KS	Great Bend	Win, unknown score
May 3	Ellingwood KS	Ellingwood	Loss, 2–1
May 7	Madison KS	Unknown	Unknown
May 8	Burlington KS	Burlington	Win, 4–1
May 10	Fort Scott KS	Forth Scott Athletics	Loss, 3–1
May 11	Rich Hill MO	Rich Hill White Sox	Loss, 14–12
May 16	Olathe KS	Olathe	Loss, 7–3
May 17	Kansas City KS	Stock Yards	Loss, 13–3
May 18	Lexington MO	Merchants	Win, 4–0

May 19	Lexington MO	Tigers	Loss, 18–2

Table 4. 1907–8 Los Angeles Nanka

Date	Place	Opponent	Result
September 9, 1907	Seal Gardens	Florence Grahams	Loss, 12–0
November 25, 1907	San Gabriel	San Gabriel	Loss, 12–5
December 2, 1907	Pasadena	Esperanto	Win, 14–12
December 9, 1907	Pasadena	Esperanto	Loss, 16–6
March 8, 1908	Praeger Park	Wells-Fargo	Loss, 10–1
March 22, 1908	Highland Park	Highland Schoolboys	Loss, 9–4
June 14, 1908	Prager Park	Pacific Stars	Loss, 8–4
June 21, 1908	Arcadia Diamond	Santa Anitas	Loss, 6–2
July 4, 1908	Venice Beach	Venice Athletic Club	Win, 19–3
November 2, 1908	Wash. & Alameda	Electric Laundry	Loss, 11–8
November 29, 1908	Sierra Madre	Sierra Madre	Loss, 10–4

Table 5. 1909 Japanese Base Ball Association California Games

Date	Place	Opponent	Result
April 17	Riverside	Riverside	Loss, 17–0
April 18	Joy Park	LA Giants	Loss, 9–3
April 22	Los Angeles	LA High School	Loss, 15–9

Table 6. 1911 Japanese Base Ball Association Barnstorming Season

Date	Place	Income	Result
April 8	Pomona CA	$40.00	Unknown
April 19	Whittier CA	$14.75	Loss, 3–2
April 23	San Bernardino CA	$44.50	Loss, 3–1
April 30	LA Giants	$4.70	Unknown
May 7	LA Giants	$5.80	Loss, 7–0
May 11	Needles CA	$59.80	Unknown
May 12	Holbrook AZ	$24.75	Unknown
May 13	Gallup NM	$89.20	Unknown
May 14	Albuquerque NM	$125	Loss, 10–5

May 15	Santa Fe NM	$25	Loss, 8–3
May 16	Las Vegas NM	$94.70	Loss, 11–2
May 18	Raton NM	$41.15	Unknown
May 20	Trinidad CO	$125.25	Loss, 8–0
May 22	Garden City KS	$24.75	Win, 5–3
May 23	Dodge City KS	$38.05	Loss, 7–2
May 24	Hutchinson KS	$13.80	Loss, 6–5
May 25	Halstead KS	$11.40	Loss, 19–2
May 26	Strong City KS	$30	Win, 8–6
May 27	Leavenworth KS	$40	Loss, 13–6
May 28	Kansas City Giants KS	$66.30	Loss, 7–0
May 30	St Louis MO	$56.20	Loss, 9–3
May 31	Mt. Olive IL	$36.25	Loss, 10–1
June 1	Flat River IL	$30.45	Unknown
June 2	Farmington IL	$10	Unknown
June 3	Jerseyville IL	0	No game
June 4	Greenfield IL	$30	Loss, 8–2
June 6	White Hall IL	$13.45	Loss, 13–8
June 6	Murrayville IL	$12.90	Unknown
June 7	Beardstown IL	$15.40	Loss, 10–9
June 8	Petersburg IL	$42.48	Loss, 23–14
June 9	Mason City IL	$35	Loss, 7–2
June 10	Minier IL	$15.95	Loss, 9–4
June 11	Bloomington IL	$22	Loss, 4–1
June 12	Chenoa IL	$7.80	Loss, 10–2
June 13	Pontiac IL	$52.50	Loss, 7–1
June 14	Minonk IL	$25	Loss, 9–4
June 15	Roanoke IL	$35	Loss, 13–10
June 15	Eureka IL	$35	Unknown
June 17	Wenona IL	$16.75	Unknown
June 18	Streator IL	$70.10	Win, 4–1
June 19	Oglesby IL	$45.35	Unknown
June 20	Earlville IL	$45.60	Loss, 12–3
June 21	Princeton IL	$25	Loss, 12–10
June 22	Henry IL	$40.05	Loss, 4–2

June 24	Chillicothe IL	$15	Rain
June 25	Farmington IL	$50.45	Win, 6–3
June 26	Lewiston IL	$36.45	Loss, 4–3
June 27	Vermont IL	$25	Win, 16–13
June 28	Cuba IL	$53.49	Loss, 4–2
June 29	Bushnell IL	$60.50	Win, 9–7
June 30	Farmington IL	$49.14	Win, 8–4
July 1	Abingdon IL	$24.04	Unknown
July 2	Macomb IL	$65.85	Loss, 9–8
July 3	Golden IL	$11.10	Unknown
July 4	Versailles IL	$27.47	Loss, 17–8
July 4	Mt. Sterling IL	$43.85	Win, 10–4
July 5	Bowen IL	$15	Win, 19–7
July 6	Carthage IL	$23.40	Loss, 9–2
July 7	Canton IL	$19.10	Unknown
July 8	Monticello IL	$31.10	Unknown
July 9	Quincy IL	$30.90	Loss, 9–5
July 10	La Belle MO	$25	Unknown
July 11	La Belle MO	$33.25	Unknown
July 12	Edina IL	$36.75	Unknown
July 13	Keokuk IL	$13	Loss, 4–1
July 14	Kahoka MO	$33.20	Loss, 5–4
July 15	Farmington IL	$15.45	Unknown
July 16	Fort Madison IL	$32.80	Win, 16–6
July 17	Mt. Pleasant IA	$40.36	Loss, 5–4
July 18	Fairfield IA	$40.55	Loss, 3–2
July 19	Winfield IA	$42.50	Loss, 4–3
July 20	Wapello IA	$43.65	Loss, 9–3
July 21	Washington IA	$72.40	Loss, 7–2
July 22	Eldon IA	$15.60	Unknown
July 23	Oskaloosa IA	$65.05	Unknown
July 24	What Cheer IA	$25.15	Loss, 3–0
July 25	Williamsburg IA	$28.40	Loss, 3–2
July 26	Mt. Vernon IA	$21.30	Unknown
July 27	Marion IA	$25	Loss, 8–5

July 28	Monticello IA	0	Rain
July 29	Cascade IA	0	Rain
July 30	Oelwein IA	$90.15	Loss, 9–2
July 31	Fayette IA	$25	Unknown
August 1	Postville IA	$32.35	Unknown
August 2	Calmar IA	$49.25	Unknown
August 3	Britt IA	$29.75	Unknown
August 4	Lehigh IA	$24.40	Win, 3–1
August 5	Webster City IA	$49.40	Loss, 6–4
August 6	Boone IA	$73.90	Loss, 7–0
August 7	Jefferson IA	$53.15	Win, 4–0
August 8	Panora IA	$20.80	Unknown
August 9	Colfax IA	$26.40	Win, 5–1
August 10	Monroe IA	$16.13	Loss, 3–2
August 11	Pella IA	$43.40	Win, 9–0
August 12	Bussey IA	$15.70	Loss, 4–3
August 13	Avery IA	$24.60	Loss, 15–10
August 13	Buxton IA	$79.75	Win, 6–4
August 14	Buxton IA	$35.58	Tie, 4–4
August 15	Hocking IA	$31.85	Win, 2–1
August 16	Albia IA	$28.15	Loss, 16–9
August 17	Corydon IA	$4.50	Unknown
August 18	Centerville IA	$62.60	Win, 1–0
August 19	Humeston IA	$31.05	Tie, 4–4
August 20	Creston IA	$57.85	Win, 8–6
August 21	Corning IA	$37.10	Loss, 3–1
August 22	Nodaway IA	$32.15	Unknown
August 23	Red Oak IA	$55.54	Win, 7–1
August 24	Malvern IA	$47.50	Unknown
August 25	Neola IA	$18	Win, 10–9
August 26	Council Bluffs IA	$26.90	Loss, 8–5
August 27	Atlantic IA	$34.40	Win, 8–2
August 28	Exira IA	$32.55	Loss, 13–7
August 29	Manilla IA	$20	Loss, 23–9
August 30	Coon Rapids IA	$14.95	Loss, 16–4

August 31	Rippey IA	$3.30	Unknown
September 1	Grand Junction IA	$8.75	Loss, 10–8
September 2	Madrid IA	$25.85	Loss, 5–3
September 3	Des Moines IA	$58.05	Loss, 3–0
September 4	Newton IA	$17.70	Loss, 8–5
September 5	New Sharon IA	$34.35	Win, 19–4
September 7	Sigourney IA	$19.90	Unknown
September 8	Hedrick IA	$25	Win, 2–1
September 9	Richland IA	$16.90	Loss, 7–5
September 10	Ottumwa IA	$68.55	Unknown
September 11	Centerville IA	$25	Win, 5–1
September 12	Centerville IA	$25	Loss, 12–2
September 13	Unionville IA	$25	Unknown
September 14	Unionville IA	$13.35	Unknown
September 15	Trenton MO	0	Rain
September 16	Novinger MO	0	Rain
September 17	Macon MO	$22.40	Unknown
September 18	Macon MO	$4.80	Unknown
September 19	Paris MO	$12.90	Unknown
September 20	Auxvasse MO	0	Rain
September 21	Wellsville MO	$50.25	Win, 12–1
September 22	Montgomery MO	$22.20	Unknown
September 23	Warrenton MO	$34.20	Unknown
September 24	St Louis MO	$92.40	Loss, 3–2
September 27	St Louis MO	$7.60	Unknown

Table 7. 1911 Waseda University American Tour

Date	Opponent	Result
April 19	Waseda alumni	Win, 19–0
April 19	Stanford University	Loss, 11–2
April 20	Santa Clara College	Loss, 10–1
April 22	University of California	Win, 4–1
April 24	Sacred Heart College	Loss, 10–9
April 26	Pensacola Naval Training Ship	Loss, 4–3

April 27	Mission High School	Tie, 5–5
April 29	Brooke Realties of Sacramento	Loss, 3–1
May 1	University of Utah	Win, 6–4
May 3	University of Colorado	Loss, 4–3
May 6	University of Chicago	Loss, 6–4
May 9	Monmouth College	Win, 3–2
May 10	Knox College	Loss, 8–3
May 13	Northwestern University	Win, 4–1
May 20	Ames College	Win, 3–2
May 20	Ames College	Loss, 1–0
May 23	University of Iowa	Win, 2–0
May 24	University of Iowa	Loss, 2–0
May 26	University of Minnesota	Loss, 3–2
May 27	University of Minnesota	Loss, 8–2
May 29	University of Wisconsin	Loss, 8–0
May 30	University of Wisconsin	Loss, 3–2
June 1	University of Illinois	Loss, 13–1
June 3	University of Chicago	Loss, 9–6
June 6	Beloit College	Loss, 2–1
June 9	University of Indiana	Win, 3–0
June 10	University of Indiana	Loss, 3–2
June 12	Purdue University	Loss, 5–1
June 17	University of Chicago	Loss, 12–11
June 19	Oberlin College	Loss, 2–0
June 20	Tellings of Cleveland	Loss, 5–3
June 22	Simon Pures of Buffalo	Loss, 14–6
June 23	Simon Pures of Buffalo	Loss, 3–2
June 24	Trinity College	Loss, 5–4
June 29	All Stars of Pawtucket	Loss, 11–3
July 1	Manhattan College	Win, 10–4
July 3	Metropolitans of New York	Loss, 6–1
July 4	Yonkers Field Club	Loss, 6–2
July 6	New York City Fire Department	Loss, 4–0
July 7	Maryland Athletic Club	Loss, 13–2
July 8	University of Pennsylvania	Win, 11–8

July 18	Boston & Montana Club of Butte	Loss, 6–5
July 19	N. Pacific Crescents of Missoula	Win, 3–2
July 20	C. M. Payne of Spokane	Win, 9–7
July 21	C. M. Payne of Spokane	Loss, 13–2
July 22	C. M. Payne of Spokane	Win, 4–2
July 25	Victors of Seattle	Loss, 4–0
July 26	Old Baby	Win, 11–6
July 27	Pfisters of Tacoma	Loss, 4–0
July 28	Tacoma Columbians	Win, 21–1
July 28	Seattle Nippon	Win, 10–0
July 29	Seattle Knights of Columbus	Loss, 3–2
July 31	Mainlands of Vancouver	Win, 4–0

Table 8. 1911 Keio University American Tour

Date	Opponent	Result
May 4	University of California	Tie, 3–3
May 6	University of Utah	Win, 11–0
May 8	Salida co	Win, 5–2
May 9	Denver University	Win, 6–2
May 10	St. Mary's College	Loss, 2–1
May 11	Kansas University	Loss, 10–8
May 12	Stars, Kansas City mo	Win, 7–6
May 13	University of Missouri	Loss, 10–0
May 15	St. Louis University	Loss, 10–0
May 16	James Millikin University	Loss, 5–2
May 17	Wabash College	Loss, 9–3
May 19	University of Cincinnati	Win, 6–4
May 20	Columbus oh	Loss, 16–6
May 21	Dayton oh	Loss, 16–5
May 22	Wittenberg University	Win, 10–3
May 23	Ohio Wesleyan	Win, 5–4
May 24	University of West Virginia	Loss, 8–4
May 25	McKeesport pa	Win, 3–2
May 26	Georgetown University	Loss, 3–2

May 27	Fordham University	Win, 11–7
May 28	Pullmans of Buffalo	Loss, 7–1
May 29	Syracuse University	Loss, 13–0
May 30	Allegheny College	Win, 7–4
June 2	University of Michigan	Loss, 20–5
June 3	University of Michigan	Loss, 3–1
June 4	Elkhart IN	Win, 4–1
June 6	Notre Dame University	Loss, 9–5
June 7	University of Wisconsin	Win, 4–2
June 8	Ripon College	Win, 2–1
June 9	Grand Rapids	Win, 8–4
June 10	Ashland WI	Win, 5–4
June 11	Ashland WI	Win, 3–1
June 13	University of North Dakota	Loss, 8–6
June 14	University of North Dakota	Win, 4–3
June 17	Spokane	Loss, 11–3
June 18	Knights of Columbus	Win, 14–3
June 18	Seattle Nippon	Win, 5–0
June 20	Olympia	Tie, 7–7
June 21	Multnomah Club of Portland	Loss, 11–3
June 22	Albany Colts	Loss, 5–3
June 23	Eugene All Stars	Loss, 4–0
June 25	Sacramento Athletic Club	Loss, 6–4
June 26	Pacifics (Issei)	Win, 20–1
June 27	U.S. Naval Training Station	Win, 6–3

Appendix B

Known Issei Baseball Clubs, 1904–10

Fuji Athletic Club, San Francisco, ca. 1903–ca. 1907
  Evidence: photograph, oral tradition

Kanagawa Doshi Club, San Francisco, ca. 1904–ca. 1907
  Evidence: photograph, oral tradition

Japanese Base Ball Club of Los Angeles, 1904–5
  Evidence: newspapers, oral tradition
  Becomes Nanka

Nippon, Seattle, ca. 1904/6–1910s
  Evidence: newspapers, box scores, photographs

Guy Green's Japanese Base Ball Club, Lincoln, Nebraska, 1906
  Evidence: newspapers, box scores, photographs

Nanka, Los Angeles, 1907–10s
  Evidence: newspapers, box scores, photographs
  Becomes Japanese Base Ball Association

Union Steam Laundry, Tacoma, 1907–10
  Evidence: photograph

Keis Gijiku Club, Spokane, 1907
  Evidence: newspaper article; no proof of games played
  Manager: Youshi K. Nakamura

Mikado, Seattle, 1908–10s
  Evidence: newspapers, box scores, photographs

Sakura (Hollywood), 1908–10s
  Evidence: oral tradition

Nihon Hayato/Sanshu, 1908–10s
  Evidence: oral tradition, photograph

Mikado's, Denver, 1908–11
  Evidence: newspapers, box scores, photographs

Asahi Athletic Club, Alameda, 1908
  Evidence: newspapers

Unknown name, organized late 1908–9, Kota (or Kato) Suyematsu
  Evidence: newspaper article; no proof of games played

Columbians, Tacoma, before 1910
  Evidence: newspapers, box scores, photographs

Cherry (Nisei), Seattle, 1909–12
  Evidence: newspapers, oral tradition, photographs
  Becomes Asahi in 1912

Japanese Base Ball Association, 1909–1911
  Evidence: newspapers, oral tradition, photographs

Appendix C

Partial Rosters of Selected Issei Teams

Japanese Base Ball Club of Los Angeles, 1904–5

Toyo Fujita, Hanzaburo Harase, Takejiro Ito (president), Ken Kitsuse, Tozan Masko, Atsuyoshi "Harry" Saisho, Kotan Saito, Yoshio Sato, Zatsuga.

Guy Green's Japanese Base Ball Club, Lincoln, Nebraska, 1906

Toyo Fujita, Kato, Umekichi "Kitty" Kawashima, Kimo, Ken Kitsuse, Tozan Masko, Shoichi Motohashi, Naito, Nishi, Kotan Saito, Junjiro Uyeda, Tetsusaburo "Tom" Uyeda.

Non-Japanese: Doctor, Charlie Farrell, Sandy Kissell, Lewis, Seguin (Sego), Dan Tobey, Roy Whitcomb (Noisy).

Nanka, Los Angeles, 1907–10s

Toyo Fujita, Shinji Hatae, Harutsugu, Umekichi "Kitty" Kawashima, Shichiji Kikuchi, Ken Kitsuse, Takeshi Kitsuse, Isamu Maeda, Tozan Masko, Senichi Morii, Oya, Atsuyoshi "Harry" Saisho, Tadashi Saisho, Kotan Saito, Sato, Sera, Riichiro Shiraishi, Minori "John" Sohara, Kiichi "Onitei" Suzuki, Tokuzoe Uneichi.

Sakura, Hollywood, 1908–10s

Kuro Ashina, Toribuchi Hiro, Kiyotomi Ito, Kaihara, Matoba Kameshige, Katagiri, Ihei Kawanishi, Mataichi Kusunoki, Shoichi Motohashi, Kojima Shichiro, Riichiro Shiraishi, Kiichi "Onitei" Suzuki, Kantaro Yamashita.

Nihon Hayato/Sanshu, Los Angeles, 1908–10s

Hiroshi Higashimura (3b), Shoji Inoue (c), Kiyoji, Takaji Kubo (ss), Takao Makimoto (2b), Hikoji Mokuta (p), Takehiko Oyama (cf), Naota Tajitsu (rf), Yuzo Uchida (1b), Toshiyasu Yamauchi (lf).

Mikado's, Denver, 1908–11

George Aoki (p), T. Horiuchi (utility), M. Ito (c), B. Iwasaki (p), Joe Katow (lf), Umekichi "Kitty" Kawashima (2b), D. Kimura (ss), W. Oya (cf), S. Sato (utility), B. Tada (3b), E. Toda (p), Takatomo "Bob" Uyeda (rf), Tetsusaburo "Tom" Uyeda (1b).

Non-Japanese: Booth, Green, Lindemeyer, Pitling, Roy Whitcomb.

Japanese Base Ball Association, 1909

Toyo Fujita (1b), Shin Hashido (2b and captain), Takejiro Ito (president), B. Iwasaki (p), Shichiji Kikuchi (cf), Ken Kitsuse (ss), Isamu Maeda (p), Takao Makimoto (inf), Tozan Masko (mgr), Atsuyoshi "Harry" Saisho (c), Riichiro Shiraishi (rf), Minori Sohara (3b), Kiichi "Onitei" Suzuki (lf).

Non-Japanese: Bell, Tally.

Japanese Base Ball Association, 1911

Toyo Fujita (1b), Umekichi "Kitty" Kawashima (of), Ken Kitsuse (ss), Takaji Kubo (of), Hikoji Mokuda (p), Shoichi Motohashi (2b), Atsuyoshi "Harry" Saisho (mgr), Kesaichi "Arthur" Shiomichi (mgr), Minori Sohara (of), Riichiro Shiraishi (utility), Kiichi "Onitei" Suzuki (3b), Tokutaro Tachiyama (utility).

Non-Japanese: James G. Blain (Oyama), Hobart (Oyama), Kenton, Louis Lockhart (Fushima), A. S. Padilla (Yama), Shields, William Watkins (Naga), Wheeler.

Notes

Introduction

1. *Haven Weekly Journal*, April 21, 1906, 5.

2. Hotchkiss, *Diamond Gods*; S. E. Johnson, "Importance"; Nagata, "Los Angeles Nippons"; Nakagawa, *Japanese American Baseball* and *Through a Diamond*; Nomura, "Beyond the Playing Field"; Regalado, *Nikkei Baseball* and "Sport and Community"; Staples, *Kenichi Zenimura*.

3. The beginnings of Japanese immigrant baseball in Hawaii have been examined by Nakagawa, *Through a Diamond*; Okihiro, *AJA Baseball*.

4. Although this spelling may look odd today, Tozan Masko referred to his team as the "Mikado's" in his letters and advertising.

1. Saisho the Dreamer

1. Quoted in *Indianapolis Star*, April 5, 1925, 65.

2. List or Manifest of Alien Passengers: SS *Gaelic*, April 5, 1903, California Passenger and Crew Lists, 1882–1959, Ancestry.com; *San Francisco Call*, April 8, 1903.

3. Soennichsen, *Miwoks to Missiles*, 89.

4. Soennichsen, *Miwoks to Missiles*, 89.

5. List or Manifest of Alien Passengers: SS *Gaelic*, April 5, 1903, California Passenger and Crew Lists, 1882–1959, Ancestry.com; *San Francisco Call*, April 8, 1903.

6. Quoted in Soennichsen, *Miwoks to Missiles*, 89.

7. Wilson and Hosokawa, *East to America*, 29.

8. Spickard, *Japanese Americans*, 25.

9. Japan Bureau de la Statistique Générale, *État de la Population*, 102.

10. Del Mar, *Around the World*, 208.

11. Chamberlain, *Handbook for Travelers*, 482.

12. This school changed its name several times when the Kitsuse brothers attended. In 1898 its name was changed from Kagoshima Prefectural Jinjo Middle School to Kagoshima Prefectural Daiichi Jinjo Middle School. The following year it was renamed Kagoshima Prefectural Daiichi Middle School and again to Kagoshima Prefectural Kagoshima Middle School in 1901.

2. The National Pastime in Japan

1. Vanner, *Dawlish Chronicles*.

2. *Japan Weekly Mail*, November 4, 1871.

3. *New York Herald*, December 18, 1871, 7.

4. Donnithorne, *Western Enterprise*, 270–71.

5. U.S. Bureau of Census, *1870 Federal Census*, 123.

6. The school's frequent name changes led to seemingly contradictory statements about where Wilson taught. The school was known as Kaisei Gakko in 1868, Daigaku Nanko in 1869–70, Nanko in 1871, Daiichi Daigaku-ku Dai Ichiban Chugaku in 1872, Kaisei Gakko (again) in 1873, and Tokyo Kaisei Gakko from 1874 to 1877. Ikuo Abe, "Muscular Christianity," 34; *San Francisco Bulletin*, September 1, 1971, 3.

7. No primary source supports the 1872 date for Wilson's introduction of baseball to Japan. The date, accepted by nearly all baseball scholars, is based on the recollections of one of Wilson's former students (named Kokyusai) published in the July 23, 1896, issue of *Nihon*.

8. Information on the Yeddo Royal Japanese Troupe's baseball games was researched and compiled by Bill Staples.

9. *Daily Morning Chronicle*, June 5, 1872, 4.

10. *Baltimore Sun*, June 8, 1872, 4; *Daily Morning Chronicle*, reprinted in *Chicago Evening Post*, June 14, 1872, 4; *Daily National Republican*, June 8, 1872, 4.

11. *News Journal*, June 18, 1872, 3.

12. *News Journal*, June 17, 1872, 2.

13. Ikuo Abe, "Muscular Christianity," 20.

14. *Japan Weekly Mail*, January 16, 1875, 1. U.S. Passport Applications Number 25324, issued October 16, 1872.

15. Quoted in *New York Clipper*, December 23, 1876, 307.

16. *New York Clipper*, December 23, 1876, 307.

17. After returning to Japan, in 1875–80 Makino attended Tokyo Kaisei Gakko, where Horace Wilson still taught. It is likely that Makino also played baseball with Wilson.

18. Y. Suzuki and Sakai, *Besuboruto okajoki*.

19. Kaneko, "Who Was the First?"

20. Guthrie-Shimizu, *Transpacific Field of Dreams*, 19–22.

21. Hirose, *Nihon no yakyushi*, 57–58.

22. Benesch, *Inventing the Way*, 79.

23. Quoted in Roden, "Baseball," 521.

24. Roden, "Baseball," 524.

25. Quoted in Roden, "Baseball," 529–30.

26. *Japan Weekly Mail*, July 11, 1896, 41.

27. Quoted in Miyazaki Omiya Senior High School, *One Hundred Years*.

28. Tanimura, *Miyazakiken yakyushi*.

29. Tanimura, *Miyazakiken yakyushi*.

30. Tanimura, *Miyazakiken yakyushi.*
31. *Miyazaki Shimpo Daily News*, November 6, 1900.
32. Miyazaki Omiya Senior High School, *One Hundred Years.*
33. Tanimura, *Miyazakiken yakyushi.*

3. The New World

1. Saisho, "Autobiography."
2. Leland Stanford Junior University, *Thirteenth Annual Register*, 56.
3. Leland Stanford Junior University, *Thirteenth Annual Register*, 58–59.
4. Leland Stanford Junior University, *Thirteenth Annual Register*, 65.
5. California Passenger and Crew Lists, 1882–1959, M1410-San Francisco, 1893–1953, Roll 007:341, Ancestry.com.
6. Daniels, *Politics of Prejudice*, 11.
7. Noguchi, *Story*, 36.
8. Noguchi, *Story*, 36.
9. Markino, "My Experiences," 110.
10. Gulick, *American Japanese Problem*, 52.
11. Although Saisho wrote in his memoirs that he attended Stanford for less than a semester, there is no record of his enrollment as a student. Records of Special Students do not survive, making it likely that he attended the school in that capacity.
12. Ichioka, *Issei*, 28.
13. Gulick, *American Japanese Problem*, 16.
14. Goyette, "How Racism Created America's Chinatowns."
15. Quoted in Daniels, *Politics of Prejudice*, 21.
16. Quoted in Sarasohn, *Issei*, 67.
17. *Houston Post*, November 23, 1906, 6.
18. McNally," How I Became a Ranchman," 299.
19. U.S. Immigration Commission, *Reports*, 48.
20. Saisho, "Autobiography."
21. *San Francisco Chronicle*, July 31, 1904, 43; *Daily Pacific Commercial Adver-tiser*, September 17, 1904, 6; *Honolulu Advertiser*, October 3, 1904, 10.
22. Ichihashi, *Japanese in the United States*, 58.
23. Daniels, *Politics of Prejudice*, 26
24. Daniels, *Politics of Prejudice*, 24.
25. *San Francisco Chronicle*, February 23, 1905, 1.
26. Daniels, *Politics of Prejudice*, 25.
27. Quoted in Daniels, *Politics of Prejudice*, 27.
28. *San Francisco Chronicle*, May 15, 1905, 7.
29. Quoted in Daniels, *Politics of Prejudice*, 28.
30. Dower, *War without Mercy*; Gulick, *American Japanese Problem*; R. Lee, *Orientals*; Maynard, *World War Two*; Ogawa, *From Japs to Japanese.*
31. Quoted in Sarasohn, *Issei*, 59–60.

4. Issei Baseball

1. Details of Masko's life come from family records provided by Senichi Mashiko and from M. Suzuki, *Inta mauten*, 141–43. For the reader's sake, I will spell his last name "Masko" throughout the book, except when direct quotations spell his name differently.

2. *Record-Union*, May 1, 1896, 9.

3. Zhao and Park, *Asian Americans*, 588–89.

4. Sanborn-Perris, *Insurance Maps*.

5. Methodist Episcopal Church, *Eighty-Third Annual Report*.

6. Niiya, *Japanese American History*, 311.

7. On Japanese in Los Angeles, see Mason, *Japanese in Los Angeles*; Modell, *Economics and Politics*.

8. Much of my discussion of the is taken from K. Hayashi, *Rafu Shimpo*.

9. Matsumoto, *Kashū jinbutsu*, 316–17.

10. Harase, "Nijyugonenmae," 17.

11. Harase, "Nijyugonenmae," 17.

12. Harase, "Nijyugonenmae," 17.

13. *Los Angeles Herald*, May 17, 1905, 10.

14. Matsumoto, *Kashū jinbutsu*, 316–17.

15. *Los Angeles Herald*, August 20, 1890, 5.

16. *Los Angeles Herald*, February 15, 1895, 11.

17. Quoted in Japanese Chamber of Commerce of Southern California, *Japanese in Southern California*, 361.

18. Regalado, *Nikkei Baseball*, 17–23; Okihiro, ᴀᴊᴀ *Baseball*.

19. Nakagawa, *Japanese American Baseball*, 45–47.

20. *Washington Post*, June 7, 1897, 8.

21. *Sporting Life*, July 3, 1897, 5.

22. Svinth, "Japanese Professional Wrestling Pioneer."

23. *New York Times*, February 10, 1905.

24. *Elmira Gazette and Free Press*, February 11, 1905.

25. *Sporting Life*, February 25, 1905, 8; *Salt Lake Herald*, February 22, 1905, 7.

26. *Sporting Life*, February 18, 1905, 18.

27. *Oakland Tribune*, February 24, 1905, 9.

28. *Sporting Life*, February 25, 1905, 8.

29. Cieradkowski, "Shumza Sugimoto."

5. Waseda Arrives

1. On Isoo Abe, see Ikuo Abe, "Muscular Christianity," 14–38; Gavin: "Abe Isoo and Baseball," 452–70, and "Poverty"; Tipton, "In a House Divided."

2. Gavin, "Abe Isoo and Baseball," 458–59.

3. *Los Angeles Herald*, July 17, 1894, 1, 4.

4. Quoted in Shibazaki, "Seattle and the Japanese–United States Baseball Connection," 9.

5. Gavin, "Abe Isoo and Baseball," 457–58; Kiku, "Japanese Baseball Spirit," 42.

6. Gavin, "National Moral Education," 323–33; Powles, "Abe Isoo the Utility Man."

7. Gavin, "Abe Isoo and Baseball," 464–65.

8. Quoted in *Stanford Daily*, May 1 1905, 6.

9. *Chicago Daily Tribune*, April 23, 1905, A1; *San Francisco Call*, April 26, 1905, 10.

10. Shibazaki, "Seattle and the Japanese–United States Baseball Connection," 11–12.

11. Quoted in Shibazaki, "Seattle and the Japanese United States Baseball Connection," 12.

12. Quoted in Shibazaki, "Seattle and the Japanese–United States Baseball Connection," 13.

13. *San Francisco Call*, April 21, 1905, 10.

14. *San Francisco Examiner*, April 21, 1905, 9.

15. *San Francisco Chronicle*, April 21, 1905, 9.

16. Izumitani Sukekatsu to Izumitani Yukatsu, April 21, 1905, ISC.

17. Izumitani Sukekatsu to Izumitani Yukatsu, April 21, 1905, ISC.

18. Izumitani Sukekatsu to Izumitani Yukatsu, April 28, 1905, ISC.

19. *San Francisco Examiner*, April 23, 1905, 55.

20. Izumitani Sukekatsu to Izumitani Yukatsu, April 28, 1905, ISC.

21. *Los Angeles Herald*, April 28, 1905, 10.

22. *San Francisco Call*, May 14, 1905, 42.

23. *San Francisco Chronicle*, April 28, 1905, 4.

24. *San Francisco Chronicle*, April 28, 1905, 4.

25. *Oakland Tribune*, April 26, 1905, 11.

26. *San Francisco Call*, April 29, 1905, 7; *Los Angeles Examiner*, May 19, 1905, 12.

27. *Daily Californian*, May 26, 1905, 3.

28. Isoo Abe, "Diary."

29. *Los Angeles Times*, April 30, 1905, 17.

30. *Pacific Commercial Advertiser*, May 11, 1905, 6.

31. *San Francisco Call*, April 20, 1905, 51.

32. *Pacific Commercial Advertiser*, May 11, 1905, 6.

33. *San Francisco Call*, May 3, 1905, 10.

34. *San Francisco Examiner*, May 3, 1905, 9.

35. *San Francisco Chronicle*, May 3, 1905, 8.

36. Maynard, *World War Two*.

37. Isoo Abe, "Diary."

38. *Los Angeles Times*, May 5, 1905, sec. 2, 3; *Los Angeles Herald*, May 6, 1905, 6.

39. Quoted in *Daily Palo Alto*, May 1, 1905, 6.

40. *San Francisco Call*, May 14, 1905, 42.

41. Quoted in *Seattle Daily Times*, May 21, 1905, 18.

42. *San Francisco Examiner*, May 16, 1905.

6. Waseda Tour Continues

1. *Los Angeles Herald*, May 17, 1905, 10.
2. *Los Angeles Examiner*, May 16, 1905.
3. *Los Angeles Times*, May 18, 1905; *Los Angeles Examiner*, May 18, 1905.
4. *Los Angeles Times*, May 18, 1905.
5. *Los Angeles Examiner*, May 18, 1905.
6. *Los Angeles Examiner*, May 19, 1905.
7. *Los Angeles Times*, May 19, 1905, sec. 2, 3.
8. *Seattle Daily Times*, June 6, 1905, 14.
9. *Los Angeles Times*, May 19, 1905, sec. 2, 3.
10. *Los Angeles Examiner*, May 20, 1905, 12.
11. Isoo Abe, "Waseda daigaku," 3.
12. *Sporting Life*, June 10, 1905, 19.
13. *Los Angeles Examiner*, May 21, 1905, 41.
14. *Los Angeles Times*, May 21, 1905, sec. 3, 1.
15. *Los Angeles Herald*, May 21, 1905, 6.
16. *Los Angeles Herald*, May 21, 1905, 6.
17. *Los Angeles Examiner*, May 21, 1905, 41.
18. *Los Angeles Herald*, May 21, 1905, 6.
19. *Los Angeles Examiner*, May 21, 1905, 41.
20. *Los Angeles Herald*, May 23, 1905, 10.
21. *Daily Californian*, May 26, 1905, 3.
22. *Los Angeles Times*, May 25, 1905, sec. 2, 3.
23. *Los Angeles Herald*, May 18, 1905.
24. *Seattle Daily Times*, May 21, 1905, 18.
25. *Los Angeles Times*, May 22, 1905, sec. 1, 12.
26. *Daily Californian*, May 26, 1905, 3.
27. *Daily Californian*, May 26, 1905, 3.
28. *Daily Californian*, May 26, 1905, 3; May 27, 1905, 5.
29. *Daily Californian*, May 29, 1905, 6.
30. *Daily Californian*, May 29, 1905, 6.
31. *Fresno Morning Republican*, June 1, 1905.
32. *Fresno Morning Republican*, May 32, 1905.
33. *Fresno Morning Republican*, June 1, 1905.
34. Isoo Abe, "Diary."
35. *Morning Oregonian*, June 8, 1905, 7.
36. "The Igorrote Tribe from the Philippines," 4.
37. *Seattle Daily Times*, June 9, 1905, 5.
38. *Seattle Daily Times*, June 8, 1905, 11.
39. *Seattle Daily Times*, June 10, 1905, 5.
40. *Seattle Daily Times*, June 12, 1905, 9.
41. Quoted in Shibazaki, "Seattle and the Japanese–United States Baseball Connection," 26.

42. *Tacoma Daily News*, June 13, 1905, 7.

43. Soden, "Ernest C. Tanner."

44. *Los Angeles Times*, May 22, 1905, sec. 1, 12.

45. Quoted in Japanese Chamber of Commerce of Southern California, *Japanese in Southern California*, 361.

46. Bruce, "Baseball and the National Life," 105.

47. Lieb, "Baseball," 393.

48. Reprinted as "Baseball Field the Real Melting Pot," *Sporting News*, April 26, 1917, 4.

49. Quoted in Azuma, *Between Two Empires*, 47.

7. Guy Green's 1906 Club

1. Green, *Nebraska Indians*, 7–8.

2. The following section on town baseball is based on Seymour, *Baseball: The People's Game*, 188–212, 258–75. When *Baseball: The People's Game* was first published by Oxford University Press in 1990, Harold Seymour was listed as the sole author. Later it was revealed that Harold's wife, Dorothy Seymour Mills, was actually the book's primary author. In subsequent editions the book's authors are listed as Dorothy Seymour Mills and Harold Seymour. In this volume, the references to *Baseball: The People's Game* with page numbers refer to the original 1990 edition.

3. Quoted in Seymour, *Baseball: The People's Game*, 196.

4. Seymour, *Baseball: The People's Game*, 188.

5. Green, *Nebraska Indians*, 7–8.

6. *Nebraska State Journal*, June 26, 1897, 8.

7. *Nebraska State Journal*, April 24, 1909, 6.

8. Green, *Nebraska Indians*, 117–19.

9. Green, Letter to Prospective Opponents.

10. *Washington Evening Journal*, April 16, 1900, 3.

11. Jeffrey P. Beck quoted in Green, *Nebraska Indians*, xviii.

12. *Headlight*, April 25, 1901, 4.

13. *Tecumseh Chieftain*, May 4, 1901, 4.

14. Green, Letter to Prospective Opponents.

15. Green, Letter to Prospective Opponents.

16. *Fort Wayne Sentinel*, January 31, 1912, 8.

17. Miller, "Great Sushi Craze."

18. *Tip Top Weekly*, July 15, 1905, and July 22, 1905; O'Connor, "Sports and Popular Literature," 768.

19. Ueda family photographs in author's collection.

20. Ueda, "Tree of Dreams."

21. Yooichi Ueda, email message to author, February 1, 2017.

22. Yooichi Ueda, email message to author, February 1, 2017.

23. Uchiyama, *Yamaguchi-ken*, 15.

24. Cedarville College, *1916 Cedrus Yearbook*, 76.

25. Cedarville College, *1897 Cedrus Yearbook*, 17.

26. *St. Louis Post-Dispatch*, February 11, 1935.

27. *St. Louis Post-Dispatch*, February 11, 1935.

28. Quoted in *St. Louis Post-Dispatch*, February 11, 1935.

29. FBI Report on Tetsusaburo Uyeda, February 5, 1942, S.L. File No. 65–55, AED.

30. Tetsusaburo Uyeda to Edward J. Ennis, January 3, 1944, AED.

31. *Los Angeles Herald*, February 12, 1905, 3.

32. *Covington Friend*, June 22, 1906.

33. *St. Louis Post-Dispatch*, February 11, 1935.

34. Akahori, *Nanka Nihonjin*, 17–21.

35. Quoted in Akahori, *Nanka Nihonjin*, 17–21.

36. Quoted in Akahori, *Nanka Nihonjin*, 17–21.

37. Quoted in Akahori, *Nanka Nihonjin*, 17–21.

38. Quoted in Akahori, *Nanka Nihonjin*, 17–21.

39. Quoted in Akahori, *Nanka Nihonjin*, 17–21.

40. Green, *Nebraska Indians*, 117–18.

41. Quoted in Akahori, *Nanka Nihonjin*, 17–21.

42. *Lincoln Daily Evening News*, April 7, 1906, 2.

43. Quoted in Akahori, *Nanka Nihonjin*, 17–21.

44. Portions of this announcement appear in the *Warren Review*, June 14, 1906, 1, and *Covington Friend*, June 22, 1906.

45. Quoted in Akahori, *Nanka Nihonjin*, 17–21.

46. Quoted in Akahori, *Nanka Nihonjin*, 17–21.

47. Quoted in Akahori, *Nanka Nihonjin*, 17–21.

8. The 1906 Barnstorming Tour

1. I recreated the season by searching newspaper databases and following up with page-by-page examinations of local papers in areas the team visited. In this manner I located 150 games. Most games are represented by single-line entries with the opponent and final score. Accounts of the games are rare, and box scores even scarcer. Even in the detailed articles the Japanese-born players are rarely discussed as individuals. Instead they are lumped together in blanket statements, such as, "The Japs play good ball and understand the game." As a result, we know little about the experiences of the individual ballplayers.

2. *Marshall County Index*, April 20, 1906, 1.

3. *New York Times*, May 28, 2013, D3.

4. *Irving Leader*, April 20, 1906, 1.

5. *Topeka State Journal*, April 17, 1906, 5; April 18, 1906, 10; April 19, 1906, 2.

6. *Topeka State Journal*, April 10, 1906, 4.

7. *Topeka Daily Capital*, April 20, 1906, 6; *Topeka State Journal*, April 20, 1906, 9.

8. *Topeka Daily Capital*, April 20, 1906, 6; *Topeka State Journal*, April 20, 1906, 9.

9. U.S. War Department, *Annual Report*, 102.

10. *Emporia Gazette*, April 27, 1906, 1.

11. *Fort Riley Guidon*, April 15, 1906, 2.

12. *Junction City Union*, April 21, 1906, 2.

13. *Junction City Union*, April 20, 1906, 1.

14. *Fort Riley Guidon*, April 29, 1906, 1; *Junction City Union*, April 23, 1906, 2.

15. Green, *Nebraska Indians*, 136.

16. *Minneapolis Messenger*, April 26, 1906, 6; *McPherson Weekly Republican*, May 4, 1906, 1.

17. *Salina Daily Union*, April 25, 1906, 3.

18. *Salina Evening Journal*, April 27, 1906, 2; *Salina Daily Union*, April 27, 1906, 3.

19. *Haven Weekly Journal*, April 21, 1906, 1, 5, 8; April 26, 1906, 1; *Hutchinson News*, April 25, 1906, 8; April 26, 1906, 5.

20. Schmidt, "Golden Age," 38–59.

21. *Stark County News*, June 20, 1906, 1.

22. *Newport Hoosier State*, June 20, 1906, 5.

23. *Mt. Vernon Daily Register*, June 9, 1906, 3; *Jewell Record*, September 20, 1906, 5.

24. *Toledo Democrat*, June 14, 1906, 5.

25. Strecker, "Grover Baichley."

26. *Toledo Democrat*, June 21, 1906, 5; U.S. Bureau of Census, *1910 Federal Census*.

27. *Toledo Democrat*, June 14, 1906, 5.

28. *Toledo Democrat*, June 21, 1906, 5.

29. *Dwight Journal*, July 19, 1906, 4.

30. *Newport Hoosier State*, June 27, 1906.

31. *Quincy Daily Whig*, August 5, 1906, 2.

32. *St. Louis Republic*, January 10, 1904, 63.

33. *Los Angeles Herald*, September 17, 1910.

34. *Los Angeles Herald*, September 17, 1910.

35. *Colfax Press*, June 28, 1906, 6; July 5, 1906, 1.

36. *Muscatine Journal*, August 13, 1906.

37. *Evansville Courier and Press*, June 12, 1906, 5.

38. *Covington Friend*, June 15, 1906.

39. *Covington Friend*, June 29, 1906, 1.

40. *Bradford Stark County Republican*, July 26, 1906, 8.

41. *Carthage Republican*, August 3, 1906, 5; August 10, 1906, 5; *Carthage Republican*, August 8, 1906, 3.

42. *Carthage Republican*, August 15, 1906, 1.

43. *Waverly Journal Enterprise*, August 3, 1906, 1; *Newport Hoosier State*, May 27, 1906.

44. *Bloomington Weekly Pantagraph*, June 29, 1906, 5.

45. *Stark County News*, June 13, 1906, 1; June 20, 1906, 1; July 4, 1906, 1; July 11, 1906, 1, 4; July 18, 1906, 1; July 25, 1906, 7.

46. *Stark County News*, July 11, 1906, 1.

47. Quotes in the next several paragraphs are from *Stark County News*, July 25, 1906, 7.

48. *Des Moines Register*, August 26, 1906, 18.

49. *Des Moines Register*, September 13, 1906, 6.

50. *Des Moines Register*, August 25, 1906, 8; *Pocahontas Record*, August 16, 1906, 3.

51. *Perry Daily Chief*, August 26, 1906, 1.

52. *Perry Chief Reporter*, August 22, 1906, 8.

53. *Perry Chief Reporter*, August 29, 1906, 3–4.

54. *Alta Advertiser*, September 28, 1906, 9; *Atlantic Cass County Democrat*, October 4, 1906.

55. *Journal Enterprise*, August 3, 1906, 1.

56. *Windsor Gazette*, June 21, 1906, 1.

57. *Pontiac Leader*, July 11, 1906, 5.

58. *Hancock County Democrat*, September 6, 1906, 1; *Des Moines Register*, September 5, 1906, 7.

59. *Garner Signal*, September 5, 1906, 1; *Hancock County Democrat*, September 6, 1906, 1; *Des Moines Register*, September 5, 1906, 7.

60. *Garner Signal*, September 5, 1906, 1; *Hancock County Democrat*, September 6, 1906, 1.

61. *Des Moines Register*, September 15, 1906, 8.

62. *Alta Advertiser*, September 28, 1906, 1.

63. *Perry Daily Chief*, August 26, 1906, 1.

64. *Dow Advocate*, September 7, 1906, 5.

65. *Hancock County Democrat*, September 6, 1906, 1.

66. *Essex Independent*, October 12, 1906, 4.

67. There are also forty days between April 15 and October 10 where no game results were located. Newspaper accounts provide clues to how the team did on these missing dates. The *Waverly Journal Enterprise* wrote that Green's team was 87-17 following a win on July 30. As the team has a confirmed 63-12 record with thirty-seven unaccounted-for days to that point, this report could be correct. Yet an August 30 article in the *Des Moines Register* claims that the squad won its hundredth game the previous day against Pocahontas. The team has a verified record of 25-4 with just one unaccounted-for day from July 31 to August 29, a statistic that if added to the record printed in the *Waverly Journal Enterprise* brings the total to 112 wins and 21 losses, greater than the 100 wins stated in the *Des Moines Register*. Therefore one of the newspapers is in error. From August 30 to October 7 Green's Japanese had 34 verified wins and 4 losses, plus four unaccounted-for days. Newspaper claims that the team had won 21 straight as of September 12 and 16 straight as of October 1 suggest that

the team had won at least 2 more games during this period. Therefore the team played a minimum of 154 games (with a 134-20 record) if we rely on the *Des Moines Register*'s total or at least 171 games (with a 146-25 record) based on the *Waverly Journal Enterprise*'s account.

68. *Brown County Republican*, August 10, 1906, 1.

69. *Perry Daily Chief*, August 26, 1906, 1.

70. *Pella Chronicle*, August 23, 1906, 1.

71. *Maryville Daily Forum*, February 11, 1947, 2.

9. Mikado's Japanese Base Ball Team

1. Ichihashi, *Japanese in the United States*, 246.

2. U.S. Immigration Commission, *Reports*, 308.

3. Masko, Mikado's Base Ball Team Correspondence.

4. Masko, Mikado's Base Ball Team Correspondence.

5. Masko, Mikado's Base Ball Team Correspondence.

6. *Evening News*, April 6, 1908.

7. *Cleveland Plain Dealer*, April 5, 1908, 18.

8. *Evening Independent*, April 3, 1908.

9. As quoted in *Salt Lake Tribune*, July 12, 1908, 18.

10. *Leavenworth Post*, May 6, 1908, 4.

11. Quoted in Hosokawa, *Colorado's Japanese Americans*, 35.

12. *Denver Rocky Mountain News*, March 22, 1908, 18.

13. *Denver Rocky Mountain News*, March 19, 1908, 8.

14. *Denver Post*, February 3, 1908, 4.

15. *Denver Times*, February 21, 1908, 7.

16. *Denver Rocky Mountain News*, April 20, 1908, 6.

17. *Colorado Springs Gazette*, April 19, 2008, 12.

18. *Denver Rocky Mountain News*, April 20, 1908, 6.

19. *Denver Rocky Mountain News*, April 20, 1908, 6.

20. *Denver Rocky Mountain News*, April 20, 1908, 6.

21. *Denver Times*, April 20, 1908.

22. *Denver Post*, April 20, 1908, 12.

23. *Denver Post*, April 21, 1908, 9; *Denver Rocky Mountain News*, April 21, 1908, 8.

24. *Daily News*, April 22, 1908.

25. *Baltimore Sun*, December 30, 1931, 6.

26. Quoted in *San Francisco Call*, July 18, 1907.

27. Quoted in *New York Times*, December 17, 1907, 2.

28. *Oakland Tribune*, July 13, 1907, 9; July 12, 1908, 28.

29. *Evening Telegram* (Garden City), April 6, 1908, 1; April 10, 1908, 2.

30. *Evening Telegram* (Garden City), April 16, 1908, 1.

31. *Evening Telegram* (Garden City), April 25, 1908, 1.

32. *Evening Telegram* (Garden City), April 27, 1908, 1.

33. *Globe-Republican* (Dodge City), April 30, 1908, 1.

34. *Emporia Gazette*, May 8, 1908, 6.

35. Quoted in *Evening Telegram*, May 6, 1908, 4.

36. *Kinsley Mercury*, May 15, 1908, 6.

37. *Emporia Gazette*, May 2, 1908, 1.

38. *Fort Scott Daily Tribune and Fort Scott Daily Monitor*, April 28, 1908, 8; May 2, 1908, 2.

39. *Fort Scott Daily Tribune and Fort Scott Daily Monitor*, May 11, 1908, 7.

40. *Fort Scott Daily Tribune and Fort Scott Daily Monitor*, May 11, 1908, 7.

41. *Fort Scott Daily Tribune and Fort Scott Daily Monitor*, May 11, 1908, 3, 7.

42. Masko, Mikado's Base Ball Team Correspondence.

43. *Lexington Intelligencer*, May 23, 1908, 3.

44. Dixon and Hannigan, *Negro Baseball Leagues*, 33.

45. *Indianapolis Freeman*, September 12, 1914.

46. *Lexington Intelligencer*, May 23, 1908, 8.

47. *Topeka Daily Capital*, May 25, 1908, 1.

48. *Denver Post*, June 28, 1908, 28.

10. The Japanese Base Ball Association

1. Akahori, *Nanka Nihonjin*, 3.

2. U.S. World War II Draft Registration Cards, 1942, for Kiichi Kitay Suzuki, Serial Number 1594, Ancestry.com.

3. Akahori, *Nanka Nihonjin*, 12.

4. Quoted in Akahori, *Nanka Nihonjin*, 12.

5. List or Manifest of Alien Passengers: ss *Kanagawa Maru*, June 21, 1904, Passenger and Crew Lists of Vessels Arriving at Seattle, Ancestry.com; U.S. World War II Draft Registration Cards, 1942, John Minori Sohara, Ancestry.com.

6. Quoted in Akahori, *Nanka Nihonjin*, 12.

7. Quoted in Akahori, *Nanka Nihonjin*, 11.

8. *Los Angeles Herald*, December 9, 1907; December 20, 1907.

9. Quoted in Kiku, "Japanese Baseball Spirit," 38.

10. Quoted in Akahori, *Nanka Nihonjin*, 30.

11. Balst, *Real Estate Surveys*.

12. Quoted in Akahori, *Nanka Nihonjin*, 12.

13. *Los Angeles Herald*, July 2, 1908, 3.

14. The lineup is derived from the team picture published on page 70 of the July 5, 1905, *Los Angeles Times*. On page 72 the *Times* included lineups for both the "L.A. Japanese" and Venice Athletic Club teams. Some of the names in the lineup are garbled and do not match the players in the picture. The article names the Nanka pitcher as Molda, which is not a Japanese name. Molda seems to be a muddled version of Oya.

15. *Los Angeles Times*, July 5, 1908, 72.

16. *Los Angeles Times*, July 5, 1908, 68.

17. *Los Angeles Times*, July 5, 1908, 72.

18. *Los Angeles Herald*, November 20, 1908; November 26, 1908.

19. Quoted in *Washington Evening Star*, November 2, 1908, 13.

20. *New York Sun*, October 19, 1908, 3.

21. *Los Angeles Times*, November 28, 1909, 119.

22. *Abbeville Press and Banner*, November 18, 1908, 7; *Columbus Daily Enquirer*, October 21, 1908, 9; *Cleveland Plain Dealer*, October 21, 1908, 5.

23. *Salt Lake Tribune*, July 12, 1908, 18.

24. *Anaconda Standard*, July 12, 1908, 19; *Japan Times*, September 15, 1908; *Salt Lake Tribune*, July 12, 1908, 18.

25. Quoted in *Salt Lake Telegram*, December 25, 1908, 13.

26. *Duluth News Tribune*, November 8, 1908, 2.

27. *Oregon Daily Journal*, September 20, 1908, 38.

28. *Reno Evening Gazette*, October 27, 1908, 6.

29. *Los Angeles Times*, November 13, 1908, 6.

30. Quoted in Akahori, *Nanka Nihonjin*, 11.

31. Quoted in Akahori, *Nanka Nihonjin*, 9.

32. *Oakland Tribune*, December 3, 1908, 13.

33. *Reno Evening Gazette*, October 27, 1908, 6.

34. *Yorozu Choho*, April 17, 1907; May 29, 1907; December 21, 1907; December 23, 1907; January 30, 1908; April 28, 1908; May 11, 1908; January 3, 1909; April 25, 1909.

35. *Los Angeles Times*, April 18, 1909, 93.

36. *Salina Daily Union*, March 20, 1909, 6; *Denver Rocky Mountain News*, April 5, 1909, 6.

37. *Riverside Daily Press*, April 4, 1909, 10.

38. *Riverside Daily Press*, April 6, 1909, 4; April 10, 1909, 4; April 12, 1909, 7.

39. *Riverside Daily Press*, April 19, 1909, 7; *Los Angeles Herald*, April 18, 1909, 7.

40. *Riverside Daily Press*, April 19, 1909, 7.

41. Quoted in Akahori, *Nanka Nihonjin*, 26–27.

42. McNeil, *California Winter League*, 28–29.

43. *Los Angeles Times*, April 18, 1909, sec. 5, 17.

44. *Los Angeles Herald*, April 19, 1909.

45. Quoted in Akahori, *Nanka Nihonjin*, 3.

11. "Japanese Invasion"

1. Quoted in *Columbus Republican*, September 1, 1910, 4.

2. Quoted in *Washington Post*, March 3, 1911, 5, and *Syracuse Post Standard*, March 6, 1911, 6.

3. *Enterprise News-Record*, May 14, 1910, 2.

4. Quoted in *Oxnard Daily Courier*, April 15, 1911.

5. *Sporting Life*, November 19, 1910, 1.

6. *Salt Lake Telegram*, January 17, 1911, 7.

7. Shizunobu Hamamoto, U.S. World War I Draft Registration Cards, A2191, Ancestry.com; *St. Louis Post-Dispatch*, August 1, 1929, 19; *St. Louis Star and Times*, December 4, 1945, 22.

8. *Chronicle-Telegram*, February 23, 1911, 3.

9. *Winnipeg Tribune*, February 24, 1911, 7.

10. *Altoona Times*, March 25, 1911, 8.

11. *St. Louis Star and Times*, December 4, 1945, 22.

12. *Washington Post*, January 20, 1911, 8; *Munster Times*, January 19, 1911, 3; *Nevada State Journal*, January 27, 1911, 7; *Pittsburg Post-Gazette*, April 28, 1911, 9; *Sacramento Union*, February 8, 1913.

13. Quoted in Pegues, "Japan Invades America."

14. Pegues, "Japan Invades America."

15. Pegues, "International Baseball," 127, 131.

16. *San Francisco Call*, April 19, 1911, 12.

17. *San Francisco Examiner*, April 21, 1911; *San Francisco Call*, April 14, 1911.

18. *Missouri Sharp Shooter*, May 19, 1911, 6.

19. Pegues, "Japan Invades America."

20. *Muskogee Times-Democrat*, May 16, 1911; *Seattle Star*, June 1, 1911, 2; June 2, 1911, 2; June 3, 1911, 2; June 5, 1911, 2; June 7, 1911, 2; June 8, 1911, 2.

21. Niese, "Voyage," 15.

22. Reprinted in *Charlotte Evening Chronicle*, March 7, 1911, 3.

23. Reprinted in *Charlotte Evening Chronicle*, March 7, 1911, 3.

24. *Decatur Herald*, May 8, 1911.

25. *Los Angeles Herald*, May 10, 1909, 6; May 12, 1909, 4; *Los Angeles Times*, May 14, 1909, 16; May 16, 1909, 94.

26. *Salt Lake Herald*, July 28, 1907, 8; March 25, 1908, 10; *Salt Lake Tribune*, May 1, 1908, 9; May 7, 1908, 10.

27. *Deseret Evening News*, July 18, 1908, 9.

28. *Deseret Evening News*, July 9, 1908, 2.

29. *Deseret Evening News*, July 11, 1908, 4.

30. *Salt Lake Herald*, July 24, 1909, 8.

31. *Salt Lake Tribune*, July 25, 1909, 7.

32. *Salt Lake Telegram*, July 8, 1909, 7; *Los Angeles Herald*, October 13, 1909, 13.

33. *Salt Lake Herald-Republican*, November 7, 1909, 10; *Los Angeles Herald*, October 27, 1909, 12.

34. *Salt Lake Herald-Republican*, November 21, 1909, 7.

35. *Salt Lake Herald-Republican*, November 22, 1909, 7.

36. *Los Angeles Herald*, December 2, 1909, 12.

37. *Los Angeles Herald*, December 9, 1909.

38. *Los Angeles Herald*, December 9, 1909; *Los Angeles Herald*, December 18, 1909; *Salt Lake Telegram*, December 11, 1909, 19.

39. *Salt Lake Herald-Republican*, December 19, 1909, 6; *Los Angeles Herald*, December 19, 1909, 30.

40. *Los Angeles Herald*, December 19, 1909, 30.

41. *Los Angeles Herald*, December 20, 1909, 6.

42. *Salt Lake Tribune*, December 20, 1909, 9; *Los Angeles Examiner*, December 20, 1909, 9.

43. *Los Angeles Times*, December 20, 1909, 16; *Salt Lake Telegram*, December 20, 1909, 7.

44. *San Diego Union*, November 4, 1909,10.

45. *San Diego Union*, January 14, 1910, 10.

46. *San Diego Union*, February 19, 1910, 7; February 28, 1910, 6.

47. *San Diego Union*, February 28, 1910, 6; *San Diego Evening Tribune*, February 28, 1910, 5.

48. *Los Angeles Times*, June 12, 1910, sec. 7, 9.

49. *Los Angeles Times*, July 17, 1910, sec. 7, 7; *Los Angeles Herald*, October 11, 1910, 8.

50. U.S. World War I Draft Registration Cards, 1917–18, Tokutaro Tachiyama, Ancestry.com; Horikiki, "Baseball History."

51. JBBA, 1911 Ledger Book, 16.

52. *Whittier News*, April 20, 1911.

53. *Los Angeles Times*, April 20, 1911, sec. 3, 1.

54. *San Bernardino Sun*, April 25, 1911, 5.

55. Quoted in *Los Angeles Times*, April 20, 1911, sec. 3, 1.

56. *San Bernardino Sun*, April 25, 1911, 5.

57. *Los Angeles Times*, May 11, 1911, sec. 3, 1.

12. Ballplayers and Diplomats

1. *Chicago Tribune*, May 7, 1911, 25; May 8, 1911, 10.

2. *Chicago Tribune*, May 5, 1911, 6.

3. *Chicago Tribune*, May 7, 1911, 23.

4. *Monmouth Republican Atlas*, May 11, 1911, 1; *Knox Student*, May 11, 1911, 635.

5. Quoted in Gillespie, "History of Baseball"; McKenna, "Goro Mikami."

6. Sayama, *Mystery*. Evidence suggests that the nickname "Jap Mikado" may have been a transcription error of "the Jap Mikami."

7. *Des Moines Sunday Register*, January 8, 1995, 31; Young, *J. L. Wilkinson*, 18.

8. *Waterloo Evening Courier and Reporter*, March 26, 1914, 14; *Aurelia Sentinel*, August 14, 1914, 1.

9. *Chicago Daily Herald*, May 3, 1912, 16.

10. *Omaha Evening World Herald*, May 29, 1915, 7; June 1, 1915, 12.

11. Gillespie, "History of Baseball"; McKenna, "Goro Mikami."

12. *Iowa City Citizen*, May 22, 1911, 1; May 23, 1911, 2; May 24, 1911, 2.

13. *Inter Ocean*, June 18, 1911, 15.

14. Quoted in *Iola Register*, May 12, 1911, 3.

15. Quoted in *Iola Register*, May 12, 1911, 3.

16. *Tipton Tribune*, June 13, 1911.

17. Quoted in *Iola Register*, May 12, 1911, 3.

18. Quoted in *Indianapolis Star*, June 12, 1911, 3; *St. Louis Star and Times*, June 11, 1911, 3.

19. *Cincinnati Post*, May 18, 1911, 6.

20. *Iowa City Citizen*, May 22, 1911, 1; *Indianapolis Star*, June 11, 1911.

21. *Bloomington Daily Student*, June 10, 1911, 3; *Sporting Life*, May 13, 1911, 4.

22. *Dubuque Telegraph-Herald*, May 5, 1911, 4.

23. *Albuquerque Morning Journal*, May 18, 1911.

24. *Albuquerque Morning Journal*, May 14, 1911.

25. JBBA, 1911 Ledger Book, 16.

26. Quoted in Sutter, *New Mexico Baseball*, 41.

27. *Albuquerque Morning Journal*, May 15, 1911, 3.

28. Halper, "A Lady Sporting Editor."

29. Endo, "Persistence of Ethnicity."

30. *Des Moines Register*, March 18, 1911, 1; March 24, 1911, 1.

31. *Chronicle News*, May 22, 1911.

32. JBBA, 1911 Ledger Book.

33. *Garden City Evening Telegram*, May 23, 1911, 1.

34. *Hutchinson Daily Gazette*, May 25, 1911, 3.

35. *Leavenworth Times*, May 27, 1911, 8.

36. *Leavenworth Times*, May 27, 1911, 8.

37. *Leavenworth Times*, May 28, 1911, 8.

38. Dixon and Hannigan, *Negro Baseball Leagues*, 87–88.

39. Negro Leagues Database, Seamheads.com.

40. *Kansas City Star*, May 29, 1911, 10.

41. *Wisconsin Rapids Daily Tribune*, May 17, 1911, 1.

42. *Kansas City Star*, May 13, 1991, 7.

43. *Indianapolis Freeman*, June 10, 1911, 7.

44. JBBA, 1911 Ledger Book.

13. Barnstorming across America

1. This discussion of Sundown Towns is based on Loewen, *Sundown Towns*.

2. *Argus*, June 9, 1911, 7.

3. *Lewistown Evening Record*, June 27, 1911, 4.

4. *Hutchinson Daily Gazette*, May 25, 1911, 3.

5. *Minonk Dispatch*, June 15, 1911, 1.

6. *Earlville Leader*, June 22, 1911, 1.

7. *Petersburg Observer*, June 9, 1911, 1; *Bloomington Pantagraph*, June 10, 1911, 1; June 12, 1911, 6.

8. *Henry Times*, June 22, 1911, 1.

9. *Cuba Journal*, June 29, 1911, 1.

10. *Minier News*, June 16, 1911, 1, 4.

11. Pope, *Patriotic Games*.

12. *Quincy Whig*, July 6, 1911, 3; *Mt. Sterling Democrat Message*, July 5, 1911, 2.

13. *Mt. Sterling Democrat Message*, July 1, 1911, 6.

14. *Mt. Sterling Democrat Message*, July 5, 1911, 2.

15. *Mt. Sterling Democrat Message*, July 12, 1911, 1.

16. *Mt. Sterling Democrat Message*, July 5, 1911, 2.

17. Quotes here and in the next several paragraphs are from *New York Times*, July 5, 1911, 4.

18. *Buffalo Courier*, May 29, 1911, 9.

19. *Buffalo Courier*, June 19, 1911, 8.

20. *Buffalo Courier*, June 23, 1911, 8; June 24, 1911, 11; *Buffalo Commercial*, June 23, 1911, 6.

21. *Hartford Courant*, June 24, 1911, 17.

22. *New York Times*, July 2, 1911; July 7, 1911, 10; *The Sun*, July 5, 1911, 7.

23. *New York Tribune*, May 28, 1911, 12.

24. A. G. Spalding, *Spalding's Official Base Ball Guide*, 99.

25. *Washington Post*, May 22, 1911, 4.

26. *Washington Post*, May 26, 1911, 8.

27. *Washington Post*, May 27, 1911, 11.

28. *Washington Evening Star*, May 27, 1911, 11; *Washington Post*, May 27, 1911, 8.

29. *Baltimore Sun*, July 8, 1911, 10.

30. *Baltimore Evening Sun*, July 8, 1911, 6.

31. *Logansport Reporter*, July 12, 1911, 8.

32. *Washington Times*, July 11, 1911, 4.

33. *Anaconda Standard*, July 18, 1911, 2; *Butte Daily Post*, July 17, 1911, 5–6.

34. *Butte Daily Post*, July 19, 1911, 6.

35. *Butte Daily Post*, July 19, 1911, 6.

36. *Butte Daily Post*, July 19, 1911, 6.

37. *Butte Daily Post*, July 17, 1911, 6; July 19, 1911, 6; *Anaconda Standard*, July 19, 1911, 2.

38. *Eugene Morning Register*, July 25, 1911, 2.

39. *Vancouver Daily World*, August 1, 1911, 18.

40. Pegues, "Japan Invades America."

14. End of a Dream

1. *Evening Democrat*, July 12, 1911.

2. *Evening Democrat*, July 17, 1911.

3. *Hutchinson Daily Gazette*, May 25, 1911, 3.

4. *Oelwan Daily Register*, July 28, 1911.

5. *Kansas City Gazette Globe*, July 18, 1911, 4.

6. *Bridgeport Times and Evening Farmer*, August 5, 1911, 1.

7. *News Dispatch*, August 10, 1911, 2.

8. *Oelwan Daily Register*, July 28, 1911, July 31, 1911; *Audubon County Journal*, August 24, 1911, 1; *Mt. Pleasant Daily News*, July 17, 1911, 4.

9. *Oelwan Daily Register*, July 28, 1911; *Neola Gazette Reporter*, August 30, 1911, 8; *Williamsburg Journal-Tribune*, July 27, 1911, 5.

10. *Williamsburg Journal-Tribune*, July 27, 1911, 5.

11. *Oelwan Daily Register*, July 28, 1911, July 31, 1911; see also *Mt. Pleasant Daily News*, July 17, 1911, 4.

12. *Audubon County Journal*, August 31, 1911, 1.

13. *Audubon County Journal*, August 31, 1911, 1.

14. *Mt. Pleasant Daily News*, July 17, 1911, 4.

15. *Webster City Freeman*, August 8, 1911, 1.

16. *Webster City Freeman*, August 8, 1911, 1.

17. *Boone News Republican*, August 7, 1911, 5; *Humeston New Era*, August 23, 1911.

18. *Audubon County Journal*, August 31, 1911, 1.

19. *Jefferson Bee*, August 9, 1911.

20. *Centerville Daily Citizen*, August 19, 1911, 4; *Centerville Semi-Weekly Journal*, August 22, 1911, 1; Suzuki quoted in Akahori, *Nanka Nihonjin*, 4.

21. *Boone News Republican*, August 5, 1911, 8.

22. In author's collection.

23. *Pella Chronicle*, August 17, 1911, 1; *Neola Gazette Reporter*, August 30, 1911, 8.

24. JBBA, 1911 Ledger Book. Monetary figures pertaining to the JBBA in the remainder of this chapter are also from this source.

25. *Audubon County Journal*, August 31, 1911, 1.

26. Quoted in *Des Moines Register*, September 3, 1911, 31.

27. Durand, *Thirteenth Census of the United States*.

28. *Centerville Iowegian*, September 12, 1911, 4.

29. *Macon Times-Democrat*, September 14, 1911, 5; *Macon Daily Chronicle*, September 9, 1911, 1; September 13, 1911, 1; September 16, 1911, 3.

30. *Macon Daily Chronicle*, September 18, 1911, 3.

31. *St. Louis Star and Times*, October 9, 1911, 10.

32. *St. Louis Star and Times*, September 17, 1911, 6.

33. *St. Louis Star and Times*, September 27, 1911, 6.

34. Akahori, *Nanka Nihonjin*, 27.

15. Baseball Comes of Age

1. Interview with Harry Saisho, January 14, 1970; unpublished manuscript in author's collection.

2. *Seattle Star*, July 22, 1907, 2; *Seattle Daily Times*, May 23, 1908, 7.

3. *Seattle Daily Times*, July 10, 1908, 16.

4. *Seattle Star*, September 10, 1910, 2.

5. Quoted in Shibazaki, "Seattle and the Japanese–United States Baseball Connection," 87–88.

6. Photograph, Union Laundry Baseball Team, Densho Digital Repository.

7. *Tacoma Times*, May 6, 1910, 2; photograph, Mikado Baseball Team 1911, Frank Fukuda Photograph and Ephemera Collection.

8. *Spokane Press*, September 22, 1908, 6.

9. Quoted in *Sunday Star* (Washington DC), June 30, 1907, 2.

10. *Waterloo (IA) Reporter*, August 2, 1907, 5.

11. *San Francisco Call*, June 29, 1908.

12. *San Francisco Call*, December 21, 1909; November 4, 1911; *Mansfield News*, August 31, 1911, 7.

13. *Seattle Daily Times*, March 23, 1914, 12; March 30, 1914, 14.

14. *Seattle Daily Times*, April 10, 1914, 21.

15. *Seattle Star*, April 10, 1914, 13.

16. *Seattle Daily Times*, April 10, 1914, 13.

17. Reprinted in Akahori, *Nanka Nihonjin*, 15.

18. Quoted in Akahori, *Nanka Nihonjin*, 4.

19. Suzuki quoted in Akahori, *Nanka Nihonjin*, 4; *Cumberland News*, May 27, 1914, 1.

20. Quoted in Akahori, *Nanka Nihonjin*, 4.

21. Shibazaki, "Seattle and the Japanese–United States Baseball Connection," 80; see also Regalado, "Baseball's Kakehashi."

22. Ito, *Yakyu-nenpoh*, 25–46.

23. Quoted in Akahori, *Nanka Nihonjin*, 4.

24. *Denver Rocky Mountain News*, July 9, 1911, 1; July 10, 1911, 5; *Denver Post*, July 9, 1911, 4.

25. *Denver Post*, July 19, 1914, 4; July 30, 1914, 13.

26. *Leslie's Weekly*, July 12, 1911, 69.

27. *Stark County News*, July 25, 1906, 7; *Covington Friend*, September 26, 1906, 1.

28. *Denver Post*, June 19, 1914, 15; June 22, 1914, 5.

29. *Denver Post*, May 11, 1913, 36; October 13, 1913, 21.

30. *St. Louis Post-Dispatch*, February 11, 1935.

31. *Denver Post*, August 31, 1913, 22.

32. *Denver Post*, August 31, 1913, 22.

33. *Denver Rocky Mountain News*, May 29, 1915, 13.

34. *Salt Lake Telegram*, October 4, 1917, 4.

35. Stevens, *Way of Judo*.

36. *Japan Advertiser*, February 27, 1921, 7.

37. *Japan Advertiser*, March 5, 1921.

38. *Japan Advertiser*, May 8, 1921, 4.

39. *Japan Advertiser*, May 8, 1921, 4.

40. *Japan Advertiser*, May 8, 1921, 4.

41. *Bremerton Searchlight*, August 10, 1921.

42. *Japan Advertiser*, August 23, 1921, 12.

43. *Japan Advertiser*, August 30, 1921, 10; November 6, 1921, 10; November 13, 1921, 14.

44. Interview with Harry Saisho, January 14, 1970; unpublished manuscript in author's collection.

45. *Japan Advertiser*, September 30, 1921, 5.

46. The following discussion is derived from Nagata, "Japan Trip Journal."

47. Benesch, *Inventing the Way*.

48. *Los Angeles Times*, November 23, 1921, sec. 3, 1. The *Times* article states that the team played eight games in Japan, winning four. Yoichi Nagata in "Japan Trip Journal" has recovered the scores from seven of these games, showing that the actual record was 1-6, with the result of one game unknown.

49. *Nichi Bei Times* quoted in Nagata, "Japan Trip Journal"; Akahori, *Nanka Nihonjin*, 2.

50. Nagata, "Los Angeles Nippons," 100.

51. Nakagawa, *Japanese American Baseball*, 50, 61.

52. Regalado, *Nikkei Baseball*, 89, 94.

16. Incarceration

1. *St. Louis Post-Dispatch*, December 3, 1941, 27.

2. Tetsusaburo Uyeda to Edward J. Ennis, January 3, 1944, AED.

3. Quoted in *St. Louis Post-Dispatch*, February 11, 1935.

4. Pascoe, *What Comes Naturally*, 90–91.

5. State of Missouri, *Revised Statutes*, Section 8280.

6. Email from Tom Tucker, Tetsusaburo's grandson, July 17, 2018.

7. FBI Report on Tetsusaburo Uyeda, File No. 65–55, December 31, 1941, 8, AED.

8. Alien Enemy Control, Summary of FBI Report in the Case of Tetsusaburo Uyeda, February 14, 1942, 1, AED.

9. Report before the Alien Enemy Hearing Board in the Matter of Tetsusaburo Uyeda, February 26, 1942, AED.

10. U.S. Bureau of Census, *1940 Federal Census*; *St. Louis Post-Dispatch*, September 26, 1926, 5; May 9, 1937, 27.

11. Reeves, *Infamy*, 3.

12. *St. Louis Post-Dispatch*, December 8, 1941, 18; January 16, 1942, 25; FBI Report on Tetsusaburo Uyeda, File No. 65–55, December 31, 1941, AED.

13. *St. Louis Post-Dispatch*, February 23, 1942, 2.

14. Memorandum to Chief of Review Section on Tetsusaburo Uyeda, March 11, 1942, AED.

15. *St. Louis Post-Dispatch*, January 30, 1948, 3.

16. "Transcript of Testimony and Proceedings before the Grand Jury, Harry C. Blanton," USVPM; Wikipedia, "Pacific Movement"; Gallicchio, *African American Encounter with Japan and China*.

17. *St. Louis Post-Dispatch*, October 1, 1932, 1, 5.

18. Memorandum to the Chief of Review Section on Tetsusaburo Uyeda, November 1, 1944, AED.

19. W. F. Kelly to Edward Ennis, March 21, 1945, AED.

20. *St. Louis Post-Dispatch*, December 20, 1945, 3.

21. Tetsusaburo Uyeda to Edward J. Ennis, March 10, 1944, AED.

22. *St. Louis Post-Dispatch*, March 12, 1956, 17; American Foreign Service, Report of the Death of an American Citizen: Takatomo Uyeda, Ancestry.com.

23. Saisho, "Autobiography." This autobiography is written in the third person. I have put it back into the first person.

24. Nishi, telephone interview with author, June 2, 2016.

25. "Oral History Interview with Giro Saisho, August 19, 2006, Camarillo, California." Go For Broke National Education Center Oral History Project, http://www.ndajams.omeka.net/files/show/1017.

26. Interview with Harry Saisho, January 14, 1970; unpublished manuscript in author's collection.

27. Reeves, *Infamy*, 18.

28. *Brawley News*, January 2, 1942.

29. *Brawley News*, January 8, 1941.

30. Quoted in Reeves, *Infamy*, 45.

31. Quoted in Reeves, *Infamy*, 37.

32. Quoted in Reeves, *Infamy*, 33–34.

33. In this book I have used the terminology for the relocation camps adopted by the Smithsonian's American History Museum.

34. Quoted in Reeves, *Infamy*, 40–41.

35. Mataye Saisho Nishi, telephone interview with author, June 2, 2016.

36. "Oral History Interview with Harry Akune, September 18, 1999." Go For Broke National Education Center Oral History Project, http://www.ndajams.omeka.net/files/show/920.

37. Mataye Saisho Nishi, telephone interview with author, June 2, 2016.

38. "Oral History Interview with Giro Saisho, August 19, 2006."

39. "Oral History Interview with Giro Saisho, August 19, 2006."

40. Mataye Saisho Nishi, telephone interview with author, June 2, 2016.

41. "Oral History Interview with Giro Saisho, August 19, 2006."

42. Quoted in Staples, *Kenichi Zenimura*, 119–25.

43. Quoted in Nakagawa, *Through A Diamond*, 86.

44. Nakagawa, *Through A Diamond*, 132.

45. Quoted in Reeves, *Infamy*, 168.

46. *Oberlin Alumni Magazine*, Winter 2013, 12–17.

47. Saisho, "Autobiography."

48. Saisho, "Autobiography."

49. Saisho, "Autobiography."

50. Mataye Saisho Nishi, telephone interview with author, June 2, 2016; Taro Saisho, telephone interview with author, February 23, 2014.

51. Quoted in Akahori, *Nanka Nihonjin*, 8.

52. Akahori, *Nanka Nihonjin*, 2, 37.

53. Interview with Harry Saisho, January 14, 1970; unpublished manuscript in author's collection.

54. Saisho, "Autobiography"; interview with Harry Saisho, January 14, 1970; unpublished manuscript in author's collection.

55. Quoted in *Albuquerque Journal*, March 18, 1911.

Bibliography

Archival Sources

AED. World War II Alien Enemy Detention and Internment Case Files, Tetsusaburo "Thomas" Uyeda, Case 146-13-2-42-36, Record Group 60, General Records of the Department of Justice, 1790–2002, National Archives II, College Park MD.

Akahori Family Papers. Charles E. Young Research Library, Special Collections, UCLA.

Ancestry.com. Draft Registration Records [database online].

———. Immigration Records [database online].

Densho Digital Repository. http://ddr.densho.org.

Frank Fukuda Photograph and Ephemera Collection. University of Washington Libraries Special Collections, Seattle WA.

Green, Guy W. Letter to Prospective Opponents, April 2, 1908. In author's collection.

ISC. Izumitani Sukekatsu Collection. Prince Chichibu Memorial Sports Museum, Tokyo.

JBBA (Japanese Base Ball Association). 1911 Ledger Book. In author's collection.

Masko, Tozan. Mikado's Base Ball Team Correspondence. In author's collection.

Saisho, Atsuyoshi Harry. "An Autobiography of Atsuyoshi Harry Saisho, as Told to Shigemoro Tamashiro." Translated by Toshiaki Katoh, 1972. Unpublished manuscript in author's collection.

Ueda, Yoshimi. "Tree of Dreams." Unpublished essay in author's collection.

USVPM. U.S. v. Pacific Movement of the Eastern World, January 27, 1943. U.S. District Court, Eastern District of Illinois, Record Group 21, Criminal Case File, Case No. 15840, Box 1, Folder 1, National Archives and Records Administration, Chicago.

Published Sources

Abe, Ikuo. "Muscular Christianity in Japan: The Growth of a Hybrid." In *Christianity and the Colonial and Post-Colonial World*, edited by John Macaloon, 14–38. London: Taylor and Francis, 2013.

Abe, Ikuo, Yasuharu Kiyohara, and Ken Nakajima. "Sport and Physical Education under Fascistization in Japan." *InYo: The Journal of Alternative Perspectives on the Martial Arts and Sciences*, June 2000.

Abe, Isoo. "Diary of the 1905 Tour." In *Saikin Yakyūjutsu*, edited by Shin Hashido.
Tokyo: Hakubunkan, 1905.

——— . "Waseda daigaku yakyi senshu tobeiki-14." *Tokyo Asahi Shimbun*,
June 22, 1905.

Adachi, Pat. *Asahi: A Legend in Baseball*. Etobicoke ON: Coronex, 1992.

Akahori, Masaru. *Nanka Nihonjin yakyushi* [History of Japanese baseball in
Southern California]. Los Angeles: Town Crier, 1956.

Ashwill, Gary. "Agate Type: Reconstructing Negro League and Latin American
Baseball History." https://agatetype.typepad.com/agate_type/.

Ayer, N. W. *American Newspaper Annual and Directory 1911*. Philadelphia: N.
W. Ayer & Son, 1911.

Azuma, Eiichiro. *Between Two Empires*. New York: Oxford University Press, 2005.

Baldassaro, Lawrence, and Richard A. Johnson, eds. *The American Game: Baseball and Ethnicity*. Carbondale: Southern Illinois University Press, 2002.

Balst, G. W. *Los Angeles 1910 Balst's Real Estate Surveys*. Los Angeles: G. W.
Balst, 1910.

Beck, Jeffrey P. "Introduction." In *The Nebraska Indians and Fun and Frolic with
an Indian Ball Team*, by Guy W. Green, xi–lv. Jefferson NC: McFarland, 2010.

Benesch, Oleg. *Inventing the Way of the Samurai*. Oxford: Oxford University
Press, 2014.

Beran, Janice A. "Diamonds in Iowa: Blacks, Buxton, and Baseball." *Journal of
Negro History* 75, nos. 3/4 (Summer–Autumn 1990): 81–95.

Bruce, H. Addington. "Baseball and the National Life." *The Outlook*, May 17,
1913, 105.

Brunson, James E., III. *The Early Image of Black Baseball*. Jefferson NC: McFarland, 2009.

Cedarville College. *1897 Cedrus Yearbook*. Cedarville OH: Cedarville College, 1897.

——— . *1916 Cedrus Yearbook*. Cedarville OH: Cedarville College, 1916.

Chamberlain, Basil Hall. *Handbook for Travelers in Japan*. London: John Murray, 1903.

Cieradkowski, Gary. "Shumza Sugimoto: A False Spring or Lost in Translation?" *Infinitecardset.com* (blog), February 10, 2015. http://infinitecardset
.blogspot.com/2015/02/192-shumza-sugimoto-false-spring.html.

Crepeau, Richard C. *Baseball: America's Diamond Mind*. Lincoln: University of
Nebraska Press, 1980.

Daniels, Roger. *Coming to America*. New York: Harper Perennial, 1991.

——— . *The Politics of Prejudice*. Berkeley: University of California Press, 1962.

Del Mar, Walter. *Around the World through Japan*. London: Adam and Charles
Black, 1904.

Dixon, Phil, and Patrick J. Hannigan. *The Negro Baseball Leagues: A Photographic History*. Mattituck NY: Amereon House, 1992.

Donnithorne, G. C. Allen. *Western Enterprise in Far Eastern Economic Development*. New York: Routledge, 2013.

Dower, John W. *War without Mercy: Race and Power in the Pacific War*. New York: Pantheon, 1986.

Durand, Dana. *Thirteenth Census of the United States Taken in the Year 1910: Statistics for Iowa*. Washington DC: Government Printing Office, 1913.

Duss, Peter, and Kenji Hasegawa, eds. *Rediscovering America: Japanese Perspectives on the American Century*. Berkeley: University of California Press, 2011.

Eberle, Mark E. *Kansas Baseball 1858–1941*. Lawrence: University Press of Kansas, 2017.

Elias, Robert, ed. *Baseball and the American Dream*. Armonk NY: M. E. Sharpe, 2001.

Endo, Russell. "Persistence of Ethnicity: The Japanese of Colorado." Paper presented at the Symposium on Ethnicity on the Great Plains, Lincoln, Nebraska, 1978.

Fitts, Robert K. *Banzai Babe Ruth*. Lincoln: University of Nebraska Press, 2012.

——— . "Baseball and the Yellow Peril: Waseda University's 1905 American Tour." In *Base Ball 10: New Research on the Early Game*, edited by Don Jensen, 141–59. Jefferson NC: McFarland, 2018.

Fleitz, David. *Louis Sockalexis: The First Cleveland Indian*. Jefferson NC: McFarland, 2002.

Franks, Joel. *Asian Pacific Americans and Baseball: A History*. Jefferson NC: McFarland, 2008.

——— . *The Barnstorming Hawaiian Travelers*. Jefferson NC: McFarland, 2012.

Furukawa, Eiji. *Minami Kashū to Kagoshima Kenjin*. Tokyo: Bunsei Shoin, 2003.

Gainty, Denis. *Martial Arts and the Body Politic in Meiji Japan*. New York: Routledge, 2013.

Galbraith, Michael. "Legendary 1896 YC&AC vs. Ichiko Baseball Games." *Galbraith Press* (blog), May 18, 2016. https://galbraith.press/legendary-1896-ycac-vs-ichiko-baseball-games/.

——— . "The Origins of Baseball in Japan." Baseball Japan.org. https://www.baseballjapan.org/common/news_doc/news_doc_1165_0001.pdf.

Gallicchio, Marc. *The African American Encounter with Japan and China*. Chapel Hill: University of North Carolina Press, 2000.

Gavin, Masako. "Abe Isoo and Baseball." In *Rethinking Japanese Modernism*, edited by Roy Starrs, 452–70. Boston: Global Oriental, 2012.

——— . "National Moral Education: Abe Isoo's Views on Education." *Japanese Studies* 24, no. 3 (2004): 323–33.

——— . "Poverty and Its Possible Cures: Abe Isoo and Kawakami Hajime." 2007. http://epublications.bond.edu.au/hss_pubs/232.

Gillespie, Paul. "History of Baseball: Japan's First Pro Ballplayer in America." *From Deep Right Field* (blog), October 26, 2011. http://fromdeeprightfield .com/history-of-baseball-japans-first-pro-ballplayer-in-america/.

Goto, Chimpei. *The Japanese Balldom of Hawaii*. Privately published, Honolulu, 1919.

Gould, Stephen Jay. *The Mismeasure of Man*. New York: Norton, 1981.

Goyette, Braden. "How Racism Created America's Chinatowns." *Huffpost*, November 11, 2014. https://www.huffingtonpost.com/2014/11/11/american -chinatowns-history_n_6090692.html.

Green, Guy W. *The Nebraska Indians and Fun and Frolic with an Indian Ball Team*. Edited by Jeffrey P. Beck. Jefferson NC: McFarland, 2010.

Gulick, Sidney L. *The American Japanese Problem: A Study of the Racial Relations of the East and the West*. New York: Charles Scribner's Sons, 1914.

Guthrie-Shimizu, Sayuri. "For Love of the Game: Baseball in Early U.S.-Japanese Encounters and the Rise of a Transnational Sporting Fraternity." *Diplomatic History* 28, no. 5 (2004): 637–62.

——. *Transpacific Field of Dreams*. Chapel Hill: University of North Carolina Press, 2012.

Guttmann, Allen, and Lee Thompson. *Japanese Sports: A History*. Honolulu: University of Hawaii Press, 2001.

Halper, Donna. "A Lady Sporting Editor: How Ina Eloise Young Covered Baseball and Made History." Paper presented at Nine Spring Training Baseball Conference, Tempe, Arizona, March 2015.

Harase, Hanzaburo. "Nijyugonenmae no *Rafu Shimpo*" [Recollections of the *Rafu Shimpo*]. Translated by Keiko Nishi Komei. *Rafu Shimpo*, October 1, 1927, 17.

Hashido, Shin, ed. *Saikin Yakyūjutsu*. Tokyo: Hakubunkan, 1905.

Hayashi, Brian. *"For the Sake of Our Japanese Brethren": Assimilation, Nationalism, and Protestantism among the Japanese of Los Angeles, 1895–1942*. Palo Alto CA: Stanford University Press, 1995.

Hayashi, Katie Kaori. *A History of the Rafu Shimpo*. Osaka: Union Press, 1997.

Heaphy, Leslie A. *The Negro Leagues 1869–1960*. Jefferson NC: McFarland, 2003.

Hirose, Kenzo. *Nihon no yakyushi*. Tokyo: Nihon Yakyūshi Kankōkai, 1964.

Horikiri, Edward Toru. "Baseball History of Issei." *Discover Nikkei*, July 28, 2014. http://www.discovernikkei.org/ja/journal/2014/7/28/issei-yakyu/.

Horne, Gerald. *Facing the Rising Sun: African Americans, Japan, and the Rise of Afro-Asian Solidarity*. New York: New York University Press, 2018.

Hosokawa, Bill. *Colorado's Japanese Americans: From 1886 to the Present*. Boulder: University Press of Colorado, 2005.

Hotchkiss, Ron. *Diamond Gods of the Morning Sun*. Victoria BC: Friesen, 2013.

Ichihashi, Yamato. *Japanese in the United States*. Palo Alto CA: Stanford University Press, 1932.

Ichioka, Yuji. *The Issei*. New York: Free Press, 1988.

Ichioka, Yuji, and Eiichiro Azuma. *A Buried Past II*. Los Angeles: UCLA Asian American Studies Center, 1999.

Ichioka, Yuji, Yasuo Sakata, Nobuya Tsuchida, and Eri Yasuhara. *A Buried Past*. Berkeley: University of California Press, 1974.

"The Igorrote Tribe from the Philippines." *Lewis and Clark Journal*, October 1905, 4.

Ikegami, Eiko. *The Taming of the Samurai*. Cambridge MA: Harvard University Press, 1995.

Ikei, Masaru. *Hakkyū taiheiyō o wataru: Nichi-bei yakyū kōryūshi*. Tokyo: Chuo Koron Sha, 1976.

Inoue, Shun. "Budo: Invented Tradition in the Martial Arts." In *The Culture of Japan as Seen through Its Leisure*, edited by Sepp Linhart and Sabine Fruhstuck, 83–93. Albany: State University of New York Press, 1998.

Irwin, Wallace. *Letters of a Japanese Schoolboy*. New York: Doubleday, 1909.

Ito, Takuo, ed. *Yakyu-nenpoh*. Tokyo: Mimatsu Shouten, 1915.

Japan Bureau de la Statistique Générale. *État de la population de l'Empire du Japon*. Tokyo: Cabinet Imperial, 1911.

Japanese Chamber of Commerce of Southern California. *Japanese in Southern California: A History of 70 Years*. Los Angeles: Japanese Chamber of Commerce of Southern California, 1960.

Jensen, Don. "John McGraw." SABR Baseball Biography Project. https://sabr .org/bioproj/person/fef5035f.

Johnson, Roxana. "Be Good Americans: The Message of the Japanese-American Courier." *The Great Depression in Washington State*. Pacific Northwest Labor and Civil Rights Projects, University of Washington, 2010. http://depts .washington.edu/depress/japanese_american_courier_americanism.shtml.

Johnson, Sarah Elizabeth. "The Importance of Baseball to Japanese-American Communities and Culture on the West Coast during the Pre-War Years and World War II." *Footnotes: A Journal of History* 2 (2018): 213–35.

Kanai, Shigeo, and Bensho Ito. *Hokubei no Nihonjin*. San Francisco: Kanai Tsushaku Jimusho, 1909.

Kaneko, Gemma. "Who Was the First Japanese Player on an American Baseball Team?" MLB.com, April 13, 2018. https://www.mlb.com/cut4/who-was -the-first-japanese-baseball-player-in-the-usa-c271935604.

Kashiwamura, Keikoku. *Hokubei tosa taikan. Jokan, kashu Nihonjin hattenchi no bu*. Tokyo: Bunsei Shoin, 2007.

Kawakami, Santaro Hirofumi. *Samurai yakyū umi o wataru: Abe Isō to Meiji 38nen sōdai yakyūbu beikoku hatsuensei*. Saga, Japan: Shoshikusabōbō, 2015.

Keaveney, Christopher T. *Contesting the Myths of Samurai Baseball: Cultural Representations of Japan's National Pastime*. Hong Kong: Hong Kong University Press, 2018.

Kiku, Koichi. "Bushido and the Modernization of Japanese Sports." In *This Sporting Life: Sports and Body Culture in Modern Japan*, edited by William

Kelly and Atsuo Sugimoto, 39–54. New Haven: Yale CEAS Occasional Publications, 2007.

——— . "The Japanese Baseball Spirit and Professional Ideology." In *Japan, Sport and Society*, edited by Joseph Maguire and Masayoshi Nakayama, 35–54. New York: Routledge, 2006.

Kimura, Yukiko. *Issei*. Honolulu: University of Hawaii Press, 1988.

Kurashige, Scott. *The Shifting Grounds of Race: Black and Japanese Americans in the Making of Multiethnic Los Angeles*. Princeton NJ: Princeton University Press, 2008.

Kusaka, Yuko. "The Development of Baseball Organizations in Japan." *International Review for the Sociology of Sport* 22 (1987): 263–78.

Kyle, Donald G., and Robert B. Fairbanks, eds. *Baseball in America and America in Baseball*. College Station: Texas A&M University Press, 2008.

LaFeber, Walter. *The Clash*. New York: Norton, 1997.

Lee, Robert G. *Orientals*. Philadelphia: Temple University Press, 1999.

Lee, Shelley Sang-Her. *Claiming the Oriental Gateway*. Philadelphia: Temple University Press, 2011.

Leland Stanford Junior University. *Thirteenth Annual Register, 1903–04*. Palo Alto CA: Stanford University, 1904.

Lieb, Frederick G. "Baseball—The Nation's Melting Pot." *Baseball Magazine* 31 (August 1923): 393.

Loewen, James W. *Sundown Towns: A Hidden Dimension of American Racism*. New York: New Press, 2005.

Macaloon, John. *Muscular Christianity and the Colonial and Post-Colonial World*. New York: Routledge, 2008.

Markino, Yoshio. "My Experiences in San Francisco." *McClure's Magazine* 36 (1911): 110.

Mason, William M. *The Japanese in Los Angeles*. Los Angeles: Los Angeles County Museum of Natural History, 1969.

Matsumoto, Motomitsu. *Kashū jinbutsu taikan: Nanka no maki* [Japanese Who's Who in California]. Tokyo: Bunsei Shoin, 2003.

Maynard, James. *World War Two, America's Divine Mission and the Formulation of the Japanese "Other": A Study of Wartime Propaganda as a Tactical Weapon and a Euphemism for Racial Discrimination*. Amazon Digital Services, 2014.

McKenna, Brian. "Charlie Grant." SABR Baseball Biography Project. https:// sabr.org/bioproj/person/bd564010.

——— . "Goro Mikami." SABR Baseball Biography Project. https://sabr.org /bioproj/person/85880465.

McNally, Andrew. "How I Became a Ranchman in California." *Country Life in America*, 1904, 297–301.

McNeil, William. *The California Winter League*. Jefferson NC: McFarland, 2002.

Methodist Episcopal Church. *Eighty-Third Annual Report of the Missionary Society of the Methodist Episcopal Church from the Year 1901*. New York: Methodist Episcopal Church, 1901.

Miller, H. D. "The Great Sushi Craze of 1905, Part 1." Eccentricculinary.com. http://eccentricculinary.com/the-great-sushi-craze-of-1905-part-1/.

Mitsumori, Nisuke. "Nisuke Mitsumori." In *The Issei: Portrait of a Pioneer*, edited by Eileen Sunada Sarasohn, 59–60. Palo Alto CA: Pacific Books, 1983.

Miyazaki Omiya Senior High School. *One Hundred Years of Omiya Senior High School*. Miyazaki: Omiya Senior High School, 1999.

Mochizuki, Ken, and Dom Lee. *Baseball Saved Us*. New York: Lee & Low, 1993.

Modell, John. *The Economics and Politics of Racial Accommodation: The Japanese of Los Angeles 1900–1942*. Chicago: University of Illinois Press, 1977.

Mori, Anori. *Life and Resources in America*. Washington DC: N.p., 1871.

Mullan, Michael L. "Ethnicity and Sport: The Wapato Nippons and Pre–World War II Japanese American Baseball." *Journal of Sport History* 26, no. 1 (Spring 1999): 82–114.

Nagata, Yoichi. "The Japan Trip Journal of Sherman Indians." *Baseball Legend Magazine* 4 (2014): 38–41.

———. "The Los Angeles Nippons Baseball Club, 1926–1941." In *More Than a Game: Sport in the Japanese American Community*, edited by Brian Niiya, 100–109. Los Angeles: Japanese American National Museum, 2000.

Nakagawa, Kerry Yo. *Japanese American Baseball in California*. Charleston SC: History Press, 2014.

———. *Through a Diamond: 100 Years of Japanese American Baseball*. San Francisco: Rudi, 2001.

Nakane, Kazuko. *Nothing Left in My Hands: The Issei of a Rural California Town, 1900–1942*. Berkeley CA: Heyday Books, 1985.

Nash, John S. "The Forgotten Golden Age of Mixed Martial Arts—Part IV: Ultimate Fighting of the Belle Époque." *Bloody Elbow*, October 31, 2011. https://www.bloodyelbow.com/2011/10/31/2521315/the-forgotten-golden-age-of-mixed-martial-arts-part-iv-ultimate.

Nichibei Shimbun. *Japanese American Yearbook 1905*. San Francisco: Nichibei Shimbun, 1905.

———. *Japanese American Yearbook 1908*. San Francisco: Nichibei Shimbun, 1908.

———. *Japanese American Yearbook 1910*. San Francisco: Nichibei Shimbun, 1910.

———. *Japanese American Yearbook 1911*. San Francisco: Nichibei Shimbun, 1911.

Niese, Joe. "Voyage to the Land of the Rising Sun." *Nine* 22, no. 1 (2013): 11–19.

Niiya, Brian, ed. *Japanese American History: An A-to-Z Reference from 1868 to the Present*. Los Angeles: Japanese American National Museum, 1993.

———, ed. *More Than a Game: Sport in the Japanese American Community*. Los Angeles: Japanese American National Museum, 2000.

Noguchi, Yonejiro. *The Story of Yone Noguchi*. Philadelphia: George W. Jacobs, 1915.

Nomura, Gail M. "Beyond the Playing Field: The Significance of pre–World War II Japanese American Baseball in the Yakima Valley." In *Bearing Dreams, Shaping Visions*, edited by Linda A. Revilla, Gail M. Nomura, Shawn Wong, and Shirley Hune, 15–32. Pullman: Washington State University Press, 1993.

O'Connor, Gerry. "Sports and Popular Literature." In *The Guide to United States Popular Culture*, edited by Ray B. Browne and Pat Browne, 767–69. Madison: University of Wisconsin Press, 2001.

Ogawa, Dennis. *From Japs to Japanese: The Evolution of Japanese-American Stereotypes*. Berkeley CA: McCutchan, 1971.

Okihiro, Michael. *AJA Baseball in Hawaii*. Honolulu: Hawaii Hochi, 1999.

Pascoe, Peggy. *What Comes Naturally: Miscegenation Law and the Making of Race in America*. New York: Oxford University Press, 2010.

Pearce, Ralph M. *From Asahi to Zebras*. San Jose CA: Japanese American Museum of San Jose, 2005.

Pegues, J. J. "International Baseball." *Independent* 70 (January 19, 1911): 126–31.

——— . "Japan Invades America: A Japanese University Baseball Team Coming to Try Conclusions with Our College Boys." *Collier's Outdoor American*, April 15, 1911, 21.

Pollock, Alan J. *Barnstorming to Heaven*. Tuscaloosa: University of Alabama Press, 2006.

Pope, S. W. *Patriotic Games: Sporting Traditions in the American Imagination, 1876–1926*. Knoxville: University of Tennessee Press, 2007.

Powers-Beck, Jeffrey. "'A Role New to the Race': A New History of the Nebraska Indians." *Nebraska History* 85 (2004): 186–203.

Powles, Cyril. "Abe Isoo the Utility Man." In *Pacifism in Japan: The Christian and Socialist Tradition*, edited by Nobuya Bamba and John F. Howes, 143–67. Kyoto: Minerva, 1978.

Rafu Shimpo. Rafu Shimpo Yearbook 1907. Los Angeles: Rafu Shimpo, 1907.

——— . *Rafu Shimpo Yearbook 1914*. Los Angeles: Rafu Shimpo, 1914.

Rawitsch, Mark H. *No Other Place: Japanese American Pioneers in a Southern California Neighborhood*. Riverside CA: Department of History, University of California, 1983.

Reaves, Joseph. *Taking in a Game: A History of Baseball in Asia*. Lincoln: University of Nebraska Press, 2004.

Reckner, James R. *Teddy Roosevelt's Great White Fleet*. Annapolis MD: Naval Institute Press, 1988.

Reeves, Richard. *Infamy: The Shocking Story of the Japanese American Internment in World War II*. New York: Henry Holt, 2015.

Regalado, Samuel O. "Baseball's Kakehashi: A Bridge of Understanding and the Nikkei Experience." In *Mapping an Empire of American Sport: Expansion, Assimilation, Adaptation and Resistance*, edited by Mark Dyreson, J. A. Mangam, and Roberta J. Park, 60–75. New York: Routledge, 2013.

———. "Invisible Baseball: Japanese Americans and Their Game in the 1930s." In *Baseball in America and America in Baseball*, edited by Donald G. Kyle and Robert B. Fairbanks, 32–51. College Station: Texas A&M University Press, 2008.

———. *Nikkei Baseball*. Urbana: University of Illinois Press, 2013.

———. "Sport and Community in California's Japanese American 'Yamato Colony' 1930–1945." *Journal of Sport History* 19, no. 2 (Summer 1992): 130–43.

Riess, Steven A. *Touching Base: Professional Baseball and American Culture in the Progressive Era*. Urbana: University of Illinois Press, 1983.

Roden, Donald F. "Baseball and the Quest for National Dignity in Meiji Japan." *American Historical Review* 85, no 3 (1980): 511–34.

———. *Schooldays in Imperial Japan*. Berkeley: University of California Press, 1980.

Sakata, Yasuo. *Fading Footsteps of the Issei*. Los Angeles: UCLA Asian American Studies Center, 1992.

Sanborn-Perris. *Insurance Maps of San Francisco*. Vol. 1. New York: Sanborn-Perris, 1899.

Sarasohn, Eileen Sunada, ed. *The Issei: Portrait of a Pioneer*. Palo Alto CA: Pacific Books, 1983.

Sayama, Kazuo. *The Mystery of "Jap Mikado": First Japanese in American Professional Baseball*. Tokyo: Tankobon, 1996.

Scheinin, Richard. *Field of Screams: The Dark Underside of America's National Pastime*. New York: Norton, 1994.

Schmidt, Ray. "The Golden Age of Chicago Baseball." *Chicago History* 29 (1999): 38–59.

Seymour, Harold. *Baseball: The People's Game*. New York: Oxford University Press, 1990.

Sheppard, Derek. "A Team of Their Own." *Kitsap Sun*, April 6, 2008. http://archive.kitsapsun.com/news/local/suquamish-baseball-a-team-of-their-own-ep-422154134-358640001.html/?page=1.

Shibazaki, Ryoichi. "Seattle and the Japanese–United States Baseball Connection, 1905–1926." Master's thesis, University of Washington, 1981.

Shimada, Akira. *Meiji 44-nen keiō yakyūbu Amerika ōdan jikki: Dendō iri Shimada Zensuke no shōgai*. Tokyo: Baseball Magazine, 1995.

Soden, Dale. "Ernest C. Tanner (1889–1956)." BlackPast.com, August 1, 2008. https://www.blackpast.org/aaw/vignette_aahw/ernest-c-tanner-1889-1956/#sthash.uqvamJhs.dpuf.

Soennichsen, John. *Miwoks to Missiles: A History of Angel Island*. Tiburon CA: Angel Island Association, 2001.

Sogawa, Masao, and Yoshimatsu Matsueda. *Nikkei imin jinmei jiten hokubei hen*. Tokyo: Nihon Tosho Sentā, 1993.

Spalding, Albert G. *America's National Game*. San Francisco: Halo Books, 1991.

———. *Spalding's Official Base Ball Guide*. New York: American Sports Publishing, 1912.

Spalding, John E. *Always on Sunday: The California Baseball League, 1886 to 1915*. Manhattan KS: Ag Press, 1992.

Spickard, Paul. *Japanese Americans*. New Brunswick NJ: Rutgers University Press, 1996.

———. *Mixed Blood: Intermarriage and Ethnic Identity in Twentieth-Century America*. Madison: University of Wisconsin Press, 1989.

Staples, Bill, Jr. "Early Baseball Encounters in the West: The Yeddo Royal Japanese Troupe Play Ball in America, 1872." https://billstaples.blogspot.com.

———. *Kenichi Zenimura: Japanese American Baseball Pioneer*. Jefferson NC: McFarland, 2011.

State of Missouri. *The Revised Statutes of the State of Missouri 1909*. Jefferson City MO: Hugh Stephens Printing, 1909.

Stevens, John. *The Way of Judo: A Portrait of Igoro Kano and His Students*. Boston: Shambhala, 2013.

St. George Stubbs, Lewis. *Shoestring Glory: Semi-Pro Ball of the Prairies*. Winnipeg MB: Turnstone Press, 1996.

Strecker, Geri. "Grover Baichley." SABR Baseball Biography Project. https://sabr.org/bioproj/person/588aaf60.

Super, Eleanor, and George Blakeslee. *Japan in American Public Opinion*. New York: Macmillan, 1937.

Sutter, L. M. *New Mexico Baseball: Miners, Outlaws, Indians and Isotopes, 1880 to the Present*. Jefferson NC: McFarland, 2010.

Suzuki, Matsuhiko. *Inta mauten doho hattatsushi*. Denver: Denba Shimposha, 1910.

Suzuki, Yasumasa, and Kenji Sakai. *Besuboruto okajoki: Nipponde hajimete kabuwo nageta toko Hiraoka Hiroshi*. Tokyo: Shogakukan, 2005.

Svinth, Joseph R. "Japanese Professional Wrestling Pioneer: Sorakichi Matsuda." *InYo: The Journal of Alternative Perspectives on the Martial Arts and Sciences*, November 2000; updated January 2005.

———. "Professor Yamashita Goes to Washington." *Akido Journal* 25, no. 2 (1998): 37–42.

Takaki, Ronald. *Issei and Nisei*. New York: Chelsea House, 1989.

Tanimura, Hirotake. *Miyazakiken yakyushi*. Miyazaki, Japan: Miyazaki Art Creators Association, 1967.

Tipton, Elise K. "In a House Divided: The Japanese Christian Socialist Abe Isoo." In *Nation and Nationalism in Japan*, edited by Sandra Wilson, 81–96. New York: Routledge, 2002.

Toyama, Chotoku. "The Japanese Community in Los Angeles." Master's thesis, Columbia University, 1926.

Uchiyama, Y., ed. *Yamaguchi-ken koto yakyushi*. Yamaguchi, Japan: Yamaguchi Prefectural High School Baseball Association, 1984.

U.S. Bureau of Census. *1870 Federal Census, San Francisco, California Ward 11, 1st District.* https://www.archives.gov/research.

———. *1900 Federal Census.* https://www.archives.gov/research.

———. *1910 Federal Census.* https://www.archives.gov/research.

———. *1920 Federal Census.* https://www.archives.gov/research.

———. *1930 Federal Census.* https://www.archives.gov/research.

———. *1940 Federal Census.* https://www.archives.gov/research.

U.S. Immigration Commission. *Reports of the Immigration Commission, Immigrants in Industries, Part 25: Japanese and Other Immigrant Races in the Pacific Coast and Rocky Mountain States.* Vol. 1. Washington DC: Government Printing Office, 1911.

U.S. War Department. *Annual Report of the Secretary of War.* Vol. 3. Washington DC: Government Printing Office, 1907.

Uzawa, Yoshiko. "Hashimura Togo Went to War: Yellowface, the Yellow Peril, and the Philosophy of Propaganda." *Nanzan Review of American Studies* 30 (2008): 189–202.

Vanner, Antoine. *The Dawlish Chronicles.* http://dawlishchronicles.com/usas-first-korean-war-1871/.

Walz, Eric. *Nikkei in the Interior West.* Tucson: University of Arizona Press, 2012.

Wei, William. *Asians in Colorado.* Seattle: University of Washington Press, 2016.

Whirty, Ryan. "Two Cultures Meet on the Diamond for the First Time?" *The Negro Leagues Up Close* (blog), November 5, 2016. https://homeplatedontmove.wordpress.com/2015/11/05/two-cultures-meet-on-the-diamond-for-the-first-time/.

White, Kenneth R. "Baseball and the American Character: Exploring the Influence of the National Pastime on the Origins of the Contemporary American Identity." *Proceedings of the National Conference on Undergraduate Research*, 2015, 172–81. http://www.ncurproceedings.org/ojs/index.php/NCUR2015/article/view/1515.

Whiting, Robert. *The Samurai Way of Baseball.* New York: Warner Books, 2005.

———. *You Gotta Have Wa.* New York: Macmillan, 1989.

Wikipedia. "Pacific Movement of the Eastern World." Last modified December 22, 2018. https://en.wikipedia.org/w/index.php?title=Pacific_Movement_of_the_Eastern_World&oldid=874910663.

Wilson, Robert, and Bill Hosokawa. *East to America.* New York: William Morrow, 1980.

Wu, Frank H. *Yellow.* New York: Perseus, 2002.

Yancey, Diana. *Life in a Japanese American Internment Camp.* San Diego: Lucent Books, 1998.

Young, William. *J. L. Wilkinson and the Kansas City Monarchs: Trailblazers in Black Baseball.* Jefferson NC: McFarland, 2016.

Zhao, Xiaojian, and Edward J. Park. *Asian Americans: An Encyclopedia of Social, Cultural, Economic, and Political History.* Vol. 1. Santa Barbara CA: Greenwood, 2013.

Index